AN INTRODUCTION

TO THE

Geography and History of India

AN INTRODUCTION

TO THE

Geography and History of India,

AND

THE COUNTRIES ADJACENT.

Edited by

A. R. SYMONDS, M.A

GYAN

Published by

Gyan Publishing House
5, Ansari Road
Daryaganj, New Delhi-110002
Phone: 011-47034999, 9811692060
E-mail: books@gyanbooks.com

Distribution Network
gyanbooks.com
India, USA, Canada, UK, Australia, France

ISBN: 978-81-212-8979-5 (PB)
First Published, 1843

2nd Impression 2023

Printed at: Gyan Press, Delhi.

AN INTRODUCTION TO THE GEOGRAPHY AND HISTORY OF INDIA

EDITOR: A. R. SYMONDS

AN INTRODUCTION

TO THE

Geography and History of India,

AND

THE COUNTRIES ADJACENT.

EDITED BY

THE REV. A. R. SYMONDS, M. A.

WADHAM COLLEGE—OXFORD.

Head Master of Bishop Corrie's Grammar School.

MADRAS:

PRINTED BY P. R. HUNT, AMERICAN MISSION PRESS,
FOR BISHOP CORRIE'S GRAMMAR SCHOOL.
1843.

PREFACE.

THE authorities, which have been chiefly made use of by the able author of this work, are Hamilton, Murray, Elphinstone and Burnes: but he has also brought to bear much valuable research and practical knowledge of his own. The plan was originally undertaken with a view to furnish Native students with fuller information respecting their own country than can be obtained in the books to which they have usually access, but from want of leisure it remained a long time unfinished. This the author was eventually induced to resume and to enlarge, and having been re-written, it was given over to the editor who made a few trifling additions and alterations, the better to adapt it to school use, and has now conducted it through the press. Whatever merit therefore on the one hand this work possesses, belongs it will be perceived entirely to the author, while on the other hand the editor fears he must ask for much indulgence for many errors which have occurred in the course of printing. These, however, have been remedied as far as possible by supplying a copious list of corrigenda, and in a second edition, to which he will immediately apply himself, every pains will be taken to render the book as complete as possible.

The editor would take this opportunity of earnestly requesting all who may make use of this work, particularly those engaged in education, to furnish him with any hints that may occur to them for improving the book in any respect whatever.

It may be well to observe, that general utility has been kept in view in the putting together of this work. To those interested in India, resident as well here as in England, it will be found it is hoped a pleasing compendium of information. To travellers also in India, and especially to young officers and others who arrive newly in the country, and who generally stand much in need of something of the kind, it may prove a convenient hand book. To render it the more useful in this respect, the travelling distances have been very generally given, as well as glossaries explanatory of the Hindoostanee and other words in common use, and of the terminations of names of places. A copious Index also has been added, so as to make the book serve in a considerable degree the purpose of a gazetteer. It has been, however, above all with a view to supply a desideratum so long felt, of a suitable school book on India, that the present work has been brought out, and most earnestly does the editor trust it will contribute to an increasing study, as well as to an increased knowledge of the Geography and History of India, about which there is so general and lamentable an ignorance. To further this object, a Map of India has been published of moderate size and price to accompany the book. For the original design and drawing of this map the editor is indebted to his friend the Rev. G. W. Mahon, Chaplain of Fort St. George, to whom he would take this opportunity of offering his best thanks, both in his own name, and in that of the Committee of Bishop Corrie's Grammar School, to whom the copyright of the Map has been presented by him, as indeed has also the copyright of the book by the author for the benefit of the school.

The editor has only to observe in conclusion that in the arrangement of Provinces, Towns, &c. the principle has been followed throughout, as far as practicable, of entering them in order from west to east, commencing at the north of each country or province.

Black Town, Madras,
August 15, 1843.

CONTENTS.

CORRIGENDA.

Teachers and others are requested to make the necessary corrections with the pen.

Page	*Line*	*For*	*Read*
20	22	each	Ooch
29	14	Kootbood	Kootb-ood
42	2	Mahrattee	Mahratee, *and so wherever it occurs.*
47	18	Sirmorees	Sirmoorees
51	22	Sikhim	Sikkim
52	24	cardamums	cardamoms
57	27	Utok	Utuk
58	18	Akbar	Akber
58	24	Juhun	Juhan
59	9	Sikhs, Singhs	Sikhs or Singhs,
61	39	accidently	accidentally
63	1	work	word
65	13	beseiged	besieged
66	11	Aligurh	*omit this Division.*
67	14	Aligurh	*omit.*
68	8	Jumna	Jumma
68	35	Patan	Parthan, *and so throughout.*
69			*omit Aligurh, which transfer to page* 90, *between Agra and Cowl.*
73	6	Mainkoor	Manikpoor
77	18	Tata	Tatta
77	30	150,000	15,000
87	24	Boonde	Boondee
89	14	Anoopshuhr, Cowl	Anoopshuhr, Aligurh, Cowl,
91	8	7,000	70,000
92	3 & 21	seige	siege
93	26	1700. When	1700, when
95	3	Sind	Indus
100	5	Kattwar	Kattiwar
100	24	Kattwad	Kattivad
105	29	Johrejas	Jahrejas
108	21	party,	*omit the comma.*
112	12	Leronje	Seronje
117	21	Kasee rao	Kasee rao,
119	20	Tunsa	Tonsa
120	24	iron-diamonds	iron. Diamonds
122	29	Kusee	Kasee
124	33	Karroje	Kanoje
128	13	Gunduh	Gunduk
128	21	Shajaood	Shuja-ood
128	22	Alikhan	Ali Khan
130	9	them	the latter
130	27	subdued. Several	subdued, several
132	9	aujiya	anjiya
135	3	Serajood	Suraj-ood
136	7	beseiged	besieged
136	8	Surajood	Suraj-ood
137	10	Bunya	Bunga
137	14	Bungalee	Bungalu
138	6	individual	individuals
138	32	Tipera	Tippera
140	13	Akbar	Akber
140	18	Jaffeer	Jaffer
140	18	1576	1756
140	19	Sura jood	Suraj-ood
142	31	Bijeen	Bijnee

CORRIGENDA.

Page	Line	For	Read
146	27	Cassey	Cassay
147	16	Doodputtee	Doodputlee, *and so throughout.*
148	28	Murjeet	Marjeet
154	9	savages	ravages
155	29	Chunteesgur	Chouteesgur
157	7	Byrgur	Byragur
166	15	Balishwar	Balishwur
168	1	The town, &c.	*omit this sentence.*
168	29	Ooreas	Ooreeas
169	11	Khoonds	Khonds
170	3	Mukhum	Mukhun
170	14	Subadar	Soobadar
170	30	Zumeendaries	Zumeendarees
171	21	Aurungabad ; Bheer,	Aurungabad and Bheer
174	7	Kanneri	Kenneri
175	11	Shah-ginj	Shah-gunj
177	2	Bhamance	Bahmenee, *and so throughout.*
179	24	Mahrattee. Goojrattee,	Mahratee. Goojratee
183	18	Kummum-nait	Kummum-mait
189	18	Ooppoo-Ellore	Ooppoo-Elloor
192	18	district	districts
192	35	latter part	middle
194	20	Severudroog	Severndroog
195	31	Severudroog	Severndroog
197	34	island	islands
201	10	Jessaye	Dessaye
201	34	Mahratta	Mahrattas
202	—	Balaghat,CededDistricts.	Balaghat Ceded Districts.
203			*The heading of pages* 203 *and* 205 *should be* Ceded Districts.
205	13	Karnatuk	Kurnatuk
205	14	Karnata	Kurnatu
218			Name *to be inserted in margin.*
225	29	1936	1639
226	9	raja Sahib	Raja Sahib
229	7	Sadrungaputtanum	Sadrungaputtunum
229	16	Nuli,	Buli,
230	1	the most splendid settlement	one of the most splendid settlements
232	25	Wynaad, Palghat	Wynaad and Palghat
233	15	bebee	beebee, *and so throughout.*
238	13	Beer and Veer	Beer or Veer
241	12	exceeding	amounting to
242	1	Trichinopoly	Trichinopoly,
249	29	Ekhojee	Ekkojee
254	14	Koochee	Kochee
262	2	chalk	chank
265	12	Kevetta	kwetta
268	21	climate	climates
274	5	porportion	proportion
274	27	Yahoodee	Yuhoodee
279	27	Eyool	Eyoob
283	2	Khoosh	Koosh
283	3	Koondoor	Koondooz
283	5 & 8	Merue	Merve
286	—	Kohan	Kokan
291	—	Khoondooz	Koondooz, *and so throughout.*
298	8	Kalmuck	Kalmuk, *and so throughout.*
301	23	Lakdack	Lahdack
309	12	Peehelee	Pechelee
324	10	Debor	Deb or
336	3	Keenduem	Kienduem
338	28	Merqui	Mergui, *and so throughout.*
353	20	these	the
357	8	moved	moored
359	30	which overflowed	which is overflowed
361	26	Jahore	Johore

CHAP. I.

§ 1.

Explanations.

GEOGRAPHY (from the Greek γη *gē*, earth, and γραφω *graphō*, to write) is the description of the earth which we inhabit.

In its fullest range it comprehends a description of the surface of the earth, its figure or shape, formation, and extent,—its divisions, natural and artificial,—its productions, animal, vegetable, and mineral,—together with a notice of its inhabitants, as to their number, constitution, history, politics, religion, manners, and customs. It also treats of the earth as part of the solar system, and explains the use of globes, charts and maps, &c.

The earth is also called the World, and the Globe, both which words signify *a round body;* and the earth is so called because it is round like an orange.

The earth is composed of two things, namely, land and water. About one-third of the globe is land, and all the rest is water. The land is divided into various parts. The principal are called continents, islands, peninsulas, isthmuses, and promontories, or capes.

The name of *Continent* (from the Latin *conti-*

neo, to hold together) is given to those large portions of land which are not interrupted by sea.

There are two *great* continents—viz. the Old Continent, also called the Old World, because the only one known to the ancients, comprising Europe, Asia and Africa; and the New Continent, or New World, consisting of America, which was not known to Europeans until A. D. 1492; when it was discovered by Columbus.

Europe, Asia, Africa, and America, are also separately spoken of as continents.

An *Island*, or isle, is a portion of land smaller than a continent, entirely surrounded by water, as Ceylon, the Isle of France, Java, Britain.

A *Peninsula* (from the Latin *pene*, almost, and *insula*, an island) is a portion of land almost but not quite surrounded by water, as Malaya, Morea, Corea.

An *Isthmus* is a narrow neck of land by which two other portions of land are joined together, as the Isthmus of Suez, which joins Asia and Africa, the Isthmus of Panama which joins North America to South America, and the Isthmus of Kraw joining Malaya to the continent of Asia.

A *Promontory* (from the Latin *pro*, in front of, and *mons*, a mountain) is strictly a tract of high land stretching out into the sea, and its extremity next the sea is called properly a *cape* (from the Latin *caput*, a head) or *headland*. This distinction, however, is not always observed, and these names therefore are often used indifferently. Thus the southern end of India is called a cape, namely, Cape Comorin. The southern end of Africa is called a cape, namely the Cape of Good Hope, with many others.

The *Water* is divided into the following principal parts, oceans, seas, gulfs, bays, straits, rivers, and lakes.

An *Ocean* is the largest portion of water.

There are three great oceans, namely, the Pacific Ocean, the Atlantic Ocean, and the Indian Ocean.

The Pacific Ocean (from the Latin *pacificus*, peaceful) is so called because the Europeans who first sailed there thought it was more quiet and safe than the other oceans.

The Atlantic Ocean is so called because it runs along the coast of Africa, the chief portion of which was formerly known as the country of Atlas. The Atlantic Ocean is also called the Western Ocean.

The Indian Ocean is so named from India.

A *Sea* is a portion of water smaller than an ocean, and more enclosed by land, as the Mediterranean Sea, between Europe and Africa, the Red Sea, between Arabia and Africa, and the Black Sea, between Europe and Asia.

A *Gulf* is a portion of the sea, running up into the land and almost surrounded by it, as the Persian Gulf between Persia and Arabia, the Gulf of Siam, the Gulf of Mexico in America.

A *Bay* is like a gulf, but when the mouth is small, the name of gulf is generally used, and when the mouth is broad and large, and the sea does not run far into the land, the name of bay is applied. Thus, the sea between India and Ava is called the Bay of Bengal. When it is very small it is called by different names such as *creek* or *cove*, and when it affords shelter for shipping, a *harbour* or *haven*.

A *Strait*, or Channel, is a narrow passage of water joining two other portions of water together, as the Straits of Ormus which join the Persian Gulf to the Arabian Sea, the Straits of

Babelmandel which join the Red Sea to the Arabian Sea, the Straits of Gibraltar which join the Mediterranean Sea to the Atlantic Ocean, the Straits of Ramisseram between India and Ceylon, and the Dardanelles which connect the Grecian Archipelago with the Sea of Marmora.

A *River* is a stream of water which begins at some place in the land, and runs into the sea or into some other river or lake, as the Ganges which begins or rises near the Himalaya mountains, and runs into the Bay of Bengal, after a course of 1500 miles.

Sometimes a river, before falling into the sea, spreads out into several channels, forming a triangle. The land enclosed by these is often called the *delta* of the river—from its resembling the form of the Greek letter Δ so named.

Thus the land enclosed by the several mouths of the Nile in Egypt, is called the Delta of the Nile. Thus too, the Ganges spreads out into various channels beginning at about 200 miles from the sea, and the space lying between the eastern and western branches is called the Delta of the Ganges.

A *Lake* is a large portion of water entirely surrounded by land, as the Chilka lake near Jugganath—the Pulicat lake, near Madras.

Thus it will be seen that oceans in the water correspond or are analogous to continents in the land, seas and gulfs to peninsulas, straits to isthmuses, lakes to islands, and bays and creeks to promontories.

There are various other names given to different parts of land and water, an explanation of which may be found in the Glossary.

§ 2.

The earth is, in its shape, spherical, (from the

Greek σφαιρα *sphaira*, a globe) *i. e.* round like an orange, being slightly flattened at the top and bottom. The top or upper end is called the North Pole—the bottom or lower end, is called the South Pole.

The circumference of the earth, that is, its measurement round the middle, is about 24,856 English miles. Its diameter, that is, its measurement through from pole to pole, is about 7,917 miles.

In order to distinguish one part of the earth from another, so as to know about what particular part of it we are speaking, we suppose a number of lines to be drawn on the face of the globe.

The first of them is drawn round the middle of the globe and divides it into two equal parts, and is therefore called the *equator*.

It is also known by the name of the *equinoctial line*, (from the Latin *equa*, equal, and *nox*, night) because when the sun arrives directly over it there is equal day and night of twelve hours each over the whole earth. It is often called, shortly, the *line*.

The two equal parts into which the equator divides the earth, are called the northern and southern hemispheres.

Hemisphere (from the Greek ημι *hemi*, half, and σφαιρα *sphaira*, sphere, or globe) means *half sphere, or globe*.

The distance of any place from the equator towards either pole is called its *latitude*.

From the equator to the north pole is *north latitude*. From the equator to the south pole is *south latitude*.

The supposed lines drawn on the face of the globe are also called circles. Each circle is divided into 360 parts, named degrees—a half circle is therefore 180, and a quarter circle 90 degrees.

Every degree is also divided into 60 parts, called miles or minutes.

The degree is marked thus ° and the mile or minute thus ′ so that 54° 31′ will signify 54 degrees and 31 minutes.

From the equator to the pole is a quarter of a circle, or ninety degrees.

Latitude is measured from any part of the equator all round to either of the poles, and therefore there are ninety degrees of north latitude and ninety of south latitude.

Places on the equator are not considered as having latitude ; but are described as on the line, as Siak in Sumatra.

The next great division is a line drawn round the globe through the poles, which divides the globe into two parts, called the eastern and western hemispheres.

This line is called a *meridian* (from the Latin *medius*, mid, and *dies*, day) because when the sun comes to the meridian of any place, not within the polar circles, it is mid-day or noon at that place.

In general each country chooses its own meridian to count from—thus, the English draw a line through the poles, passing through their observatory at Greenwich, close to London, and call that line the *first meridian*.

The distance of any place to either side of this meridian is called its *longitude*.

As this meridian goes round the earth through the poles, it cuts the equator into two half circles. Each half circle has 180 degrees. Counting from the first meridian at Greenwich round the globe to the eastward, until we reach the same meridian on the opposite side, we reckon 180°, and so far we count *east longitude*. Then, counting from the first meridian round the globe to the westward, until we reach the same meridian on the opposite side, we reckon again 180°, and so far we count *west longitude.*

Now it must be remembered,

1st. That the distance of any place north or south of the equator is called its latitude, and is counted as far as 90°, which will bring us to the poles.

2d. That the distance of any place east or west from the first meridian is called its longitude, and is counted as far as 180°, which will bring us to the first meridian again, on the opposite side, where east and west longitude meet.

3d. As the equator is the line from which we begin to count latitude, therefore, a place situated on any part of the equator has no latitude.

4th. As the English meridian, commonly called the Meridian of Greenwich is the meridian from which we begin to count longitude, therefore, a place situated on any part of that meridian has no longitude.

Now, when a place is said to be in 15° 42′ *north latitude,* 80° 30′ *east longitude,* we mean that its distance north of the equator is 15 degrees and 42 minutes, and that its distance to the east of the English meridian is 80 degrees and 30 minutes,—which two measurements show us the exact situation of the place on the globe.

§ 3.

In order to teach correct notions respecting the earth, various representations of it have been constructed, which are called globes, and maps, or charts.

A globe is a round ball representing the earth according to its real shape as a sphere.

A map or chart is a representation of it upon

a plane. It is a sort of picture of the surface of the earth or of a part of it.

Upon these are drawn the various lines before mentioned. Those drawn from pole to pole, or in a map from the top of it to the bottom, mark the longitude. The circles drawn above and below the equator, or in a map the lines drawn from side to side, mark the latitude, and are called parallels of latitude because they are circles or lines parallel to the equator from which latitude is measured.

On a globe, or a round map, the figures for the longitude are marked on the equator, in a square map, at the top and bottom. The figures for latitude are marked, for a globe, upon the brazen meridian in which it is suspended, in a round map, upon the outer circle, in a square map, upon the sides.

In looking at a map, if the figures for longitude count to the right then the longitude is east, if they count to the left the longitude is west. If the figures for latitude count towards the top the latitude is north, if towards the bottom, south.

Sometimes maps are marked to show which is the north, but when there is no such mark, then the top of the map is the north.

These four, north, south, east, and west, are the chief points of the compass. They are also called the *cardinal points*.

The word compass means circle, namely that circle which is made round any person by the ***horizon***.

The horizon (from the Greek *οριζω* ***horizo***, to bound or limit) is that part where the view is bounded or limited to the eye, and where the sky seems to any person to join the earth all around him.

If a person stand with the rising sun in a line with his right arm, the north is straight in front of him, the south straight behind him—the right hand side, where the sun rises, the east, and the left hand side, where the sun sets, the west.

These four cardinal points divide the circle into four parts or quarters, each quarter is divided into eight points—in all, thirty-two points in the compass or circle.

The middle point between north and east is north east, between east and south, south east, between south and west, south west, and between west and north, north west.

There are four remarkable parallels of latitude.

1. The tropic of cancer.
2. The tropic of capricorn.
3. The arctic circle.
4. The antarctic circle.

The tropics are 23½ degrees from the equator, the tropic of cancer on the north side of it, and the tropic of capricorn on the south.

The arctic and antarctic circles are 23½ degrees from their respective poles. The former from the north, the latter from the south pole. They are also called the *polar circles*.

These four circles divide the globe into five parts called *zones*, or belts; which, in reference to their respective degrees of heat or cold, are thus named: One, *torrid*, i. e. hot, from the Latin *torridus*—two, *temperate*, i. e. moderate heat or cold, and two, *frigid*, i. e. cold (from the Latin *frigidus*.) The torrid zone is between the two tropics and is therefore 47° in extent, the frigid zones are between the polar circles and the poles, and are each consequently 23½° in extent, the temperate zones are between the torrid and the frigid zones, and are 43° in extent.

These different degrees of heat and cold, as also the changes of the seasons, and the succession of day and night, are the consequence of the earth's relation to the sun. In the course of 365 days the earth performs a revolution round the sun, during which at one part of its course, the north pole, and at another, the south pole, is turned towards the sun, and this produces spring, summer, autumn, and winter. Situated as the earth is in respect to the sun, the rays of the sun must always fall more directly or vertically upon the equator and the parts on each side of it, and so cause greater heat in those parts than in others. Hence the reason of the hot climate of India. The course of the earth round the sun is shown on the globe by the *ecliptic* circle. In the course of 24 hours, also the earth performs a revolution of its own, on its own *axis*, as it is called. Thus each side becomes in turn exposed to the sun, and withdrawn from it, and this causes day and night—but for a full explanation of these things, a book on Astronomy must be studied.

CHAP. II.

The World.

Divisions. THE world used generally to be divided into four principal parts, called, but not properly, *quarters*—namely, Europe, Asia, Africa, and America. To these, however, must be added two other important divisions, viz. Australia, or the continent of the south, (from the Latin *Australis*, southern) consisting of New Holland and the adjacent islands, and Polynesia, or the Many Isles, (from the Greek πολλη *pollē*, many, and νησος *nēsos*, island) consisting of those numerous groups of islands in the Pacific Ocean.

It is also to be observed that there are in the Polar Seas several large islands not included in any of the above divisions.

Population. The total number of inhabitants on the whole earth is estimated to be about eight hundred millions. Of these there are in Asia, including Australia and Polynesia, about six hundred millions. In Africa about thirty millions, America, thirty millions, and in Europe, one hundred and forty millions.

Religion. There are two principal divisions of the inhabitants of the World as to *religion*,—one consisting of those who possess a Revelation from God in His word, the other of those who have none. The first division is composed of Christians and Jews. The second of all others. There are supposed to be about two hundred millions of Christians, three millions of Jews, sixty millions of Mahomedans, and the remainder different divisions of Heathens.

Varieties of the human race. Originally the whole human race sprung from a single pair, namely, Adam and Eve—and after the destruction of the world by the flood, A. M. 1656, the earth was repeopled from only three pairs, namely, the three sons of Noah, Shem, Ham, and Japheth, and their wives.—Among the inhabitants of our world, however, though thus de-

Varieties of the human race.

scended from the same source, there exists an almost infinite variety, as to colour, size, shape; in short as to their mental, moral, and physical construction generally. These varieties have been investigated by many scientific men in order to ascertain their nature and cause, and the most eminent of them have come practically to the same conclusion, namely, that all the varieties of the human race may be reduced to three *primary* divisions—the Caucasian, Mongolian, and Ethiopian. Each of these indeed admits of several subdivisions, but still every one of the numerous differences in the great family of man may be classed under one or other of the above named three branches of the human race.

The Caucasian race, whose original seat is supposed to have been, as the name implies, that lofty chain of mountains between the Black and Caspian Seas, is distinguished by a fair skin, red cheeks, copious, soft, flowing hair, generally curled or waving—ample beard—small, oval, and straight face, with the features very distinct, expanded forehead—large and elevated cranium—narrow nose—and small mouth. These are the prominent characteristics of the race, but in proportion as its various branches, which diverge in every direction from the Caucasian Alps, recede from their original seat, so do their peculiarities become modified, altered, and finally lost. In mental and moral qualifications this race stands first, and from it have sprung the most civilized and powerful nations of both ancient and

Varieties of the human race.

modern times, as for instance, the Greeks and Romans in the former period, the English and French in the latter.

To this variety four branches may be assigned. 1st, The Pelasgic, extending over the greater part of Europe and Western Asia. 2nd, The Syrian, which takes a southerly direction and includes that portion of Asia formerly inhabited by the Assyrians, Chaldeans, and ancient Egyptians. 3rd, The Indian, which passes to the east and loses itself among the Natives of Hindoostan. 4th, The Scythian or Tartaric, spreading over the more northern parts of Asia. The Caucasian race becomes mingled with the Mongolian in the inhabitants of Finland, Lapland, and the central parts of Tartary.

The Mongolian variety has these characteristics:—Skin of an olive yellow—hair thin, coarse, and straight—little or no beard—broad flattened face with the features running together—small and low forehead—square shaped cranium—wide and small nose—very oblique eyes—and thick lips. In moral and intellectual energies, as well as in stature, this race is inferior to the Caucasian. Its origin appears to have been in the mountains of Altai, whence it has spread over the whole of central and northern Asia, losing itself among the Esquimaux on the one hand, and the Caucasian Tartars on the other. It further extends to the Eastern Ocean and includes the Japanese, the Coreans, and a large proportion of the Siberians. Its limits to the south do not appear to

Varieties of the human race.

extend below Northern Hindoostan, the northern parts of Bengal, Bootan, and Assam.

The third leading variety of the human race is the Ethiopian or Negro:— Skin black—hair short, black, and woolly—skull compressed on the sides and elongated towards the front—forehead low, narrow, and slanting—cheek bones very prominent—jaws projecting, so as to render the upper front teeth oblique—eyes prominent—nose broad and flat—lips, especially the upper one, particularly thick. In point of intellect and moral feelings, the African or Ethiopian race is the lowest in the scale of mankind. Different branches of it spread over the whole of the African continent, excepting those parts bordering the north and east of the great desert occupied by the Caucasian Syrians.

Under this head may be included two other variations, which though their differences are not so decidedly marked, as in the three just described, have yet sufficient peculiarities to deserve distinct description, and are reckoned by some as primary divisions. These are the American and Malay. In the American variety, the skin is dark and more or less red—hair black, straight, and strong, with the beard small—face and skull very similar to the Mongolian, but the former not so flattened—eyes sunk, forehead low, nose and other features somewhat projecting. In moral and intellectual character, far inferior to the Caucasian and Mongolian, though superior to the African. This race, as its

Varieties of the human race.

name imports, extends over the whole of the New World, blending with the Mongolian at the north,—the Esquimaux and other Polar races appearing to unite in themselves the characteristics of both the Mongolian and American varieties. The Malay varies in the colour of the skin from a light tawny to a deep brown, approaching to black—hair black, more or less curled, and abundant—head rather narrow—bones of the face large and prominent—nose full and broad towards the tip. Under this variety are included races of men very different in organization and qualities, but still presenting such general points of resemblance as to forbid their being classed under any of the former varieties. In point of extent this variety includes the inhabitants of Malaya, Sumatra, and of the numerous islands in the Indian Archipelago and Pacific Ocean.

Causes of these varieties.

On the causes of these varieties much has been written, but no adequate cause has been discovered. By some they have been attributed to the effect of difference of climate, locality, food, manner of life, and disease. But these upon examination are found to be wholly insufficient to produce such variations as those just described. Climate for instance will not account for the difference of colour, since those living in the same latitude yet vary in colour. These causes, combined with intermarriages between different races, undoubtedly operate in a considerable degree in producing modifications of the great primary

Causes of these varieties.

varieties, and hence the numberless variations of a stronger or slighter kind existing in the earth. For instance in India. Here we find the Caucasian form, but, owing to climate and mode of life, with less muscular development and vigour, and presenting a colour approaching the Ethiopian. Allowing however the utmost influence to the above named causes, it still leaves the reason of the difference between the three primary divisions unaccounted for; nor do we believe it can be accounted for upon any secondary causes, and therefore, the most satisfactory as well as the most philosophical way is to resolve it simply into the *will of God.* It was the will of God that made the three sons of Noah to be the progenitors of the whole race of man, and by His immediate act one hundred years after, their descendants were caused to separate and disperse, and to speak a diversity of tongues. Is it therefore any thing unreasonable to suppose, in the absence of all secondary causes, that it was by God's immediate will that an entire diversity of races was caused to proceed from those three progenitors, knowing too, as we do, that there is no one feature more strongly impressed upon the whole of God's creation than that of *variety.*

CHAP. III.

Asia.

Extent. ASIA extends eastward from the twenty-fifth degree of east longitude to the hundred and seventieth degree of west longitude—and from the seventy-eighth degree of north to the tenth degree of south latitude.

It is about 6000 miles in breadth from the Dardanelles on the west to the eastern coast of Tartary—and about 5500 miles in length from the most northern Cape of Asiatic Russia to the most southern part of Malaya.

Boundaries. It is bounded on the north by the Arctic or Frozen Ocean—north-east by Bherring's Straits, east by the Pacific, south by the Indian Ocean—west by the Indian Ocean, Red Sea, Mediterranean, Black Sea, and Russia in Europe.

Countries. The principal countries of Asia are Tartary, which includes Asiatic Russia, Chinese Tartary, Tartary, and Tibet: Turkey in Asia, Persia, China, Arabia, Hindoostan, or India, Burma, or Ava, Siam, Cochin China, Malaya, and some islands.

The people of Asia are called by the general name of Asiatics. All religions exist among them, the Heathens being the most numerous.

CHAP. IV.

Hindoostan or India.

Extent. HINDOOSTAN is situated in the southern part of Asia, and lies between the eighth and thirty-fifth degrees of north latitude, and the sixty-eighth and ninety-second degrees of east longitude. The extreme length from north to south is about 1,900 miles, and from east to west about 1,500.

Boundaries. It is bounded on the north by the Himalaya Mountains, on the east by Assam, Arracan, and the Bay of Bengal, south by the Indian Ocean, and west by the Arabian Sea and the river Indus, separating it from Beloochistan and Afghanistan.

Divisions. Hindoostan is divided into four large portions, called, Northern Hindoostan, Hindoostan Proper, the Dekkan, and Southern India.

NORTHERN HINDOOSTAN is that part of the country which lies along the south side of the Himalaya Mountains. Its chief divisions' are 1. Cashmeer, 2. Sirmoor, 3. Gurwal, or Sreenuggur, 4. Kumaoon, 5. Nepaul.

HINDOOSTAN PROPER lies between Northern Hindoostan and the river Nurbudda, by which it is bounded on the south. It is divided into the provinces of 1. Lahore, or the Punjaub, 2. Mooltán, 3. Delhi, 4. Oude, 5. Sind, 6. Ajmeer, or Rajpootana, 7. Agra, 8. Kuch, 9. Guze-

Divisions. rat, 10. Malwa, 11. Allahabad, 12. Bahar, 13. Bengal.

THE DEKKAN is bounded on the north by the Nurbudda, and a line, drawn from the source of that river, eastward to the mouth of the Hoogly—on the south it is bounded by the rivers Kistna and Malpurba.

It is divided into the provinces of 1. Khandesh, 2. Gondwana, 3. Berar, 4. Orissa, 5. Aurungabad, 6. Beder, 7. Hyderabad, 8. the Northern Circars, and 9. Bejapoor.

SOUTHERN INDIA, the last division of Hindoostan, includes all the country to the south of the rivers Kistna and Malpurba, and ends at Cape Comorin.

Its chief provinces are the 1. Dooab, 2. Ceded Districts, 3. Northern Carnatic, 4. Kanara, 5. Mysore, 6. Baramahal, 7. Salem, 8. Central Carnatic, 9. Malabar, 10. Koorg, 11. Coimbatoor, 12. Southern Carnatic, 13. Travancore.

The Sea Coast on the west, from Bombay to Cape Comorin is usually called by Europeans the Malabar Coast, from the province of that name which was the first visited by European Navigators; and the coast on the eastern side, from the mouth of the river Kistna to Cape Comorin, the coast of Coromandel, from the ancient Hindoo kingdom of Tanjore, formerly called the *Chola desum*, that is the Chola country, or *Chola mundul*, the Chola sphere or circuit.

Rivers. There are many large rivers in Hindoostan, the principal of which are the following :—

Rivers.

1. The INDUS, called by the Natives, the Sind, and by Mahomedan writers, the Hind. It has not yet been ascertained with certainty where this river rises.

It enters Hindoostan through the mountains of Cashmeer, passes along the western side of Lahore, and running to the south through Mooltan and Sind falls into the Arabian Sea. It is said to be navigable for vessels of 200 tons as far as Lahore. Including its windings the course of this river is supposed to be not less than 1,700 miles in length.

2. The SUTLUJ, called by the Greek writers, the Hyphasis. This river issues from two lakes on the north side of the Himalaya mountains in about lat. 31° 46′ N. and long. 80° 43′ E., passes along the eastern side of Lahore and through Mooltan, and falls into the Chenab, a short distance to the northward of each, after a course of between four and five hundred miles.

3. The JUMNA. This river rises in the Himalaya mountains, to the west of the Ganges and not far from it.

It flows through the province of Sreenuggur, and enters Hindoostan Proper in the province of Delhi. It proceeds southward through Delhi and Agra, and falls into the Ganges at Allahabad. From its source to its joining the Ganges, the length of its course is about 700 miles.

4. The GANGES. This river rises on the south side of the Himalaya mountains. It is first seen in about lat. 31° N. and long. 79° E. where it

Rivers. issues from under a very low arch, at the bottom of a great mass of solid frozen snow, about 300 feet high. Its breadth at this place is about 30 feet, and the depth about one foot. It enters Hindoostan Proper near Hurdwar in the province of Delhi, about 120 miles distant from the city of Delhi. It passes through the provinces of Delhi, Agra, Oude, Allahabad, Bahar, and Bengal, and falls into the Bay of Bengal. About 200 miles from the sea, taking a straight line, or 300 miles taking the windings of the river, the Ganges sends out a number of branches. The two western-most branches, called the Kasimbazar and Julingy rivers, join together at Nuddea, 60 miles from Calcutta, and form the river Hoogly.

Near the sea, the number of branches increases, occupying from the Hoogly to the eastern mouth of the Ganges a space of about 200 miles in breadth, forming a great many islands, called Sundurbunds. The whole course of this river, following its windings, is about 1,500 miles.

5. The BRAHMAPOOTRA. This is the largest river in India. It rises on the north side of the Himalaya mountains, about lat. 32° N. and long. 82° E. It runs eastward through the country of Tibet, and after winding for a great distance through the mountains which divide Tibet from Assam, turns to the westward into Assam, and enters the province of Bengal near Rungamutty. It then passes round the western point of the Garrow mountains, after which it turns to the south and

Rivers. joins the river Megna in the district of Dacca. It then takes the name of Megna, and uniting with the Ganges near the sea, flows with it into the Bay of Bengal. The whole course of this river, following its windings, is about 1,600 miles.

In 1822, this river overflowed its banks in the district of Bakurgunj, and deluged the surrounding country. About 37,000 men and women were destroyed by the flood.

6. The NURBUDDA. This river rises in the province of Gondwana, in about lat. 23° N. and long. 82° E. It runs westward, through the provinces of Gondwana, Malwa, Khandesh and Guzerat, and falls into the sea below Baroach. Including its windings, its course is about 750 miles.

7. The TUPTEE. This river rises near the village of Batool in the northern mountains of Berar. It runs westward, through the provinces of Khandesh and Guzerat, and falls into the sea, below Surat, after a course of about 750 miles.

8. The MUHANUDDEE. This river rises in the province of Gondwana, it is supposed near Kyragur. It runs eastward, in a very winding course, of 550 miles through Gondwana and Orissa, and falls into the Bay of Bengal, in the district of Kuttack. Diamonds of good quality are found in this river.

9. The GODAVERY. This river has its source in the Western Mountains about 70 miles to the north east of Bombay. It runs eastward through the provinces of Aurungabad and Beder, and turning

Rivers. to the south east flows between the provinces of Orissa and Hyderabad, which it separates, and through the northern Circars into the Bay of Bengal. Its whole course is about 850 miles.

10. The KISTNA. This river has its source near the Western Mountains not far from Sutara, in the province of Bejapoor, and about 50 miles from the western coast of India. It flows south-easterly as far as Merrich, where it turns eastward, forms the southern boundary of Beder and Hyderabad, and flows through the northern Circars, by the district of Kondapilly, into the Bay of Bengal. Its whole course is about 700 miles.

11. The TOOMBUDRA. This river is formed by the junction of two other rivers, named the Toonga and the Budra.

The Toonga rises in the Western Mountains a little to the south of Bednore.

The Budra rises in a chain of hills, called the Baba Boodun Hills, situated to the eastward of the Western Mountains, nearly opposite to Mangalore.

The two rivers join at Koorlee, near Hoolee Oonnoor in the province of Mysore, and form one river, called the Toombudra. From this, the Toombudra winds to the north, and north east, and falls into the Kistna, a little beyond Kurnool.

12. The PENNAR. This river rises in the Hills near Nundydroog in the province of Mysore. It runs northward until near Gooty, in the Ceded Districts, when it runs to the eastward and flows

Rivers. between Northern and Central Carnatic into the Bay of Bengal, near Nellore.

13. The PALAR. This river also rises in the hills near Nundydroog, not far from the Pennar. It flows southerly through Mysore and Central Carnatic into the Bay of Bengal, which it reaches near Sadras.

14. The CAVERY. This river rises in the western hills of Koorg, near the province of Malabar, and runs eastward through Mysore, Coimbatoor, and Southern Carnatic.

At Trichinopoly it divides into two branches—the northern branch is named the Coleroon, and flows into the Bay of Bengal at Devicotta.

The southern branch retains the name of the Cavery, and flows through Tanjore by a number of channels into the Bay of Bengal.

Mountains. The most remarkable mountains in Hindoostan, are the following.

1. The HIMALAYA. These mountains, which are believed to be the highest in the world, form the northern boundary of India, separating it from Tibet. Their greatest height has not yet been determined. The highest peak which has been measured is 27,000 feet.

2. The Mountains of Kumaoon between Kumaoon and Sreenuggur.

3. The SEWALICK mountains, which separate Delhi from Sreenuggur.

4. The VINDHYA mountains which extend through Bahar, Allahabad, and Malwa, along the north side of the

Mountains. Nurbudda, almost as far as the western coast of Hindoostan.

5. The WESTERN MOUNTAINS, or Western Ghats. These extend from the Tuptee to Cape Comorin. The highest part of the range is about 6,000 feet above the level of the sea.

6. The EASTERN MOUNTAINS, or Eastern Ghats, which extend from the Kistna to near the Cavery. The highest part of the chain is about 3,000 feet above the sea.

The word *ghat* signifies a *pass* or *ford*. It is commonly used by the English in speaking of these two ranges of mountains, though properly meaning only the passes through them.

7. The NEILGHERRY mountains, forming a connecting range between the Eastern and Western Mountains, through the province of Coimbatoor. Their highest point is estimated at 8,800 feet above the sea.

Productions. There are many large forests in India. In the Western Mountains the trees grow to a very great size, particularly the Teak.

Of the various kinds of trees in India, the principal are the Teak, Banyan, Cocoanut, Palmyra, and Bamboo. The chief fruits are the Plantain, Mangoe, Lime, and Guava. The principal grain produced is Rice.

The wild animals of India, are principally Elephants, Rhinoceroses, Tigers, Bears, Leopards, Panthers, Lynxes, Hyenas, Wolves, Buffaloes, Bisons, Hogs, various species of Deer, Apes, Monkeys, Jackals, and Foxes.

Productions.

The tame animals are Camels, Horses, Asses, Oxen, Sheep, Goats, and others.

There are various kinds of birds, of which the Peacock, Vulture, Crow, and Kite are the chief.

Reptiles of almost every kind abound in India. The Cobra and the Alligator being the most formidable.

The mineral productions of India are diamonds and other precious stones, gold, in small quantities in some of the rivers, iron, and a little copper and lead.

Climate.

Situated as India is in point of latitude, and varying in height from the level of the sea to the summits of the Himalaya, it cannot but have very different degrees of heat and cold. On the general level of India, however, and within the great northern chain the climate is one of heat, especially for three months at least in the year, when hot winds prevail. In India the rain falls periodically at certain seasons called monsoons, and at those times with such violence as to exceed in quantity all that falls in England during the course of the whole year. On the Malabar Coast the rain is brought up from the Indian Ocean by a south-west wind, which prevails between June and October. On the Coromandel Coast the rain is brought from the Bay of Bengal by a north-east wind, during October and November.

Inhabitants.

The Natives of India are commonly divided by Europeans into two classes, Hindoos and Mahomedans.

Under the former appellation are in

Inhabitants. cluded all who are not Mahomedans, whether followers of the Brahminical system, or of the Jain or Booddhist, and of whatever caste. European writers also frequently designate the Hindoos of Southern India by the names of Gentoos and Malabars, meaning by the former the Telingas or Teloogoos, and by the latter the Tamil people. Throughout India, taking one country with another, it may be estimated that there are about seven Hindoos to one Mahomedan.

The total population is believed to be about one hundred and forty-one millions, of which about one hundred millions are subjects of the British Government.

Besides the Hindoos and Mahomedans, there are a number of tribes who inhabit the hills and forests, and who apparently belong to a distinct race. They are in a very rude state, and are supposed to be descended from the aborigines of the country, who were driven into the mountains and woods by the Hindoos.

They are noticed in connection with the several provinces in which they are now principally found.

It is also to be noticed that there is in India a numerous class consisting of those who are called East Indians, or Indo-Britons, descendants of European and Native parents. Also a large number of the descendants of the Portuguese, who are closely intermingled with the Natives.

Besides the British there are also many French, American, Dutch, German, and Danish residents in India. On the Malabar coast there are many Jews.

History.

Of the early history of India little is known with any certainty, the Hindoos having no historical record that deserves the name, and such records as they do possess are mixed up with so many monstrous fables that it is difficult to ascertain from them any thing upon which dependence can be placed.

From the Vedas, however, which are believed to have been compiled in the fourteenth century before the Christian era, and from the Institutes of Menu which were probably drawn up in the ninth century before Christ, there is reason to suppose that India anciently comprised several separate kingdoms, varying in power and extent, and, as appears from the Ramayana, Pooranas, and other writings, engaged in constant wars among themselves. It has been said that India was first invaded by Darius, the King of Persia, but it seems certain that he never crossed the Indus, and that the first invasion was that of the Greeks under Alexander the Great, about B. C. 327.

No permanent settlement was made by the Greeks, and from this period there is a blank in our records of Indian history until A. D. 664, when the Mahomedans made their first invasion, and entered the province of Mooltan. Several invasions followed, but no permanent dominion was established by the Mahomedans, and in A. D. 750, a general insurrection breaking out against them, they were entirely expelled, and the Hindoo Princes recovered the whole of their territories. India then continu-

History. ed under its Native Sovereigns until A. D. 1001, when the celebrated Sooltan Mahmood of Ghuznee determined upon adding it to his empire. He made no less than twelve expeditions into the country, in the course of which he overran most of the western provinces of Hindoostan Proper, and took and plundered Delhi, which, however, he afterwards restored to its Hindoo Raja.

From this time India was constantly exposed to the attacks of the Mahomedans, and, in 1193, Delhi was again taken by Kootbood Deen, who founded the first Afghan or Pathan Sovereignty, which continued until 1525, when Sooltan Baber, grandson of Tymoor, conquered Ibraheem Lodi, and founded what has been usually denominated the Mooghul Empire.

During the reign of the Pathan Sovereigns India was twice invaded by the Mahomedans of Tartary and Toorkistan, namely, in 1221 by the celebrated Mooghul, Zinghis Khan, *(Jungez Khan)* and, in 1398, by Tamerlane, *(Tymoor Lung.)*

Sooltan Baber was not a Mooghul, but from the time of Jungez Khan, all Tartars and Persians seem to have been called in India by the general name of Mooghuls, and thus the empire founded by Sooltan Baber has always been so designated, although Baber himself was a decided enemy to that people.

Under the Mooghul Sovereigns, the empire rapidly extended until it comprehended all the principal provinces of Hindoostan. In 1582, the empire was

History. divided by the emperor Akber, the grandson of Baber, into 11 soobas or provinces, namely Lahore, Mooltan, Ajmeer, Delhi, Agra, Allahabad, Bahar, Oude, Bengal, Malwa, and Guzerat, to which were afterwards added Cabool and the countries west of the Indus, and Berar, Khandesh, and Ahmednuggur in the Dekkan. Other Mahomedan governments were also established towards the south, sometimes independent, and sometimes paying tribute to the emperor of Delhi. The Mooghul empire attained its greatest extent of power and prosperity under Aurungzeb, great grandson of Akber, who reigned from 1658 to 1707. After his death one weak prince succeeded another till the invasion of India by the Persian Koolee Khan or Nadir Shah, in 1738 and 1739. From this period, the Mooghul empire rapidly decayed, the various provinces became independent principalities, some under their Mahomedan governors, others under the Mahrattas, until the city of Delhi, with a small district around, formed all that remained to the house of Tymoor. The first European settlement in India was made in 1497, when the celebrated Portuguese Navigator, Vasco de Gama, arrived at Calicut. The Portuguese soon acquired considerable influence with the Native Governments and established themselves in numerous towns and forts upon the coast from Surat to Chittagong, including Ceylon, fixing the capital of all their possessions and the seat of Government at Goa. The Portuguese were shortly followed by the Dutch, and suc-

History. cessively by the English, French, and Danes. In the wars which took place between the Portuguese and Dutch, the power of the former was nearly annihilated, and all their settlements, with the exception of Goa, were taken from them. The Dutch in their turn were supplanted by the English and French, which two nations for many years disputed the superiority, until after much warfare the ascendancy of the English was finally established. The Danes never made any extensive settlement, having merely a few ports on the coast for the purposes of commerce. Various circumstances, for the detailed account of which we must refer the student to the History of British India, led the English forward, in a manner altogether unexpected and unintended by them, until nearly the whole of Hindoostan became subject to their rule. The following is an abstract of their territorial possessions with the date of their acquisition.

A.D. 1639—Madras, with a territory five miles along shore by one mile inland.
1664—Bombay.
1691—Fort St. David (Cuddalore.)
1696—Calcutta.
1750— to 1763— The Jaghire (Jageer) a small district extending from Pulicat to Alumparva, and westward to Conjeveram, being about 100 miles along shore, and 50 inland in the widest part.
1757—The 24 Purgunnas in Bengal.

History.

A.D. 1761—Chittagong, Burdwan, and Midnapoor.
1765—Bengal, Bahar, and four of the Northern Circars.
1776—Salsette.
1781—Benares.
1787—Guntoor Circar.
1792—Malabar, Kanara, Coimbatoor, Salem, Dindigul, and the Baramahal.
1799—Seringapatam.
1800—Balaghat Ceded Districts.
1801—Rohilkhund, and various Districts in Agra, Allahabad, Oude, and other provinces.
1801—The Carnatic, comprising the whole of the territory subject to the Nabob of Arcot.
1803—Ceylon.
1803—Delhi, Agra, the Dooab, Bundelkhund, Kuttak, &c.
1803—Guzerat.
1805—Gurwal and other parts of northern Hindoostan.
1816—Kuch.
1818—The whole of the Peshwa's Dominions, Khandesh, Malwa, the town of Ajmeer, and part of Gondwana.
1834—Koorg.

The several States amongst which India is now divided may be classed as follows.

The British.
The Nizam of Hyderabad,
The Raja of Nagpore,
The King of Oude,
The Guikowar of Guzerat,
} Allies and Tributaries of the British.

History.

The Raja of Mysore, The Raja of Travancore and numerous petty Chiefs,	Allies and Tributaries of the British.
The Raja of the Punjab, The Raja of Nepaul, Ameers of Sind, Sindia (Gualioor,)	Independent.

A few small settlements on the coasts are still possessed by the French, Portuguese, and Danes, but are none of them of sufficient importance to require separate notice.

They are included in the several provinces in which they are situated.

Name.

The name "Hindoostan" is of Persian origin and signifies the "Hindoo country" from Hindoo and "istan" country or region. It is also called simply "Hind." Mahomedan writers apply the name Hindoostan only to that portion of the country which was under Mahomedan rule.

The name "India" was first given to this country by the Greeks, who so called it from the river Indus. From them therefore the name India has been adopted. Europeans also frequently apply to this country the name of "East Indies." This originated in the circumstance of the Islands on the eastern side of America having been mistaken, when they were first discovered, for part of India, which led to their being designated as the West Indies; and, afterwards, for the purpose of distinguishing between them, India was generally styled the *East Indies*.

Though designated by the one general name of Hindoostan, or India, it, in reality, consists of a number of distinct countries, differing from each other in about as great a degree as do the various countries of Europe.

Religion. The prevailing religions of India, are the Brahminical system and Mahomedanism.

The Brahminical system, or, as it is commonly designated, Hindooism, appears to have been introduced into India, and probably from the West, at a very early period.

It is first known to have existed in a small tract of country to the north-west of Delhi, whence it gradually spread, partly by conquest, and partly by colonization, throughout India.

It is taught in four books called Vedas, the Institutes of Menu, and eighteen others, called Pooranas.

The Vedas seem to have been written at different periods, but to have been compiled, in their present form, in the fourteenth century before Christ. They are written in an ancient form of Sanscrit, which none but the more learned Brahmins can understand.

The Institutes of Menu, which contain a code of laws founded upon the Vedas, are considered to have been drawn up in the ninth century before Christ.

The Pooranas were written by different authors between the eighth and sixteenth centuries of the Christian era, and they constitute the principal source from which the Hindoos are accustomed to derive their notions of religion.

Hindooism may be very briefly des-

Religion. cribed as a very complicated system of idolatry, combining a kind of vague declaration of the unity of a Supreme Being with the worship of a multitude of gods and goddesses, amounting, according to some accounts, to upwards of three hundred millions.

It is chiefly distinguished from other pagan religions by the division of the people into *castes*. The word cast, or caste, is an English word, but used only in India in the sense of a class. It is derived from the Portuguese *casta*, a breed. These, originally, were four in number, Brahmins, Kshatriyas, (or Rajpoots,) Vesiyas, and Soodras; but, in course of time, each of these has been subdivided into an indefinite number of classes, each of which maintains a scrupulous separation from the other; and, out of these subdivisions, have arisen several castes, not acknowledged as belonging to any of the four great divisions, and considered to be inferior to them all.

Those in Southern India, who are now commonly called *Pariars*, are, in all probability the descendants of the original inhabitants. Many of the most celebrated Tamil books, for example, are by Pariar authors, which could never have been the case, had not their literature been formed before the introduction of Brahminism.

There are three principal sects of worshippers, the Saivas, followers of Siva; Vaishnavas, followers of Vishnoo; and the Saktas, followers of the Suktees, or wives of the Gods.

There are two other religions, which,

Religion. although distinct from Brahminism, appear to belong to the same stock. These are the Booddhist and Jain systems.

The Booddhist system appears to have been founded by Gaotuma, a Sukya Mooni or *great saint*, a native of Kapila near Gorukpoor, in the province of Oude, about the middle of the sixth century before Christ.

The Booddhists deny the authority of the Vedas and Pooranas, and have no distinction of caste. Some of their sects are mere atheists, not acknowledging any Supreme Being; others have a confused notion of what they term a Divine Essence.

This system has few followers now in any part of India, excepting in Northern Hindoostan and Ceylon, having been generally driven out in the eighth or ninth century.

The Jains hold an intermediate place between the Booddhists and the followers of the Brahminical system, agreeing partly with both. Their system appears to have originated in the course of the sixth or seventh century of the Christian era. It spread itself chiefly in Southern India and in Guzerat and the western parts of Hindoostan Proper. They are still numerous in Guzerat, Rajpootana, and Kanara.

The Sikh religion is noticed in the account of Lahore.

Mahomedanism derives its name from its founder, Mahomed, sometimes improperly called Mahomet, who was born at Mecca, in Arabia, A. D. 569, of the family of Hashim, and of the tribe of Koreish,

Religion. who were the hereditary keepers of the principal temple of the Arabs, at Mecca, called the Kaaba. Both his parents died when he was yet a child, and, being left without the means of subsistence, he was taken into the family of his uncle, Aboo Talib, by whom he was instructed in the arts of war and commerce. At the age of twenty-five, he became the factor or agent of a rich widow, named Kadija, whom he soon afterwards married, and thus raised himself from a state of obscurity and indigence to an equality with the proudest merchants of Mecca.

Though but imperfectly educated, he was a man of considerable eloquence, and possessed of great energy of character; and influenced, partly by feelings of disgust towards the gross idolatry which then prevailed among his countrymen and partly by strong personal ambition, he formed the design of effecting a reformation, and of establishing a new religion of which he should be himself the head. For several years he had been living in retirement, during which period his mind was continually occupied with his great project. He had had, also, occasional intercourse with certain Monks, or Syrian Christians, as well as with Jewish Rabbins, all which tended to confirm him in his views. At last, about the year 609, he announced to his wife, Kadija, that he had received a mission from God, by the Angel Gabriel, and, having been acknowledged by her and some others of the family, particularly his youthful cousin Ali, he began publicly to preach the doctrine of the unity of

Religion. God, and to denounce idolatry, promising both present and future rewards to those who acknowledged that there was but one God, and that Mahomed was his prophet. For many years, though he laboured incessantly to convince his countrymen of the reality of his mission, he gained but few converts. His own tribe became bitterly opposed to him, and in A. D. 622, his uncle Aboo Talib, and his wife Kadija, having both died about three years before, Mahomed, in consequence of a plot which had been formed by the Koreish for his destruction, was compelled to fly from Mecca to Medina. From this event, called the Hijra, or flight, the Mahomedans compute their time.

Hitherto Mahomed had declared that he had no authority to use force to compel any one to embrace his religion,—but now, finding himself supported by a strong party at Medina, he announced that the angel Gabriel had commanded him to propagate the true faith by the sword. His followers were now promised the plunder of their enemies, and immediate happiness in paradise if killed in their holy war. From this moment his cause prospered, and he was soon at the head of a powerful army, which, under his able command, rapidly extended his authority on all sides. His subsequent career was most successful. He defeated his opponents in repeated battles, and, in the course of a few years, compelled the whole of the Arab tribes to submit to his Government, and to embrace his religion. He died in the 63rd year of his age, at Medina, A. D. 632.

Religion. The doctrines and precepts of Mahomed, with his pretended revelation from Heaven, are contained in a book called the Koran, which means "the reading," or that which ought to be read. By Europeans it is often incorrectly termed the Alcoran,—the prefix *al* being the Arabic article *the*.

This volume he is thought to have composed with the help of a Jewish Rabbi and two Syrian Christians, and the number of monkish legends and tales from the Talmud, which are found in different parts of the Koran, appear to put this beyond doubt. It may safely be affirmed, that whatever truth it contains is taken from the Bible.

The fundamental principle laid down is this, "There is but one God and Mahomed is his Prophet." It teaches a strict fatalism, that is, that every action and event of a man's life, whether good or bad, is absolutely predestinated. It inculcates a belief in the existence of angels, good and evil, and also of an intermediate order of creatures called génii, both good and bad. It asserts the doctrine of a general resurrection, a judgment to follow, and a future state of reward and punishment—the latter, however, being *eternal* only in the case of infidels, or unbelievers of the Koran. It was Mahomed's plan to gain converts and to keep them faithful, by holding out both present and future rewards of a sensual kind, and, accordingly, we find the pleasures of Heaven described in the Koran as being all sensual, the pains of Hell all physical, —neither are of a moral character. It is

Religion.

undoubtedly to this adaptation of the system to corrupt human nature, that Mahomedanism owes chiefly, though combined with other causes, its widely spread propagation. The Koran teaches also the meritoriousness of human actions, and hence enjoins the observance of festivals, regular prayers, (the face being turned towards Mecca,) washings, alms-giving, fasting, and pilgrimages to Mecca, as so many means of expiating sin, and earning the joys of Paradise. It forbids usury, games of chance, the use of wine, and eating blood, swine's flesh, &c.

The places of public worship are called Mosques, from the minarets or high towers of which, the people are called to prayers by appointed officers, called Muezzins. Women may not enter a mosque, but stay in the porches without. The priests and doctors, or men learned in the Koran, are called Moollas, the chief of whom has the title of Mufti, and, formerly, great power was attached to his office.

There are, amongst the Mahomedans, innumerable sects, differing in various particulars from one another, but the whole may be classed under the two great divisions of Soonnees and Shiahs.

The Soonnees, or "orthodox," (*lawful,*) insist on the supremacy of Mahomed over all created beings, and on the right succession of Aboo Bikr, Oomer, Oosman, and Ali, as the first four Caliphs, or successors of Mahomed, and they acknowledge the authority of various traditions. The Shiahs, or "heretics," reject all traditions, insisting upon the sole

Religion. authority of the Koran, and they stigmatize Aboo Bikr, Oomer, and Oosman, as usurpers, considering that the rightful successor was Ali alone, whom they hold to have been equal to Mahomed, and are accustomed to style, the Vicar of God. Both sects exist in India, the Soonees being the most numerous sect in Hindoostan Proper, and the Shiahs in the Deccan and Southern India.

The proper name of this religion is Mahomedanism, and of its followers Mahomedans, as those terms simply imply connection with Mahomed. In India, however, the Mahomedans are commonly styled *Moosulmans*, and their religion *Islam*, both derived from an Arabic root, signifying *submission*, (to God,) *peace*, *safety*. They are also frequently called *Moslems*, (Mooslims,) from the same root.

Language. Different dialects are spoken in the different provinces, as noticed in the description of each,—those of Hindoostan Proper, and part of the Deccan being principally derived from the Sanscrit, and those of Southern India being principally derived from the Tamil.

The Sanskrit is generally considered to be one of the most perfectly formed languages in the world. It has long been a dead language, and there is reason to doubt whether it ever was commonly used for colloquial purposes. It is written from left to right in a character called the Deva Nagree.

Tamil appears to have been the general language of Southern India, and to have

Language. been the original source of the Malayalim, Kanarese, Teloogoo, Mahrattee, and Ooreea. It is known to have attained a highly polished form, some time prior to the introduction of the Brahminical system, though, together with other dialects, it has since received a large admixture of Sanskrit.

The general language of the Mahomedans throughout India, with slight provincial variations, is the Hindoostanee. This is of modern origin, having been gradually formed by the mixture of the various dialects spoken by the different tribes of Mahomedan invaders, and the natives of the country. It is written sometimes in the Deva Nagree, but most generally in the Persian character.

The dialects of the various hill tribes are still, for the greater part, entirely distinct from the others, and have no written character.

CHAP. V.

NORTHERN HINDOOSTAN.

§ 1.

Cashmeer (Kasmeer.)

Boundaries. CASHMEER is bounded on the north and north-east by the Himalaya mountains, separating it from Tibet; and on the east, south, and west by Lahore.

Rivers. Its principal river is the Jelum which traverses it from east to west. There are also numerous smaller streams, and lakes, many of them navigable for boats, affording means of communication, and copiously watering the province throughout.

General Description. Cashmeer consists of a valley of an oval form, about 60 miles from north to south and 110 miles from east to west, surrounded on all sides by lofty mountains. There is a tradition, which seems from appearances to be well founded, that the whole of this valley was once the bed of a large lake. It is generally of a level surface, and is celebrated throughout Asia for the beauty of its situation, the fertility of its soil, and the pleasantness of its climate. Earthquakes are, however, frequent, and on this account the houses are usually built of wood.

Productions.

This province yields abundant crops of rice. It also produces wheat, barley, and other grains, various kinds of fruits and flowers common to Europe, as well as those generally found in Asia, sugar, wine, and a superior sort of saffron. Iron of an excellent quality is found in the mountains. Cashmeer is famous for the manufacture of very fine shawls. The wool of which these are made is brought from Tibet, and prepared in Cashmeer. The natives are likewise very clever in all kinds of lacquered ware and cabinet work, and they make the best writing paper in Asia.

Towns.

The principal towns are Cashmeer, and Islamabad.

Cashmeer, formerly called Sreenuggur, is the capital. It is situated on both banks of the river Jelum, in lat. 33° 23′ N.; long. 74° 47′ E., and contains about 150,000 inhabitants. Travelling distance from Agra, 730 miles—from Bombay, 1,300—from Calcutta 1,560—from Madras 1,900.

Islamabad is also a large town. It is situated on the north side of the Jelum, about 30 miles E. S. E. from Cashmeer.

Name.

In the memoirs of Sooltan Baber it is stated that the hilly country along the upper course of the river Sind was formerly inhabited by a race of men named Kas, and he supposes that the country of Cashmeer (Kasmeer) derives its name from them, as being the country of the *Kas*; the affix, "*meer*," being found united to various other names in the same manner, as Aj-meer, Jussul-meer, &c. By others the name is derived from Kasyapa, its first ruler.

Inhabitants.

The natives of Cashmeer, or, as they are generally denominated, Cashmerians, are partly of Hindoo and partly of Afghan and Mooghul origin. They are a stout, well formed people, of a gay and lively disposition, and much addicted to literature and poetry. The Cashmerian females have always been noted for their beauty and their fair complexions—and were formerly much sought after for wives by the Mooghul Noblemen of Delhi. The mountains are inhabited by tribes entirely distinct from the Cashmerians of the valley, but scarcely any thing is yet known about them. The total population of the valley is supposed to be about 600,000.

History.

According to tradition, the valley of Cashmeer was first drained and colonised by Kasyapa, about 2,700 years before the Christian era, and continued under the rule of a succession of Hindoo kings until conquered by the Mahomedans some time during the 11th century, when it came under the government of a long race of Tartar Princes. In 1586, it was subdued by Akber, and annexed to the empire of Delhi, with which it remained until 1750, when it was taken possession of by Ahmed Shah Abdalli of Cabool. In 1809 the Afghan Soobadar, or governor of the province, taking advantage of the disturbed state of affairs in Cabool, threw off his allegiance, and established himself as an independent sovereign.

Cashmeer has since been in a very unsettled state, exposed to invasion from Cabool, and latterly from Lahore. It is at present under the government of the Sikhs.

Religion. Mahomedanism may be considered the predominant system of religion—but there are also many Hindoos. The whole of this province is still considered holy land by the latter class.

Language. The general language of the province is styled Kasmeeree. It is a dialect derived from the Sanskrit, somewhat resembling the Mahratee. Their songs are usually written in Persian.

§ 2.

Sirmoor.

Boundaries. North, the Himalayas; east, the Jumna, separating it from Gurwal; south, Delhi; and east, the Sutluj, separating it from Lahore.

Divisions. None of any note.

Rivers. Sutluj, Paber, Tonse or Tonsa, and Jumna.

General Description. With the exception of a small portion, called the Karda Doon, the whole of this province consists of ranges of mountains, with narrow valleys and ravines. The Karda Doon is a valley in the south-eastern part, bordering upon the Jumna, consisting principally of marsh and low jungle, but capable of being rendered very fruitful. Coal is found near Nahan.

Towns. Simla, Subathoo, and Nahan.

Subathoo is a military post in lat. 30° 58′ N. long. 76° 59′ E.

Simla is a station on the hills near Subathoo, about 7,000 feet above the level of the sea, which has been recently formed by the English, who resort to it on account of its cool and healthful climate.

Nahan is situated in lat. 30° 33′ N. long. 77° 16′ E. It is a neat open town, and the capital of the Raja.

Name. The origin of the name Sirmoor is not known.

Inhabitants. The inhabitants, usually called Sirmorees, are Hindoos, including a large proportion of Rajpoots.

History. Very little is known of the history of this province—it appears to have been for many years under the government of a race of Rajpoot princes, said to have come, originally, from Jussulmeer. Towards the end of the eighteenth century it was conquered by the Goorkhas, from whom it was reconquered in 1814 by the English, who restored it to the Raja, with the exception of Karda Doon, which they retained.

Religion. The religion of the province is the Brahminical.

Language. The Khasiya dialect.

§ 3.

Kumaoon.

Boundaries. North, the Himalayas; east, Nepal, from which it is divided by the river Kalee; south, Delhi; and west, Gurwal.

Divisions. Kumaoon, Bhootant, and Painkhundee.

Rivers. Ganges on the west, and Kalee on the east.

General Description. The whole of this province is mountainous. At the foot of the hills on the Delhi side is a belt of jungle, and higher up, throughout the ranges of mountains, are forests, producing various kinds of trees, including the oak and fir. Parts of the province are open and naked, particularly about Almora.

The northern part of Bhootant, through which are several passes into Tibet, is covered with snow during more than half the year.

Productions. The productions of this province are principally a coarse kind of wheat, barley, and chenna. The tea plant grows wild, but not fit to use. In the forests are oak and fir; and gold is supposed to exist in the mountains. In the Painkhundee cedars grow of a large size, and hemp. Paper of a particular kind is manufactured from a plant in this district.

Towns. The only place of any consequence in the province is Almora, situated in lat.

Towns. 29° 35′ N. long. 79° 44′ E. about 90 miles to the northward of Bareilly. It is the modern capital of the province.

Name. The origin of the name of this province is not known.

Inhabitants. Bhooteeas and Khasiyas, with about 6,000 Brahmins scattered through the districts, but the province is very thinly inhabited.

History. This province appears to have been, in early times, an independent principality under a Brahminical government. In 1790, it was conquered by the Goorkhas, and annexed to the kingdom of Nepal, from which it was taken by the English during the war with that country in 1815; and it is now part of the British dominions.

Religion. The Brahminical system generally prevails.

Language. The Khasiya dialect is commonly spoken in this province.

§ 4.

Gurwal.

Boundaries. North, Himalaya mountains; east, Kumaoon; south, Delhi; west, the Jumna, separating it from Sirmoor.

Divisions. Gurwal, the sources of the Ganges, and Deyra Doon.

Rivers.

Ganges, called in this province, the Bhagirathi, Alcananda which joins the Bhagirathi at Devaprayaga, where the two form what is then called the Ganges and the Jumna.

General Description.

The whole of this province consists of an assemblage of hills, some covered with trees and verdure, others perfectly bare and stony, affording shelter neither for birds nor beasts. The valleys are all narrow, often little more than mere watercourses between the hills. Only a small portion of the country is either populated or cultivated, the larger part being left to the wild animals.

Productions.

There are extensive forests of oak and fir, and also copper mines of some value.

Towns.

Barahat and Sreenuggur.

Barahat, situated on the bank of the Ganges in lat. 30° 35′ N. long. 78° 22′ E., is the modern capital of the province.

Sreenuggur, the former capital, is in lat. 30° 11′ N. long. 78° 44′ E.

In the mountains, on the north-eastern side of the Deyra Doon, are the stations of Landour and Mussoorie. These have been formed by the English, who resort to them for change of air, the climate being cold and healthful.

Name.

This province is often called Sreenuggur from its former capital. The origin of the name Gurwal is not known.

Inhabitants.

The inhabitants are generally termed Khasiyas, but they claim to be considered as the descendants of Hindoos and reject the former name.

History. The province appears originally to have been under the rule of a petty raja, who, about the middle of the fifteenth century, was expelled by a Rajpoot Chief from the south, whose descendants were afterwards known as the Sreenuggur Rajas. In 1803 the province was conquered by the Goorkhas, from whom it was reconquered by the English in 1815, and by them restored to the raja, who now holds it under their protection; with the exception of the southern frontier district, called the Deyra Doon, which was retained by the English.

Religion. The religion of the inhabitants is the Brahminical.

Language. The prevailing language is the Khasee.

§ 5.

Nepal.

Boundaries. North, the Himalayas, separating it from Tibet; east, Sikhim; south, Bengal, Bahar, Oude, and Delhi; west, Kumaoon.

Divisions. Jemla, Goorkba, Nepal, Mukwanpoor, Morung.

Rivers. Kalee, Suryoo, which, joining together at Bramadee, form the Goggra, and Gunduk.

Rivers.

The Gunduck is supposed to rise in the Himalayas, and flows into the Ganges near Patna. The upper part of the river is called the Salgramee, from the stones called Salgrams which are found in it. These stones are considered sacred by the Hindoos, and are carried for sale to all parts of India. Some have been sold for as much as 2,000 rupees each.

General Description.

The lower part of the country, lying along the borders of Oude and Bahar, and which is called the Turiyanee, (*low lands*,) consists of a long belt or strip of low level land. Beyond this is a strip of nearly the same width of hills and valleys, rising gradually towards the north. The upper or northern part is composed of high mountains terminating in the Himalayas.

Productions.

Wheat, oats, barley, millet, maize, and other grains; and, in the valleys, large quantities of rice, which forms the principal article of food. Sugar and cardamums, wax, dammer, and oil. Amongst other trees, the forests produce oak and pine, with rattans and bamboos, both of enormous size. Elephants are numerous. The sheep are large and their wool good. Iron and copper are found in the hills.

The sheep and goats are used in the mountain districts to carry burdens. These animals being saddled with small bags of grain are despatched in flocks under the charge of a few shepherds and their dogs. An old ram furnished with a bell leads them.

Towns. Malebum, Goorkha, Khatmandoo, Lalitaputtun, Mukwanpoor.

Malebum stands on the west bank of the Gunduk, in lat. 28° 32′ N. long. 83° 13′ E.

Goorkha is situated in lat. 27° 52′ N. long. 84° 22′ E. This was formerly the capital of the Goorkhas, before the formation of the present kingdom of Nepal.

Khatmandoo, the capital of Nepal, stands upon the bank of a small river called the Bishenmuttee, in lat. 27° 42′ N. long. 85° E.

Lalitaputtun stands about a couple of miles to the south of Katmandoo. This is the largest town in Nepal, and contains about 25,000 inhabitants.

Name. The name of the province is said to be derived from that of its first raja.

Inhabitants. The inhabitants of Nepal are composed of a number of tribes of different origin, and differing from one another in their language and manners. The original inhabitants appear to have been of Tartar descent. They now chiefly occupy the northern parts. The tribes occupying the central and southern districts form a mixed race, partly Tartar and partly Hindoo. Of these the principal are the Goorkhas, composed mostly of Khasiyas and Mugurs, both original tribes, and the Purbuttees and Newars. The Mugurs constitute the principal military force. The Purbuttees usually inhabit the mountains and are a pastoral race; while the Newars live in the valleys, and are engaged in agriculture and commerce.

History. This country appears, in early times, to have been divided into a number of little principalities, the chiefs of which were most frequently at war with one another, but still continuing independent. About the year 1320 the district of Nepal was subdued by a Rajpoot Chief from Oude. It subsequently passed under the government of a chief of Newar origin, with whose family it remained till 1768, when it was conquered by the Goorkha Chief, Prithi Narrain. His successors prosecuted their conquests until their territory extended to the Sutluj on the west, and Bhootan on the east. Continuing their encroachments along their southern frontier also, they at last came in contact with the British provinces, until, in 1814, in consequence of an attack made by them upon two of the English stations, the latter were obliged to declare war against them. The war lasted for more than two years, and, at first, through mismanagement, the English sustained several severe defeats; ultimately, however, the English were victorious, and, in 1816, when the army, under Sir David Ochterlony, had arrived within three days' march of Katmandoo, the raja was compelled to submit, and to give up all his conquests beyond the river Kalee on the west, and Morung upon the east, within which limits it has since remained.

Religion. The prevailing religion is the Brahminical, but many of the tribes still follow a sect of Booddhism, and, latterly Mahomedanism has been introduced.

Language. A number of different dialects are spoken, of which the principal is the Purbuttee, called, in the western parts the Khasee, which appears to be derived from the Hinduwee, and is written in a character resembling the Nagree.

CHAP. VI.

HINDOOSTAN PROPER.

§ 1.

Lahore or the Punjab.

Boundaries. North, the Himalayas, Cashmeer, and the Himalayas; east, the Sutluj, separating it from Delhi; south, Mooltan; west, the Indus.

Divisions. The province is divided into a number of small districts for the purposes of government, but the two principal natural divisions may be said to be the Lower Punjab, or level country, between the rivers, and the Kohistan, or hill country, occupying the northern part.

Rivers.

The principal rivers are the Indus, Jelum, Chenab, Ravee, Beya or Beas, and Sutluj.

The Indus and Sutluj have been already described.

The Jelum, called, by the Greek writers the Hydaspes, has its source in the south-eastern corner of Cashmeer, and flowing first westward, and afterwards to the south, falls into the Chenab, after a course of about 450 miles, 100 miles above Mooltan.

The Chenab, which is the largest of the five rivers forming the Punjab, rises in the Himalayas, eastward of Cashmeer, and flowing south-westerly is joined by the Jelum at Trimoo Ghat. Lower down, about 50 miles north of Mooltan, it receives the Ravee, and a little above Ooch, it is joined by the Sutluj, or, as it is also called at this part, the Garra, whence it flows south-westerly into the Indus at Mittun. The Chenab is considered to be the Acesines of the Greeks.

The Ravee, or Hydraotes of the Greeks, rises in the Kohistan, near the Himalayas, and flowing south-westerly past the city of Lahore, joins the Chenab about 50 miles to the northward of Mooltan.

The Beya or Beas, the Hyphasis of the Greeks, also rises in the Himalayas, and falls into the Sutluj some distance above Ferozepoor.

General Description.

The Kohistan division, as implied by the name, is hilly throughout, and its productions are not numerous; the cold, for some months, being too severe for

General Description.

those of India generally, and the heat during others being too great for those of more northern climates. The declivities of the mountains, however, produce abundant crops of wheat, barley, and peas, which constitute the principal articles of food of the inhabitants.

The Punjab is generally level, and affords both pasturage and tillage. It yields wheat, barley, rice, pulses of all sorts, sugar, and tobacco. Horses of tolerably good quality are bred in great numbers, and the oxen and buffaloes are of a large powerful kind. Large quantities of fossil salt are found in many places, particularly between the Indus and the Jelum.

Towns.

Attok, Rawulpindee, Rotas, Kishtawur, Lahore, Umritsir.

Attok is a fortress situated on the eastern bank of the Indus, in lat. 33° 56′ N. long. 71° 57′ E. It is noticed as being placed on the principal route across the Indus, and as marking the point at which Alexander the Great, Tymoor, and Nadir Shah all entered India. The name Attok, (*Utok*,) means *limit* or *hindrance*. It is a place of little strength, and does not contain more than 2,000 inhabitants.

Rawulpindee is a populous and well built town, situated in lat. 35° 36′ N. long. 73° 45′ E.

Rotas, situated about 100 miles to the northward of Lahore, is a strong fortress, much celebrated in the early history of the Mahomedans in India, as one of their

Towns.

main bulwarks between Tartary and Hindoostan.

Lahore, the capital of the Punjab, is situated on the south side of the Ravee, lat. 31° 36′ N. long. 74° 3′ E.

In the earliest times of which we have any historical record, this appears to have been a place of consequence as the capital of the Rajpoot Kings of Lahore. Subsequently, in the year 1520, Sooltan Baber made it the capital of his empire, and it continued to be the seat of government for nearly a hundred years. Though the old city is now, in many parts, nearly in ruins, it still retains the vestiges of its former grandeur, and contains several magnificent edifices, particularly the palace built by the Emperor Akbar, the Shah Dura, or Mausoleum of the Emperor Juhangeer on the opposite side of the river, and the tomb of his queen, the celebrated Noor Juhan.

There is also the beautiful garden of Shah Juhun, called the Shalimar, intersected by a canal, which throws up its water in 450 fountains to cool the air.

Umritsir is situated 50 miles north-westerly from Lahore. This is properly the capital of the Sikh nation, being considered by them as their holy city. It derives its name, which signifies *the pool of immortality*, from a small tank, in the centre of which stands a temple dedicated to Gooroo Govind Singh, and containing the book of laws written by him. It is larger than Lahore, and the principal mart of the province. Many rich merchants and bankers reside here, and amongst its inhabitants are several hundred *Akalees* or priests.

Name. Lahore is the ancient Hindoo name of this province, but it is now usually denominated the Punjab, from Punj, *five*, and ab, *river*, in allusion to the five rivers by which it is traversed.

Inhabitants. The inhabitants of this province are Sikhs, Singhs, Jats, Rajpoots, and other Hindoos, of inferior castes, and Mahomedans. The latter are still numerous, but chiefly of the poorer classes. The total population is supposed to amount to between three and four millions. They are generally a robust, athletic race, and of martial habits.

History. In early times, Lahore formed an independent kingdom, which appears to have continued for many centuries under a succession of Rajpoot rajas. There is, however, no historical record upon which any reliance can be placed, prior to the times of the Mahomedans. Alexander the Great entered Lahore, by Attok, about the year B. C. 327, and captured the city of Lahore, after having defeated the raja, Porus, on the banks of the Jelum.

On the withdrawal of the Greeks, the country reverted to its own rulers, and little more is known of it till A. D. 711, when it was attacked by the Arabs who had conquered Mooltan. They do not appear, however, to have effected any permanent conquest, and were finally expelled about the year 750. The Mahomedans having, subsequently, established them-

History.

selves in Afghanistan, frequent collisions took place between them and the Hindoos on the Indus,—until, in 977, Jypal, the raja of Lahore, determined to attack them. He was twice defeated,—the second time, when he was accompanied by the rajas of Delhi, Ajmeer, Kalinjer, and Kanouj, with immense slaughter, and in A. D. 1001, the country was invaded and overrun by Sooltan Mahmood of Ghuznee. From this time Lahore was exposed to continual attacks from the Mahomedans, until it was finally subjugated and added to the Mahomedan empire of Delhi, on the dissolution of which it fell into a state of great disorder, and became the scene of frequent revolutions, until it was conquered by the Afghans, under Ahmed Shah, in 1748. It continued subject to Cabool, but with frequent revolts, until 1758, when a general insurrection of the Sikhs broke out, assisted by a large body of Mahrattas, and the province remained for some time in a state of great confusion. After the battle of Paniput, in 1761, it again submitted to the authority of Ahmed Shah; but, during these continued disturbances, the power of the Sikhs had been rapidly increasing, and after repeated conflicts with the Afghans, they at last succeeded, about the year 1768, in completely expelling them from the province. From this period, the regular government of the Sikhs may be considered to have commenced, the country being gradually settled under the government of a number of independent chiefs. It was, however, again invaded by the Afghans, under Shah Zuman, in 1795;

History. and the Sikhs were at first overcome, and driven out of the Punjab, into the Kohistan, but Shah Zuman being obliged suddenly to return to Afghanistan, which had meanwhile been invaded by the Persians, they were saved. Shah Zuman again invaded Lahore in 1797 and 1798, and at last succeeded in bringing most of the Sikh chiefs to submit to his authority. An insurrection in his own country, however, again recalled him to Cabool; and the subsequent wars amongst themselves put a final stop, on the part of the Afghans, to any further attempts at conquest in India. As late as 1805, the Sikhs were still divided into a number of petty republics. Between that period and 1812, the celebrated Runjeet Singh taking advantage of the constant feuds between the various chiefs and the distracted state of the country, succeeded, partly by force and partly by fraud, in establishing his own authority over the whole. Under the rule of this remarkable man, the constitution of the Sikh government soon passed from a pure republic into an absolute monarchy; the bounds of which he extended by successive conquests until they included Mooltan, Cashmeer, and the town of Peshawur, with part of the surrounding district. Runjeet Singh died in 1839, leaving an only son, Kurruk Singh, and a grandson, Noor Nihal Singh; besides two adopted sons, Shere Singh, and Tara Singh. He was succeeded by Kurruk Singh, who died in November, 1840; and Noor Nihal Singh, while returning from the funeral, was killed, it is said accidently, by the falling in of a

History. gate through which he had to pass. Shere Singh then obtained possession of the kingdom, which he has since continued to hold.

The title of the monarch is the Muha Raja, or the great raja. By the English he is usually styled the Ruler of the Punjab.

Religion. The religion of the Sikhs may be described as a mixture of Hindooism and Deism. It was founded about the middle of the 15th century, by a Hindoo priest, named Baba Nanuk, or Nanuk Sah, who desired to reform what he looked upon as the corruption of his religion. His system gradually spread under the influence of the Gooroos, or teachers, who succeeded him, until the time of the tenth Gooroo, Govind Singh, who, animated by the ambition of worldly, as well as religious power, entirely remodelled the Sikh constitution, and converted his followers into a body of fierce and formidable soldiers, changing their designation from Sikhs, signifying simply *disciples*, into Singhs or *lions*, which before had exclusively belonged to the Rajpoot tribes. The Sikhs revere Gooroo Nanuk, as the founder of their religion, but have still greater veneration for Gooroo Govind, as the founder of their national power. Gooroo Govind is believed to have died about the year 1708, and was the last of the Gooroos.

Their tenets are contained in a number of books written at different times, by Nanuk and others of the Gooroos, and finally arranged in one volume, called the

Religion. Grinth or Grunth, a Sanskrit work, meaning *book* or writing.

The Sikhs reject all distinction of caste, and admit converts from all classes.

Language. The language of the Sikhs is called the Punjabee. It is a mixture of Hindoostanee and Persian.

§ 2.

Mooltan.

Boundaries. North, the Punjab; east, the Punjab and Ajmeer; south, Ajmeer and Sind; west, the Indus.

Divisions. Mooltan and Buhawulpoor.

Rivers. The Chenab and Sutluj.

General Description. This province is generally level and open, in parts fertile and well cultivated, but with large tracts of arid sandy soil; and partly from natural causes, but chiefly from its having been, during many centuries, the scene of continual invasions and warfare, it has become for the greater part a poor and thinly inhabited country.

Productions. Wheat and other grains, cotton, and indigo.

Towns. Mooltan, Buhawulpoor, and Ooch.

Mooltan, one of the most ancient cities in India, stands in lat. 30° 9′ N. long.

Towns. 71° 7′ E. four miles from the left bank of the Chenab. This was, formerly, the capital of a Hindoo kingdom, and, subsequently, the residence of a viceroy of the emperor of Delhi, but it has latterly become a place of little importance. It is noted for its manufactures of silks and carpets. It contains about 6,000 inhabitants principally Mahomedans.

Buhawulpoor, which stands about 60 miles to the south-eastward of Mooltan, near the left bank of the Sutluj, here named the Garra, is a large and flourishing town, and the capital of the Khan of the district. It has an extensive manufacture of silks, which are in much request.

Ooch is situated at the junction of the Sutluj and Beya with the Chenab. It stands in a fertile plain four miles from the left bank of the river. It is an ancient city, much noted during the first invasions of the Mahomedans. It has now about 2000 inhabitants.

Name. The name Mooltan is a corruption of the two words Mali, the name of the tribe by which the place was originally inhabited, and *than*, signifying *place*, viz. *the place of the Mali.*

Inhabitants. Principally Juts, with Beloochies, Sikhs, and Hindoos. The inhabitants of Buhawulpoor style themselves Daoodpootras, or descendants of Daood, from a celebrated chief of that name.

History. Mooltan was, in early times, the seat of

History. a Hindoo sovereignty, the country of the Malis being noticed by the Greek historians. It was one of the first provinces of India invaded by the Mahomedans, who entered it as early as the year 644, and entirely subjugated it by the year 711. In 750, a general insurrection took place, and the Rajpoot tribes succeeded in entirely expelling their Mahomedan conquerors; who do not appear to have regained their footing in the province, until the time of Mahmood of Ghuznee, who beseiged and took the capital in 1005, at which period it was under the government of a rebel Afghan chief, whose grandfather, in return for the cession of the province, had joined the Hindoos in their confederacy against Subuktageen. From this time Mooltan continued generally subject to Mahomedan rulers, until it became a regular province of the Mooghul empire. In the disorders which followed upon the death of Aurungzeb, Mooltan suffered greatly from the contending parties, and was, for some years afterwards, in the course of which it was overrun and ravaged by the Mahrattas, in a very unsettled state. The Mahrattas were driven out about the middle of the eighteenth century, by Ahmed Shah Abdallee, and the province continued tributary to Cabool until 1816, when it was finally conquered by Runjeet Singh, and annexed to the kingdom of the Punjab, with the exception of the district of Buhawulpoor, which still remains a distinct principality, under a Mahomedan chief, who is styled the Khan of Buhawulpoor.

Religion. Principally Mahomedanism.

Language. Generally the dialect spoken in Lahore, and called the Punjabee.

§ 3.

Delhi.

Boundaries. North, Sirmoor, Gurwal, and Kumaoon; east, Oude, and Agra; south, Agra and Ajmeer; west, Ajmeer and the Punjab.

Divisions. This province is divided into a number of districts, of which the principal are the following: Sirhind, Suharunpoor, Meerut, Delhi, Aligurh, Rohilkhund.

Rivers. Jumna, and Ganges, with several smaller rivers.

General Description. On its northern and western frontiers this province is hilly, but otherwise it is generally level and open. In former times it was fertile and well cultivated, but having subsequently been for a series of years exposed to the ravages of numerous armies, the means of irrigation were destroyed, and large districts became almost desert from the prevalence of moving sands blown over the surface by the winds. During the last twenty years, however, the attention of the British Government has been given to the restoration of the canals, of which there were formerly three, much celebrated in this part of India, viz. Ali Murdan

General Description. Khan's, constructed during the reign of the Emperor Baber, Sooltan Feroz Shah's, and Zabita Khan's. Ali Murdan Khan's canal, running from Kurnal to Delhi, 180 miles in length, was restored in 1820, after a labour of about three years, and has produced the most beneficial effects over a large extent of country.

Productions. Its principal productions are wheat, bajra and other grains, sugar, and cotton.

Towns. The principal towns are Ferozepoor, Loodiana, Kurnal, Suharunpoor, Delhi, Meerut, Mooradabad, Rampoor, Bareilly, Aligurh, and Shahjuhanpoor.

Ferozepoor and *Loodiana* are noticed chiefly on account of their being the principal stations of the British Territories on the north-western frontier, both on the bank of the Sutluj, the former in lat. 30° 55′ N. long. 74° 35′ E. and the latter in the same latitude, long. 75° 48′ E.

Kurnal, situated about 70 miles N. W. from Delhi, is a large town, and one of the principal military stations in the province.

Delhi, the ancient capital of the Mahomedan empire in India, is situated on the bank of the Jumna, in lat. 28° 41′ N. long. 77° 5′ E. Long before the Mahomedans invaded India, Delhi appears to have been a city of considerable importance and the capital of one of the most powerful of the Hindoo Sovereigns. Under its Mahomedan sovereigns it became one of the most splendid cities in Asia, and in the time of Aurungzeb, had

Towns. a population estimated at not less than two millions. The ruins of numerous buildings, extending over a space of nearly twenty square miles, remain to attest its former magnificence, and there are still many beautiful mosques and other edifices in good preservation, particularly the Jumna Musjid, built by the Emperor Shah Juhan, and the Mausoleum of Hoomayoon. The Kootb Minar or Minaret of Kootb, which stands at a few miles distance from the city, is also a very remarkable object. This column, which is two hundred and forty-two feet in height, was built by Kootb-ood Deen, the founder of the first Afghan sovereignty of Delhi, and was intended with another, which was never completed, for the entrance of a grand mosque, parts of which may be seen around. Under the British Government, Delhi has again become a thriving town, and is one of the principal marts for the interchange of commodities between India and the countries to the north and west. Its present population is believed to be about 250,000. Travelling distance from Calcutta, 900 miles, from Madras 1372.

Fifty miles to the northward of Delhi stands the town of Paniput, celebrated in history as the scene of two of the greatest battles ever fought in India. The first was in A. D. 1525, between the army of Sooltan Baber and that of the Patan Emperor of Delhi, Ibraheem Lodi, when the latter was totally defeated and his kingdom overturned. The second was in A. D. 1761, between the Mahomedans under Ahmed Shah, the King of

Towns. Cabool, and the Mahrattas. The Mahrattas were routed with dreadful slaughter, nearly half a million, including women and children, being killed or made captive.

Meerut is a large and ancient town, about 40 miles north-east from Delhi, and one of the principal civil and military stations of the British.

Mooradabad stands on the western bank of the river Ramgunga, in lat. 28° 51′ N. long. 78° 42′ E. It is one of the most populous and flourishing commercial towns in the province.

Rampoor is situated about 20 miles to the eastward of Mooradabad. It is the residence of a Rohilla chief, styled the Nabob of Rampoor, and is celebrated on account of a severe action which took place a few miles from it in 1794, between the Rohillas and the British troops.

Bareilly, a large town, and formerly the capital of one of the Rohilla chiefs, is situated in lat. 28° 23′ N. long. 79° 16′ E. Amongst other manufactures it is noted for brass water-pots, and cabinet work.

Aligurh is a strong fortress, situated about 50 miles to the north of Agra. In 1803 it was one of Dowlet Rao Scindia's principal strongholds, and was stormed by the British troops under Lord Lake. The town is called Coel.

Name. The present name of the province has its origin in that of the ancient Hindoo city Delhi, or as it is often called by the Hindoos, Dillee. It is said to be derived from the name of its founder, Raja Dilloo.

Inhabitants. Hindoos of various tribes, and a large proportion of Mahomedans; of the latter class, there are considerable numbers in the district of Rohilkhund, called Rohillas or Patans. They are the descendants of Afghans, and retain much of the Afghan manners and appearance.

History. This province appears to have been at a very early period the seat of a Hindoo kingdom, of considerable extent and power; it was invaded by the Mahomedans under Sooltan Mahmood in A. D. 1011, when the city of Delhi was taken and plundered, but it was restored to the raja as a tributary of Ghuznee, and it continued under a Hindoo government until 1193, when it was taken possession of by Kootb-ood Deen, who established the Afghan or Patan sovereignty of Delhi. The Patan dynasty continued till 1525, when the King Ibraheem Lodi was defeated at Paniput by Sooltan Baber, who the same year captured Delhi, and founded what has since been designated the Mooghul empire, or the empire of the Great Mooghul. Under his successors, particularly the celebrated Akber, who reigned from 1556 to 1605, and Aurungzeb from 1658 to 1707, the Mooghul empire was extended on all sides until it embraced nearly the whole of India.

From that period, however, it rapidly declined. A series of weak princes filled the throne of Delhi, the provinces

History. became independent states under their several Soobadars or Viceroys, and the Mahrattas made such progress that in 1735 they burned the suburbs of Delhi itself. In 1739 the province was invaded by Nadir Shah, who plundered Delhi, after a terrible massacre of the inhabitants. In 1756 the province was again invaded by Ahmed Shah, the founder of the Dooranee kingdom of Cabool. In 1761, Shah Alum, the second, the ninth monarch from Aurungzeb, succeeded to the throne, and commenced his reign by a very unprovoked and foolish attack upon the British in Bengal and Bahar. He was entirely defeated, and subsequently came over to the British camp. He remained for some years under the protection of the British Government, who settled upon him a pension of twenty-six lacks of rupees, with a considerable tract of fertile territory; but in 1771 he decided upon returning to Delhi, where he immediately fell into the hands of the Mahrattas, who had shortly before got possession of the city. In 1788 Delhi was suddenly captured by a Rohilla leader, named Ghoolam Kadir, who seized the unfortunate emperor, and after exposing him for many weeks to every kind of insult and degradation, at last deprived him of sight by piercing his eyes with a dagger. Ghoolam Kadir was shortly after driven out and killed by the Mahrattas, and the emperor again became their prisoner. In 1803, the city was taken by the British troops under Lord Lake, and Shah Alum was once more placed under their protection. Delhi became from that pe-

History. riod a province of the British empire, and though Shah Alum and his family continued to retain their usual titles, their authority may be considered as having terminated, and they have since resided at Delhi supported by an annual allowance from the British Government.

Religion. Hindooism and Mahomedanism.

Language. Principally Hindoostanee.

§ 4.

Oude.

Boundaries. North, Nepal; east, Bahar; south, Allahabad; west, Agra and Delhi.

Divisions. Khyrabad, Baraitch, Luknow, Fyzabad, Gorukpoor, Manikpoor.

Rivers. Ganges, Goomtee, and Gogra, all flowing through the province south-easterly.

General Description. The whole surface of this province, excepting upon the northern and north-eastern frontiers, is perfectly level, well watered, and very fertile. It is one of the smallest provinces of Hindoostan Proper, but has always been one of the richest and most populous. Its length, from west to east, is about 250 miles, by 100, the average breadth from north to south.

Productions. Wheat, barley, peas, rice, and other grains; sugar, indigo, opium, and to-

Productions. bacco; saltpetre is abundant, and lapis lazuli is amongst the mineral productions.

Towns. Khyrabad, Baraitch, Luknow, Roy-Bareilly, Fyzabad, Tanda, Sooltanpoor, Gorukpoor, Mainkoor.

Luknow, the capital of the province, is situated on the south side of the Goomtee, in lat. 26° 51′ N. long. 80° 50′ E.

It is a large and populous town, divided into three distinct quarters. The first, consisting of the old native city, is extensive but meanly built and very dirty; the second, containing the king's palace and the residences of his court, is of modern origin, and the houses are for the most part in a mixed style of European and Eastern architecture; the third consists chiefly of palaces and religious edifices, erected by the former nabobs.

Travelling distance from Calcutta 650 miles. On the opposite side of the river, a few miles distant, is a large English cantonment.

Fyzabad stands on the south side of the Gogra, about eight miles to the eastward of Luknow. This was formerly the capital of the province. It is still of considerable extent, and contains a numerous population, but chiefly of the lower classes; the bankers, merchants, and others of the higher orders having removed to Luknow.

Name. The English name of this province, Oude, is a corruption of the Hindoo name *Uyodhya*, by which it is mentioned in the earliest records of Indian history.

Inhabitants. The inhabitants of this province are, generally, remarkable as a fine robust race, of an intelligent and manly character; particularly the Rajpoots, who are commonly superior in stature and appearance to Europeans. A large proportion are Mahomedans, of Afghan and Persian origin, the province having been for many centuries under a Mahomedan Government. The Bengal Army procures a considerable number of its best sepoys from this province.

History. Oude is much celebrated in Hindoo history as the kingdom of Dasaratha, the father of Rama, who is supposed, according to the Ramayana, to have extended his dominions as far as Ceylon. The distance of this province from the western frontier of India preserved it from attack by the Mahomedans, during their first invasions, but very soon after the time of Sooltan Mahmood, of Ghuznee, it was subdued by them, and thenceforward continued to form a part of the empire of Delhi, until its dissolution after the death of Aurungzeb. About the year 1730, the government of Oude was conferred by the Emperor Mahomed Shah upon one of his chiefs, named Sadut Khan, who had originally been a merchant of Khorasan; and it has ever since remained with his family. A treaty having been made with the British Government in the year 1765, Oude has been preserved from all external enemies, and

History. has consequently enjoyed a long continuance of peace and prosperity. The Governor of Oude was originally styled the Soobadar, and afterwards the Nabob. This was changed in 1814 to Vizier, (Wuzeer,) and in 1819 to Padshah, or king, by which he is now recognised.

Religion. Mahomedanism and Hindooism, the fromer the most prevalent.

Language. Hindoostanee.

§ 5.

Sind.

Boundaries. North, Afghanistan, and Mooltan; east, Ajmeer; south, Kuch and the sea; west, Beloochistan.

Divisions. Upper Sind, or the northern part of the country down to Shikarpoor, and Lower Sind, extending from Shikarpoor to the sea.

Rivers. The Indus, including its various branches.

General Description. East of the Indus, the province is almost a perfect level, and is for the greater part, except in the immediate vicinity of the river, a barren waste. West of the Indus, the face of the country varies, and on the western and north-western frontiers becomes mountainous. The climate of Upper Sind is temperate, but that of Lower Sind oppressively hot and very unhealthy.

Productions.

Upper Sind produces wheat, barley, and other grains; and Lower Sind, rice and bajree in great abundance, sugar, and indigo, saltpetre, and potash. Cattle and sheep are numerous; as also a small breed of horses and camels of a superior description.

Towns.

Shikarpoor, Sukkur, Khyrpoor, Larkhanu, Sehwun, Hyderabad, Omerkote, Tatta, Kurachee, and Meerpoor.

Shikarpoor is situated a little distance to the westward of the Indus in lat. 27° 36′ N. long. 69° 18′ E. It is the most populous town in Sind, and carries on an extensive commerce with the adjacent countries. The inhabitants are almost all Hindoos, termed Shikarpoorees, and speak a dialect of Hindoostanee, distinguished by that name.

Sukkur is chiefly noticed on account of its position on the right bank of the Indus, opposite Bukkur, a fortress built upon a rock in the middle of the river—lat. 27° 42′ N.

A few miles from Sukkur are the ruins of Alore, in early times the capital of a mighty kingdom, which extended from the ocean to Cashmeer on the north, and from Candahar on the west, to Kanoje on the east; and mentioned by the Greek Historians as the kingdom of Musicanus.

Khyrpoor is the capital of one of the three Ameers of Sind. It is a place of

Towns.

some trade, and is noted for the dyeing of cloth. It has about 150,000 inhabitants.

Hyderabad, the modern capital of the whole country, and the residence of the principal Ameer, stands on the bank of the Fulalee, a branch of the Indus, in lat. 25° 22′ N. It contains about 20,000 inhabitants. The armourers of this place are noted for the excellence of their workmanship, as also are the artificers who embroider in leather.

Omerkote is situated on the eastern frontier, about 85 miles to the eastward of Hyderabad. This was formerly the residence of an independent Rajpoot Chief, and is noted as the birth-place of the Emperor Akber.

Tata, the ancient capital of Sind, stands on the right bank of the Indus, about 130 miles from the sea, in lat. 24° 44′ N. It is believed to be the Pattala mentioned by the Greeks, and was a place of considerable importance before the Mahomedan invasion. During the existence of the Mooghul empire it continued to be much celebrated as a city of considerable commerce, and was famous for its manufactures of silk. It has since greatly decayed, and does not now contain more than 150,000 inhabitants.

It is still visited by numbers of Hindoos, being on the high road to Hinglaj in Beloochistan, a place of pilgrimage much resorted to by the people of the western provinces.

Kurachee is noted as being one of the principal seaports, and a British station. It is at the western-most mouth of the Indus, in lat. 24° 51′ N. long. 67° 16′ E.

Name.

The province derives its name from that of the river Indus, which by the Hindoos is called the Sind.

Inhabitants.

Hindoos, Juts, and Beloochees. The Juts are Mahomedans, the descendants of the original Rajpoot inhabitants of the province, converted at an early period to the Mahomedan faith, and they compose the chief military force of the country.

It is believed that the total population does not exceed one million, although in early times the province appears to have been very thickly peopled.

History.

In ancient times this province appears to have formed part of a very extensive kingdom, which embraced nearly the whole of the north-western provinces of India, governed by a raja who had his capital at Alore, near Sukkur. This kingdom still subsisted, though not with the same extent of territory, when it was first invaded by the Arabs, about the year 664. It was entirely subjugated by the Arabs in 711, and continued under their rule until 750, when a general insurrection broke out, and the Mahomedans were expelled by the Rajpoot tribe of Soomra. It then appears to have fallen under the government of two chiefs, one a Rajpoot and the other a Mahomedan of Hindoo descent, who both ruled under the title of the Jams of Sind. Hardly any thing further is known of its history from this period until the next invasion by the Mahomedans, under Mahmood of Ghuznee, in the early part of the 11th century,

History. when it was again subdued; and after many years of conflict and disorder became a regular province of the Mooghul empire. In 1737 India being then in a state of great alarm from the expected invasion of Nadir Shah, a chief of Sewistan, named Mahomed Abassee Kaloorce, succeeded in persuading the soobadar or viceroy of Sind to resign the government into his hands. Nadir Shah entered the province and drove out the Kaloorce family, but afterwards allowed them to resume their authority as his tributaries. The province continued under their rule until 1779, when a tribe of the Beloochies, named the Talpooree, rebelled against the Kaloorce Nabob, as he was then styled, and expelled him from the country, which was then divided amongst the Talpooree chiefs, and eventually formed into the three principalities of Hyderabad, Khyrpoor, and Meerpoor, under three brothers, styled the Ameers of Sind, under which dynasty it has ever since remained. In 1839, a British army entered Sind upon its route to Afghanistan, a treaty having been concluded with the Ameers for the passage of the troops through their territories, and cantonments have since been formed in Upper Sind and at Kurachee.

Religion. The prevailing religion of the province is Mahomedanism, generally of the Soonnee division, though the Ameers themselves are Shiahs.

Language. The language is termed Sindee, and resembles the Hindee dialects of Hindoostan.

§ 6.

Ajmeer, or Rajpootana.

Boundaries. North, Mooltan and Delhi; east, Delhi and Agra; south, Malwa, Guzerat and Kuch; west, Sind.

Divisions. The Bhattee Country, Bikaneer, Jussulmeer, Marwar or Joudpoor, Jeypoor, including Skikawuttee, Ajmeer, Meywar or Odeypoor, Boondee, and Kota.

Rivers. This province is destitute of rivers, except in the southern and eastern parts. The only streams of any note are the Banass, which rises in the district of Odeypoor, and flows south-westerly until it is lost in the Run of Kuch; and the Chumbul, which enters the district of Kota from Malwa, and flows northerly into the province of Agra, to the Jumna.

General Description. In its south-eastern districts this province is fertile, well watered, and hilly; but westward and northward, with a few exceptions, it is absolutely desert, the whole surface of the country being either covered with loose sand, which in some places is driven by the wind, into mounds and hillocks, some of them a hundred feet in height; or else composed of hard flat salt loam, wholly destitute of vegetation. In the midst of these burning plains, the water melon, the most juicy of all fruits, is found in astonishing pro-

General Description. fusion, and of large size. Water is procured, but in small quantity, and brackish, from wells which are frequently three hundred feet deep, though not more than three or four feet in diameter. During the hot season the passage of the desert cannot be attempted, without great risk of suffocation, from whirlwinds of driving sand.

Productions. The productions of the cultivated parts of this province, are wheat, barley, rice, sugar, cotton, indigo, and tobacco. Camels are numerous, and bullocks of a superior description. Salt is abundant, and the Odeypoor districts yield copper, lead, sulphur, and iron.

Towns. Bhatneer, Bikaneer, Jussulmeer, Nagore, Joudpoor, Jeypoor, Ajmeer, Chitore, Odeypoor, Neemuch, Boondee, Kota.

Bhatneer is the principal town of the Bhattee tribe, and is a place of some antiquity, as it is mentioned as having been taken by Tymoor in 1398. It stands on the eastern border of the great desert.

Bikaneer is situated in the midst of a very desolate tract, in lat. 27° 57′ N. long. 73° 2′ E. It is a fortified town and the capital of the raja.

Jussulmeer stands in lat. 26° 43′ N. long. 70° 54′ E.

Joudpoor is situated in lat. 26° 18′ N. long. 73° E. It is the capital of the district, and is said to be a well built town.

Travelling distance from Oojein 260 miles.

Jeypoor, the capital of the principality,

Towns.

is situated in lat. 26° 55′ N. long. 75° 37′ E. This is considered to be the handsomest, and most regularly built town in India, many of its streets being equal in appearance to those of European cities. The present town is of modern origin having been planned and built for the Raja Jey Sing, a celebrated chief in the time of the Emperor Aurungzeb, by an Italian architect.

Travelling distance from Delhi 156 miles, from Bombay 740.

Ajmeer, formerly the capital of the province, stands at the bottom of a fortified hill, in lat. 26° 31′ N. long. 74° 28′ E. This was formerly a large and opulent city, and occasionally the residence of the Emperor of Delhi. The English had a trading factory here in 1616. It was nearly ruined during the disorders which followed upon the dissolution of the Mooghul empire, and the establishment of the Mahratta power; but since its transfer to the British in 1818, it has greatly improved, and is now a handsome town, second only to Jeypoor.

At Nusseerabad, 15 miles from Ajmeer, is a British cantonment.

Chitore stands in lat. 24° 52′ N. long. 74° 45′ E. This was for many centuries the capital of the principality of Odeypoor, and much celebrated for its strength and riches. It was several times captured by the Mahomedans, but was never permanently retained by them. It is still a fine town, and contains many temples, and other buildings remarkably well constructed, particularly two towers of white marble, about 100 feet high, and

Towns. finely carved, dedicated to Siva. The fort, which was formerly considered one of the strongest in India, stands on a steep rock, overlooking the town, and about four miles in length.

Odeypoor, the present capital, is situated in lat. 24° 35′ N. long. 73° 44′ E. It stands on the border of a large lake, which on the other sides is enclosed by ranges of wild and rugged hills. The palaces and garden residences on the borders of the lake, are all of marble, highly sculptured. Images, toys, and a great variety of articles of marble, and rock crystal, are sent from this place to the neighbouring provinces.

Neemuch, situated about 40 miles to the south, eastward of Chitore, is the principal British station in this province.

Travelling distance from Delhi 372 miles.

Boondee is situated in lat. 25° 28′ N. long. 75° 30′ E. It is a handsome well built city, and the residence of the raja of the district.

Kota, the capital of the district stands on the east side of the Chumbul, about 150 miles to the south, eastward of Ajmeer. It is a large and populous place, and contains some handsome buildings of white marble.

Name. This province derives its name of Ajmeer from that of the city of Ajmeer, which was its Mahomedan capital; but it is more commonly designated as Rajpootana, or the country of the Rajpoots, from its being the seat of the principal Rajpoot principalities of India.

Inhabitants. Rajpoots, Jats, Bhatteeas, Bheels, and a small proportion of Mahomedans.

The Rajpoots are usually divided into two great tribes, the Rahtores and the Chouhan-Teesodiya. They have always been celebrated throughout India as a brave and hardy race and were always held in high estimation by the emperors of Delhi, who were accustomed to employ their chiefs in the most important military commands. They were never conquered by the Mahomedans, though they acknowledged the emperor of Delhi as their superior, and served as auxiliaries in the Mooghul armies. They are unhappily much addicted to the use of opium, the pernicious effects of which have become very apparent in the deterioration of their race, in both mind and body.

The Jats are Hindoos of a lower class, much inferior in every respect to the Rajpoots, who hold them in strict subjection, and deny the claim which they advance to be considered, of Rajpoot origin. They are generally of short stature, black, and ill-looking.

The Bhattees were originally shepherds, but have long been noted as a plundering tribe, remarkable for carrying on their depredations on foot, and for the length and rapidity of their excursions. Their chiefs were originally Rajpoots, but are now Mahomedans, as are also the majority of the people.

The total population is estimated at not more than four millions.

History. This province was, in early times, the

History. seat of one of the principal Rajpoot sovereignties in India. The raja of Ajmeer appears to have been a powerful monarch, when India was invaded by Sooltan Mahmood of Ghuznee, and was one of those, who entered into the unsuccessful confederacy with the raja of Lahore against that monarch in 1008. Subsequently, Pritwee, the raja of Ajmeer, was adopted by the raja of Delhi, his maternal grandfather, who had no son, and on whose death the two kingdoms were united. This gave great offence to the raja of Kanoje, who also was a grandson of the raja of Delhi, and brought on a war between them. The Mahomedans did not fail to take advantage of their dissensions, and in 1191 they entered the province of Delhi under Shuhab-ood-deen, afterwards known by the name of Mahomed Ghouree. They were however defeated with great slaughter by Pritwee raja, and Shuhab-ood-deen was compelled to fly with the wreck of his army to Lahore. Having obtained reinforcements from Ghuznee, Shuhab-ood-deen, in 1193, again advanced. Pritwee raja met him with a vast army, numerous allies having joined him from the other states: but his former success had rendered the raja too confident, and exposed him to a surprise which led to his total defeat. Pritwee raja was taken in the pursuit, and put to death in cold blood by the Mahomedans; Ajmeer was taken, and thousands of the inhabitants slaughtered, after which Shuhab-ood-deen made over the kingdom to a relation of Pritwee raja, under an engagement for a

History. heavy tribute. A long series of disorders followed, and the kingdom was eventually divided into a number of independent principalities which, on the establishment of the empire of Delhi, became nominally subject to the Mahomedan government. It was never thoroughly subdued, and, though numbered amongst the regular provinces of the empire, always retained a sort of independence; paying an annual tribute, and furnishing a certain number of troops to the emperor; but in other respects remaining under the rule of its own princes. This continued till the dissolution of the Mooghul empire in 1748, when the Rajpoot chiefs assumed entire independence. The province was then for many years desolated by internal wars, and by repeated invasions of the Mahrattas, who, about the beginning of the present century, were upon the point of effecting the complete conquest of the whole country, when their progress was stopped by their becoming engaged in a war with the English. The peace which followed was again broken in 1807, when a contest arose between the rajas of Jeypoor and Joudpoor, each claiming the honour of marrying the daughter of the raja of Odeypoor. Both parties called in the aid of the neighbouring Mahratta chiefs, who, while they pretended to act as their allies, in reality occupied themselves only in plundering the country. The province was thus involved in so much distress, and suffered so severely from the devastations of the Mahrattas, that the whole of the Rajpoot chiefs

History. repeatedly entreated to be admitted into an alliance with the British Government. This was for some time refused, the British Government not wishing to interfere, but consequent upon the second war between the Mahrattas and the English in 1817, it was at length conceded, and the Rajpoot principalities have ever since remained at peace, under the protection of the British Government. The province is now divided under the following chiefs. 1st, The rana of Odeypoor, mentioned in the early Mahomedan histories as the rana of Chitore, who holds the highest rank in the estimation of the Rajpoots, on account of his belonging to what is considered, by them, to be the purest family of their race, though his territories are much reduced. 2nd, The raja of Joudpoor, who is also styled the Rahtore raja, being of that tribe. 3rd, The raja of Jeypoor, formerly called Jynuggur, and also Ambher. 4th, The rajas of Jussulmeer, Bikaneer, Kota, and Boonde. Under these are a number of Thakoors, or chiefs, and others of inferior authority; each principality constituting a feudal state.

Religion. Generally Hindooism. In the western parts there are a good many Jains. The Mahomedans are in the proportion of about one to ten.

Language. Hindoostanee.

§ 7.

Agra.

Boundaries. North, Delhi; east, Oude and Allahabad; south, Malwa; west, Ajmeer.

Divisions. Narnool, Agra, Aligurh, Furrukhabad, Etaweh, Macheree or Alvar, Bhurtpoor, Gualior, Gohud, Kalpee.

The tract of country between the Ganges and Jumna, comprehending the districts of Aligurh, Furrukhabad and Etaweh, is also commonly designated the *Dooab*—from *doo* two, and *ab* river.

Rivers. Ganges, Jumna, Chumbul, and several smaller streams. The Chumbul rises in Malwa, and flows northerly and easterly into the Jumna, running between the districts of Bhurtpoor and Gualior.

General Description. Northward of the Jumna the surface of the province is in general flat and open, and for the greater part very bare of trees. Southward and westward it becomes hilly and jungly. Though traversed by several rivers, the province is not well watered, and depends greatly upon the periodical rains. The heat, during the prevalence of the hot winds, is intense, and the jungly districts very unhealthy, but at other seasons, the climate is generally temperate and occasionally cold.

Productions. Rice is grown in the vicinity of the rivers, but the general cultivation is of

Productions. dry grains, as millet, barley, gram, &c. The staple article of product is cotton. The province also yields abundance of indigo, with tobacco, sugar, saltpetre, and salt. It has the common breeds of cattle and sheep; and horses of a good description. Firewood is scarce throughout the Dooab, and expensive. The jungly districts swarm with peacocks, which are held in great veneration by the Natives. The only manufacture of note is that of coarse cotton cloths.

Towns. Narnool, Nooh, Muttra, Agra, Dholpoor, Attaer, Anoopshuhr, Cowl, Moorsaum, Secundra, Hatras, Furrukhabad, Futihgurh, Kanoje, Mimpooree, Etaweh, Bela, Alwur, Macheree, Rajgurh, Deeg, Bhurtpoor, Beeana, Gualior, Antra, Pechor, Nurwur, Bhind, Gohud, Jalown, Kalpee, and Koonch.

Narnool, situated in lat. 28° 5′ N. long. 75° 52′ E. about 90 miles south-westerly from Delhi, is the frontier town of the territories belonging to the raja of Jypoor. It is a place of considerable antiquity, but at present of little importance.

Nooh, in lat. 27° 51′ N. long. 77° 31′ E. is noted for the manufacture of culinary salt, distinguished by the name of "Salumba"—which is procured from salt springs in the neighbourhood.

Muttra, or *Mathura*, is situated on the west bank of the Jumna, in lat. 27° 31′ N. long. 77° 33′ E. This is a place of great antiquity, much celebrated in the legends of the Hindoos, by whom it is supposed to be sacred, and mentioned as an important city by the early Greek

Towns.

geographers. On account of its position, it is still considered one of the principal towns of the province, and forms an English military station. The pagodas swarm with large monkeys, peacocks, and brahminee birds, all held sacred by the Hindoo inhabitants.

Travelling distance from Delhi 98 miles, from Agra 36.

Agra stands on the southern side of the Jumna in lat. 27° 11′ N. long. 77° 53′ E. During the reign of the Emperor Akber, by whom it was greatly enlarged and embellished, Agra was made the capital of the Mooghul empire, and became one of the most splendid cities in India. The seat of government having been subsequently re-established at Delhi, Agra greatly declined, and is now much decayed. Amongst the still remaining edifices which bear witness of its former grandeur, the most remarkable is the Taj Mahal, erected by the Emperor Shah Juhan, for the celebrated Noor Juhan; and which is considered the most beautiful and perfect specimen of oriental architecture in existence, unequalled by any thing in India.

Cowl, or *Koil*, is situated in lat. 27° 54′ N. long. 78° E. two miles from the fortress of Aligurh, with which it is connected by a fine avenue of trees. It is a large busy town, and the principal civil station of the district.

Travelling distance from Agra 56 miles.

Hatras is situated in lat. 27° 37′ N. long. 75° 58′ E. It is a busy town and flourishing. Its fort, which was strong and well built, was taken in 1817 by the

Towns. British troops, (being then occupied by a refractory chief,) and destroyed.

Travelling distance from Agra 35 miles.

Furrukhabad stands at a short distance from the bank of the Ganges in lat. 27° 24′ N. long. 79° 27′ E. It is a large and populous town, containing about 7,000 inhabitants, and is a place of considerable commerce.

Travelling distance from Agra 112 miles, from Luknow 110, from Calcutta, by way of Beerbhoom, 755.

Futihgurh is situated three miles to the eastward of Furrukhabad. It is the principal residence of the civil authorities of the district, and is noted for the manufacture of tents.

Kanoje is situated in lat. 27° 4′ N. long. 79° 47′ E. about two miles distant from the bank of the Ganges, with which it communicates by means of a canal. In the remote ages of Hindoo history, Kanoje was a place of great renown, and the capital of a powerful empire, which existed at the time of the first Mahomedan invasion. Not the slightest vestige now remains of the ancient Hindoo city, all the existing buildings being of Mahomedan and modern origin.

Travelling distance from Agra 217 miles, from Luknow 75, from Delhi 214, from Calcutta 270.

Alvar, or *Alwur*, is situated in lat. 27° 44′ N. long. 76° 32′ E. at the base of a strongly fortified hill. It is the capital of the Macheree raja's territories.

Travelling distance from Agra 60 miles.

Bhurtpoor, the capital of the Bhurtpoor raja, one of the principal Jat Chief-

Towns. tains, is situated in lat. 27° 17′ N. long. 77° 23′ E. This place is much noted on account of its seige in 1805 by the English, who four times assaulted it, and were repulsed with severe loss. The raja, however, fearing to continue his resistance, sent his son to the English camp with the keys of the fort, and submitted. This chief, who so gallantly defended his capital, died in 1824, and was succeeded by his son, who also died immediately afterwards; leaving a son, then seven years of age, under the guardianship of the mother and an uncle. In 1825, a cousin of the young raja murdered the uncle, and seized the person of the raja, on which the British Government being compelled to interfere, Bhurtpoor was once more attacked by the English, and in January, 1826, was taken by assault after a seige of six weeks. The town was subsequently restored to its lawful chief.

Travelling distance from Agra 35 miles.

Beeana stands on the banks of the Ban-Gunga, in lat. 26° 57′ N. long. 77° 8′ E. It is a large and flourishing town, and was the capital of the province before Agra.

Travelling distance from Agra 65 miles.

Gualior is situated in lat. 26° 15′ N. long. 78° 1′ E. Its fortress was reputed, amongst the Natives, to be impregnable, until taken by escalade in 1780 by a detachment of British sepoys. It is now the capital of the Sindia Mahratta territories.

Travelling distance from Agra 74 miles, from Delhi 200, from Nagpoor 380, from Calcutta 800.

Towns. *Kalpee* is situated on the bank of the Jumna, in lat. 26° 10′ N. long. 79° 41′ E. It is a large and populous town, possessing an extensive trade, and noted for the manufacture of paper and sugar-candy.

Travelling distance from Agra 160 miles, from Calcutta 700.

Name. The present name of this province is derived from that of its capital.

Inhabitants. Hindoos, including the Mewatties, and Jats, and Mahomedans, among whom are many Pathans. They are generally a handsome robust race of men, much superior to the natives of the more eastern provinces. The Mewatties chiefly inhabit the Macheree country, occasionally styled,, by Mahomedan writers, *Mewat*. They have always been noted as a rude, savage people, and are robbers by profession, from which circumstance they derive their name; but latterly in consequence of the measures adopted by the British Government, their character has greatly improved. The Jats first attracted notice in Hindoostan about the year 1700. When they migrated from the banks of the Indus, and settled, chiefly as agriculturists, in various parts of the Dooab. Their subsequent progress was remarkably rapid; and during the civil wars, carried on by the successors of Aurungzeb, they found means to possess themselves of a large portion of country, in which they built forts and accumulated treasure. They successively extended their power, until it embraced the principal part of the province, but after wards lost most of their acquisitions, and by the end of the 18th century, were restricted to the territory of Bhurtpoor.

History. This was formerly one of the most important of the Hindoo provinces, containing Kanoje, Muttra, and Bindrabund, the seats of the most famous of the Hindoo kingdoms; and still greatly venerated as places of pilgrimage. On the conquest of Delhi by the Mahomedans, Agra also fell under their dominion; and during the reign of Akber, when the city of Agra was for a time the capital, it became the principal province of the Mooghul empire. After the death of Aurungzeb it fell into great disorder, and suffered much from the ravages of the Jats and Mahrattas, who for many years disputed the possession. This state of things continued until 1805, when, consequent upon the war between the English and the Mahrattas, the province was added to the British territories; the raja of Bhurtpoor and a few other chiefs holding their districts under the general control of the English Government.

Religion. Hindooism and Mahomedanism.

Language. Hindoostanee and Mahrattee.

§ 8.

Kuch.

Boundaries. North, Ajmeer, from which it is separated by the great sandy desert; east

Boundaries. Guzerat, from which it is divided by the Run; south, the Sea; west, the easternmost branch of the Sind, called the Lonee, and a salt marsh separating it from Sind.

The southern boundary is formed by an arm of the sea running inland, between Kuch and the Peninsula of Guzerat, and called the Gulf of Kuch.

Rivers. There are no rivers in this province, with the exception of the Lonee, which flows along its western frontier. During the rainy season there are many streams, but their channels are generally dry soon after the rains cease.

General Description. This province may be described as consisting of two distinct portions. One an immense salt morass, named the Run; the other an irregular hilly tract, completely insulated by the morass and the sea.

The Run, which is estimated to cover a surface of about 8000 square miles, commences at the head of the Gulf of Kuch, with which it communicates, and sweeps round the whole of the northern frontier of the province. It varies in breadth from five to eighty miles across, and during the rainy season forms a large sheet of salt water. At other times it presents a variety of appearances, being in some parts dry barren sand, in some deep swamps, in others, shallow pools and lakes, elsewhere fields of salt, and occasionally affording pasturage, and capable of cultivation. The other portion of this province is inter-

General Description.

sected by a range of rocky barren hills, running through the centre from east to west. It is almost destitute of wood, and has no water except as procured by means of wells. The whole face of the country near the hills is covered with volcanic matter, and there is said to be an extinct volcano eighteen miles to the eastward of Lukhput Bundur. In 1819 Kuch was visited by a severe earthquake, which nearly destroyed a number of towns and forts, and filled the Run with water. It appears probable that originally this province was an island.

Productions.

This province is not fertile, water being scarce and often salt, and the soil either rocky or sandy. Its productions are consequently few, the principal is cotton, which is exported in exchange for grain, from Sind and other provinces. The horses of this province are however considered the best in India. Camels and goats also thrive, but the cattle are of an inferior description. Iron and alum are found in various parts, with a species of coal, and abundance of bituminous earths. Date trees grow in some tracts, and produce fruit of good quality; but the cocoanut is reared with difficulty, even on the coast. Salt is procured from the Run, the banks of which are also much frequented by the wild ass. This animal is much larger and stronger than the domestic ass, and remarkably swift, but very fierce and quite untameable. It is sometimes caught in pits, but has never been domesticated. Its flesh is esteemed good eating.

Towns. Lukhput-Bundur, Kowra, Bhooj, Anjar, and Mandavie.

Lukhput-Bundur is situated on the bank of the Lonee, in lat. 23° 47′ N. long. 68° 56′ E. seventy-five miles westerly and northerly from Bhooj.

Kowra is remarkable for its situation in the midst of the Run, which completely surrounds it. It is in lat. 23° 46′ N. long. 69° 44′ E. thirty-eight miles to the north of Bhooj.

Bhooj, the capital of the province, is situated inland in lat. 23° 15′ N. long. 69° 52′ E. It is a modern town, having been founded by the rao of Kuch, about the commencement of the 17th century. It is tolerably well built, and contains about 20,000 inhabitants, among whom are artists remarkable for their ingenuity in working gold and silver. This town was nearly destroyed in June, 1819, by a severe earthquake.

Travelling distance from Bombay 587 miles.

Anjar is situated in lat. 23° 3′ N. long. 70° 11′ E. about ten miles from the Gulf of Kuch. It contains about 10,000 inhabitants, and is the principal town of the British district of Anjar. It was much injured in 1819 by the earthquake.

Mandavie, the principal seaport of the province, is situated on the south coast in lat. 22° 50′ N. long. 69° 33′ E. It possesses a tolerable harbour, and is a place of considerable trade with the western Coast of India, Sind, Arabia, and Africa, but it has no manufactures of any note. It is the most populous town in Kuch, containing about 35,000 inhabitants, prin-

Towns. cipally Bhattias, Banyans, and Brahmins, with some Mahomedans and others.

Travelling distance from Bhooj 40 miles.

Name. The derivation of the name is not known.

Inhabitants. In ancient times this province appears to have been occupied entirely by pastoral tribes of Hindoos. At present its inhabitants are principally Jahrejas of Sind origin, Bhattias, and other tribes of Hindoos, and a large proportion of Mahomedans. The Bhattias are a Hindoo tribe, the principal merchants of the country, actively engaged in trade with Arabia and the west of India. As a people, the inhabitants of this province, or as they are generally styled, the Kuchhees, may be described as the most degraded in India. They are noted for drunkenness and debauchery, and their treachery is proverbial. Female infanticide is universally practised by the Jahrejas, even by tribes calling themselves Mahomedans. The Kuch pilots and mariners however are noted for their skill, and claim the merit of having first instructed the Arabs in navigation and ship building, though they still follow the practice of their forefathers without improvement.

History. Nothing is accurately known of the early history of this province. It is mentioned in 1582 by Abul Fazil as an independent state, governed by a chief styled the rao of Kuch, whose authority

History. appears subsequently to have been considerably extended, as about the middle of the 18th century, the rao Dasul is said to have held garrisons in parts of Sind, Ajmeer, and the Guzerat Peninsula. After his death much confusion and anarchy ensued, and the province was the scene of numerous revolutions effected by the mercenary troops, chiefly Arabs and Sindees, until order was finally restored by the British. Owing to its poverty, and the difficulties of its situation, this petty principality continued unconquered and independent until 1819, when Bhooj was captured by the British, who were compelled to interfere to repress the banditti, who were continually issuing from the Kuch territories, and laying waste the neighbouring provinces. Since that period it has remained under the general government of the rao, subject to the control of the British, and it is garrisoned by British troops. Subordinate to the rao are a number of petty chieftains.

Religion. Hindooism and Mahomedanism.

Language. The general language of the province is styled the Kuchhee. It is a dialect derived from the Sanskrit, of which it retains many words in purity, but it is much mixed with Sindee and Goojratee. It has no peculiar written character. The language of business throughout Kuch, is the Goojratee, and the Goojratee character is used for correspondence.

§ 9.

Guzerat.

Boundaries. North, Ajmeer; east, Malwa, and Khandesh; south, Aurungabad, and the sea; west, the sea, and Kuch.

Divisions. Puttunwara, Ederwara, Doongurpoor, Banswara, Jhutwar, Chowal, Kattwar or the Peninsula, Ahmedabad, Kaira, Soont, Sunawara, Barrea, Barode, Baroach, Rajpeepla, Surat.

Rivers. Banas, Subrmuttee, Mhye or Mahe, Nurbudda, and Tuptee. The Banas flows along the north-western frontier, into the Run. The Subrmuttee rises in Ajmeer and flows southward into the Gulf of Cambay. The Mhye enters the province in the Banswara district, and flows south-westerly into the Gulf of Cambay.

General Description. The northern and eastern districts of this province are mountainous, rugged, and jungly. The central districts form an extensive plain, generally well watered, open, and fertile. The south-western portion, forming the division of Kattiwar, or Kattwad, approaches the shape of a peninsula, having an arm of the sea, called the Gulf of Cambay, on its eastern side, the sea on its south, and the Gulf of Kuch on its west. The Gulf of Cambay is about 150 miles in length. The surface of the peninsula in general is hilly.

General Description. remarkably well watered throughout, and fertile. On the north-west, Guzerat is separated from Kuch by the Run and the Banas river, and the adjacent districts consist chiefly of arid plains, or salt swamps and jungles.

Productions. Wheat, rice, and other grains; cotton, hemp, indigo, opium, sugar, honey, saltpetre, and various seed-oils; horses and cattle of a superior description, hides, and timber. There are cornelian mines in Rajpeepla, and jaspers and agates are procured in Ederwara and other hilly districts. The Kattivad supplies abundance of white clay, used by the Hindoos for the purpose of marking their foreheads. Large quantities of salt are obtained from the Run. The manufactures are principally coarse cotton fabrics and soap.

Towns. Deesa, Palhanpoor, Radhunpoor, Puttun, Eder, Ahmednuggur, Doongurpoor, Banswara, Pathree, Bejapoor, Nuwanuggur, Poorbunder, Joonagur, Puttun-Somnath, Diu, Ahmedabad, Kaira, Kuppurwunj, Cambay, Bhownuggur, Gogo, Soonth, Lunawara, Barrea, Chumpaneer, Baroda, Chandod, Jumboseer, Baroch, Nandod, Rajpeepla, Surat, Sacheen, Bulsar, Dhurmpoor, and Daman.

Deesa is situated on the Banas river, in lat. 24° 9′ N. long. 72° 8′ E. It is chiefly noticed on account of its being the most advanced military station of the British on the Guzerat frontier.

Travelling distance from Kaira 117 miles.

Towns.

Palhanpoor is situated about 12 miles to the eastward of Deesa. It is a populous town, and the capital of a small Mahomedan principality tributary to the Gaikowar. It contains about 30,000 inhabitants.

Radhunpoor is situated in lat. 23° 40′ N. long. 71° 31′ E. It is the residence of a Mahomedan chieftain, the descendant of the last Mahomedan governors of the province of Guzerat.

Puttun is situated on the south side of the Suruswate river, in lat. 23° 48′ N. long. 72° 2′ E. This was the ancient capital of Guzerat, and was formerly styled Nuhrwala.

Nuwanuggur is situated on the western coast of the Peninsula, in lat. 22° 55′ N. long. 70° 14′ E. It is a large town, the capital of a tributary chief, styled the Jam of Nuwanuggur, and is noted for various cotton manufactures.

Poorbundur, on the south-western coast of the peninsula, in lat. 21° 39′ N. long. 69° 45′ E., is a large and populous town, and one of the principal trading ports of Guzerat.

Puttun-Somnath, on the south-west coast of the Peninsula, in lat. 20° 53′ N. long. 70° 35′ E., is noted on account of its celebrity as a place of pilgrimage for the Hindoos. There was formerly a temple here, in which was an idol of very great repute. Mahmood of Ghuznee, allured by the report of its riches, attacked and captured the town in 1024, and destroyed the idol. The Brahmins entreated him to spare the image, and even offered a very large sum of money for its

Towns. ransom, but Mahmood was deaf to their solicitations. The idol was broken in pieces, when, to the agreeable surprise of the Mahomedans, an immense store of precious stones, as well as of money, was found concealed inside it. The idol was in fact the treasury of the Brahmins, who had therefore good reason for the great love they professed towards it.

Ahmedabad is situated on the banks of the Subrmuttee, in lat. 23° 1′ N. long 72° 42′ E. This was the Mahomedan capital of the province, and was formerly one of the most opulent and commercial cities in this quarter of India, but under its Mahratta rulers it was nearly ruined. It suffered greatly from the earthquake in 1819, but has since much improved. Its population is estimated at 100,000 inhabitants.

Travelling distance from Bombay 321 miles, from Delhi 610.

Kaira is situated about 40 miles to the north of Cambay, in lat. 22° 47′ N. long. 72° 48′ E. It is a large and neat town, the capital of the eastern division of the British territories in Guzerat, and the principal military station in the province.

Travelling distance from Bombay 334 miles.

Cambay is a seaport, situated at the head of the Gulf of Cambay, in lat. 22° 21′ N. long. 72° 48′ E. It is an ancient town, and was formerly of considerable commercial importance. The silversmiths at this place are still noted for their skill in embossing.

Chumpaneer is a hill fortress situated upon a large mountain or rock rising

Towns.

about 2500 feet above the surrounding level plain. At its foot there are the remains of an ancient city, the ruins of which extend for several miles round, said to have been the capital of a Hindoo principality long prior to the first Mahomedan invasion.

Baroda is situated in lat. 22° 21′ N. long. 73° 23′ E. This is the capital of the Gaikowar. It is a large and flourishing town, and contains about 100,000 inhabitants.

Travelling distance from Bombay 281 miles.

Baroch, or *Broach*, is situated on the north bank of the Nurbudda, about 25 miles from the sea, in lat. 21° 46′ N. long. 73° 14′ E. At an early period this place is noticed in history as a very flourishing seaport. It has since much declined, but still carries on a considerable coasting trade. Its present population is estimated at about 30,000 inhabitants, including a large proportion of Banyans and Parsees.

Travelling distance from Bombay 221 miles.

Surat, or *Soorut*, is situated on the south bank of the Tuptee, about 20 miles from its junction with the sea, in lat. 21° 11′ N. long. 73° 7′ E. This is one of the most ancient cities of Hindoostan, being mentioned in the Ramayana. After the discovery of the passage to India by way of the Cape of Good Hope, Surat became the principal resort of European trading vessels. Factories were established by the different European nations, and its population is said to have increas-

Towns. ed to 800,000 persons. In latter times the trade of Surat has much declined, other ports having risen into notice, and its manufactures not now being in so much request. It is now the capital of Guzerat, and the residence of the principal British authorities in the province. The town is large, but ugly and badly built; and contains about 180,000 inhabitants.

Travelling distance from Bombay 180 miles.

Sacheen, in lat. 21° 4′ N. long. 73° 5′ E. is noted as the residence of a petty chief, the head of a small principality of Siddees.

Daman, a seaport, in lat. 20° 25′ N. long. 72° 58′ E. belongs to the Portuguese. It was formerly a place of much commerce. At present it is noted chiefly for ship building.

Travelling distance from Bombay 100 miles.

Name. The origin of the name is not known. By the Natives it is usually pronounced "Goojrat."

Inhabitants. The inhabitants of this province comprise a great variety of classes, the principal of which are the following, Johrejas and other tribes of Rajpoots, Jhuts, Katties, Koolees, Bheels, Banyans, Parsees, Boras, Siddees, and Mahrattas. The Katties, according to their own traditions, are of Hindoo origin. From the earliest period of their history they have been professed thieves, considering robbery to be the express object of their

Inhabitants.

creation, and their proper and lawful mode of subsistence. The higher classes have always practised female infanticide. They chiefly inhabit the Peninsula.

The Koolees are a wild predatory tribe spread in considerable numbers throughout the province, forming numerous clans under the command of different chieftains. They have always been noted as a most turbulent race, delighting in war and bloodshed, and preferring plunder to any other means of subsistence. They are hardy and brave, and with the Bheels, were, for a long series of years, the incessant disturbers of the province, until coerced by the British into more regular habits. The Portuguese at an early period used the name *coolie* as a term of reproach, and from them it has passed in the same sense to the English. This must not be confounded with the word *cooly*, commonly used in Southern India, which is derived from the Tamil and merely means a labourer for hire. The Bheels, whose principal country is the province of Aurungabad, do not greatly differ from the Koolees, except as being still more savage and uncivilised. Probably both the Koolees and Bheels are of the same race, and it is the common belief in Guzerat, that these rude tribes are the original inhabitants of the province.

The Banyans, or *Vunyas*, are a tribe of Hindoos, the whole of whom are merchants or tradesmen.

The Parsees, or, as the name originally signified, the Persians, are the descendants of the ancient Guebres *(Gubrs)* or

Inhabitants.

fire-worshippers of Persia; the followers of the once predominant religion of the Magi, who left their country on its conquest by the Mahomedans. At first they retired to Ormus in the Persian Gulf, where they learned the art of ship-building, and also acquired some knowledge of navigation. After a few years they quitted Ormus, and proceeded to the island of Diu, on the south coast of Guzerat, from which place they afterwards removed to the Continent, landing at a place called Sejan, in about 20° N. lat. where they permanently established themselves. From this they subsequently spread over the western coast of India, and soon, from their superior intelligence and industry, acquired wealth and importance. As ship-builders especially, they are remarkably skilful. Their total number is estimated at about 200,000 families.

The Boras are a singular class of men found in all the larger towns of Guzerat, and in parts of Khandesh and the adjacent provinces, who, although Mahomedans in religion, are Jews in features, manners, and character. They form everywhere a distinct community, and are noted for their skill in trading and their extreme devotion to gain. They profess to be quite uncertain as to their own origin.

The Siddees, or Seedees, are the descendants of Abyssinians, who were formerly much employed under the Mooghul government for its naval service, and also in the army. The sailors of this province have always been consi-

Inhabitants. dered the best in India, especially those of Gogo, and other parts of Kattivad.

Bhats are more numerous in Guzerat, than in any part of India. These men may be described in general as itinerant bards. During the sway of the Native princes, even to a very recent period, they possessed unbounded influence, every chief having his bhat, and all classes looking upon their persons as sacred. They were regularly employed by the Native governments in the collection of revenue, and by individuals for the recovery of debts. In order to enforce the payment of claims, for which they had become security, these men were in the habit of performing or threatening to perform *traga*, that is, they would commit suicide, or more frequently put to death some aged female or child of their family, in presence of the party, causing them to break their engagement, and in such veneration are they held by the superstitious Natives, that in almost every case the threat would prove effectual.

The Grassias, who have been much noted in the history of this province for the last two centuries, are not a distinct tribe, but are simply plunderers of all descriptions and castes, both Mahomedans and Hindoos.

History. Of the early history of this province we have no accounts on which any dependence can be placed. According to Abool Fazil it was first invaded by the Mahomedans in 1025, when it was entered and overrun by Sooltan Mahmood of

History. Ghuznee, who conquered its native prince, named Jamund, and plundered Nuhrwala, his capital. Guzerat was subsequently annexed to the dominions of the Pathan empire of Delhi, but, in the 15th century, again became an independent kingdom under a dynasty of Rajpoot princes who had adopted the Mahomedan faith. In 1572, during the reign of Akber, this dynasty was overthrown, and the province was once more annexed to the Delhi empire. After the death of Aurungzeb in 1707, Guzerat was overrun by hordes of Mahrattas, and about 1724 was finally severed from the Mooghul dominions. Previously to this, Juwan Khan Babi had established himself as the soobadar of Guzerat, though not regularly appointed by the emperor; and his family continued with much bravery to dispute the sovereignty of the province with the Mahrattas until 1774, when Ahmedabad, their capital, was taken, and the Babi family reduced to the small principality of Rahdunpoor. The Peshwa and the Gaikowar continued to possess the greater part of the province until 1818, when the whole of the Peshwa's portion came under the authority of the British, who had before acquired some of the maritime districts, including Surat. The Gaikowar is the descendant of a Mahratta leader, who acquired his power nearly at the same period, and by the same course of proceeding as the Peshwa. Pellajee Gaikowar, the founder of the sovereignty, was a village potel, who after many struggles and intrigues succeeded in establishing his authority as an

History. independent chief. At present the province is divided between the Gaikowar and the British, with numerous minor chiefs, more or less dependent upon these powers and tributary to them, the Gaikowar himself having always been in alliance with the British, and protected by them.

Religion. Hindooism and Mahomedanism. The various rude tribes which have been noticed in this province generally consider themselves followers of the Brahminical system. They know very little, however, of Hindooism, and mostly worship the sun. Amongst the Hindoos the Jains are numerous.

Language. The general language of the province is the Goojratee. It is written in a character closely resembling the Nagree—and it may be termed the grand mercantile language of Western India.

§ 10.

Malwa.

Boundaries. North, Ajmeer, Agra, Allahabad; east, Allahabad, Gondwana; south, Khandesh; west, Guzerat.

Divisions. The province is now usually considered as consisting of three divisions: 1st, The territories of Sindia—2nd, The territories of Holkar—3rd, Those of Bhopal.

Rivers.

The principal are the Mhye, Seepra, Chumbal, Purbuttee, Kalee, Sind, and Betwa, all of which have their sources in or near the Vindhya mountains.

The Mhye flows northward into Ajmeer, where it turns to the westward through Guzerat into the Gulf of Cambay.

The Seepra flows northward into Ajmeer, where it joins the Chumbul.

The Chumbul flows northward into Ajmeer, where it turns to the eastward into Agra, and falls into the Jumna.

The Purbuttee flows northward and joins the Chumbul in Ajmeer.

The Kalee flows north-easterly into Agra, where it falls into the Jumna.

The Betwa also flows north-easterly, and falls into the Jumna, in Allahabad.

General Description.

This province consists of an elevated table land generally open, excepting towards the frontiers, but diversified with conical flat topped hills and low cross ridges. It has numerous rivers and streams flowing in opposite directions, its level being above that of all the adjacent provinces; and it enjoys a mild and healthful climate, with a rich and fertile soil.

A ridge of mountains separates it from Ajmeer on the north west, and the great Vindhyan range forms its southern frontier along the line of the Nurbudda, from which branches run up the eastern and western sides.

Productions.

Wheat, grain, peas, maize, and other grains; the first two being articles of export. Rice is also grown, but only in

Productions. small quantities. Sugar, tobacco, cotton, and a little indigo. The Malwa tobacco is the best in India, and is much sought after. The grapes also of this province have long been celebrated for their richness. But the staple article of produce is opium, the soil and climate of Malwa appearing to be particularly well adapted for the cultivation of the poppy. An immense quantity of this pernicious drug is annually supplied from this province.

Towns. Rajgurh, Khemlasa, Leronje, Mahidpoor, Oojein, Sarungpoor, Bhopal, Bhilsea, Salemow, Mundoogurh, Indoor.

Mahidpoor is a small town situated on the right bank of the Seepra, about twenty-four miles to the northward of Oojein. It is noticed on account of a great battle which was fought there on the 21st December, 1817, between the army of Mulhar rao Holkar and the British troops, when the Mahrattas were entirely defeated with great loss.

Oojein is situated on the right bank of the Seepra in lat. 23° 11′ N. long. 75° 35′ E.

This is one of the most ancient cities in India, and is particularly noted in Hindoo geography as being on the first meridian, called the Meridian of Lunka, which sometimes also takes the name of this city, and is called the Meridian of Oojein. The ancient city, which was greatly celebrated as one of the principal seats of Hindoo learning, has long since gone to ruins. The modern town which stands about a mile further to the south, was until recently the capital of the Sin-

Towns. dia Mahrattas. It is a large and populous place, and contains many handsome pagodas and other buildings, with some remarkably good sculptures. It had formerly an observatory, built by raja Jey Sing, which however has been allowed to go to ruin.

Among the inhabitants are a large proportion of Mahomedans, of the class denominated Boras.

Travelling distance from Bombay 500 miles, from Nagpoor 340.

Bhopal is situated about 100 miles to the eastward of Oojein, on the frontier of the province, having one gate in Malwa, and the opposite one in Gondwana.

It is the capital of the nabob of Bhopal, but in other respects is not a place of any particular note.

Bhilsea is a large town on the east side of the Betwa, about thirty-two miles to the north-eastward of Bhopal. It is celebrated for the tobacco of the surrounding district, which is carried to all parts of India.

Mundoogurh, or *Mandoo*, is situated in the Vindhya mountains, about 65 miles south-westerly from Oojein, in lat. 22° 23′ N. long. 75° 20′ E. This place is now in ruins and uninhabited, but it was formerly much celebrated as the capital of the Pathan sovereigns of Malwa, during the 15th and 16th centuries. It was then twenty-eight miles in circumference, and contained many splendid edifices, the ruins of which still remain.

Indoor is situated in lat. 22° 42′ N. long. 75° 50′ E. It is the capital of the Holkar Mahrattas, and is a large and populous town, but contains few buildings of any note.

Name. The origin of the name of this province is not correctly known.

Inhabitants. The inhabitants are principally Rajpoots, and Mahrattas, with a few Mahomedans, chiefly in the district of Bhopal. The mountains are occupied by Bheels and other savage tribes.

History. This province appears in very early times to have formed a kingdom of considerable note among the Hindoos, the rajas of Oojein, which was then the capital, being frequently mentioned in the Pooranas and other Hindoo records.

Early in the 13th century it was invaded by the Pathan sovereigns of Delhi, by whom it was either wholly subdued or rendered tributary. It subsequently became an independent sovereignty under an Afghan or Pathan chief, whose descendants continued in possession until about the middle of the 16th century, when the province was subdued by the emperor of Delhi, to whom it remained subject until the death of Aurungzeb in 1707. It was then invaded and overrun by the Mahrattas, and about the year 1732, it was finally separated from the Mooghul empire. Many years of the most wretched anarchy succeeded, which terminated in the formation of several distinct principalities, now chiefly comprehended in the territories of Oojein or Sindia, Indoor or Holkar, and Bhopal.

The founder of the Sindia dynasty,

History. Jyapa Sindia, was a follower of the second Peshwa of the Mahrattas, Bajee rao, by whom he was employed in various important commands. This chief's grandson was the celebrated Mahajee Sindia, a most active and enterprising leader, who, during his life time, completely controlled the whole Mahratta empire. Having formed a powerful army, disciplined by European Officers, he succeeded in subduing a large portion of Hindoostan Proper, compelled the Rajpoot states to pay him tribute, obtained possession of Delhi, and extended his dominions till they came in contact with the British territories under the Bengal Presidency. Having no son he adopted his nephew Dowlut rao Sindia, who succeeded to the throne in 1794. This chief from the moment of his succession, occupied himself in a systematic course of conquest on all sides, and in 1803 he entered into a confederacy with the raja of Nagpore against the British. In the war which ensued, and which lasted little more than four months, his troops were repeatedly defeated by Generals Lake and Wellesley, and he was compelled to agree to a peace, which deprived him of more than half of his dominions, and reduced him for some time to a state of very little importance. His country afterwards fell into a state of great confusion, partly through bad government, and partly through the increasing power of the Pindarees, whom he had at first encouraged, but was eventually quite unable to control. These were bands of mounted marauders, com-

History.

posed of all classes, Mahomedans, Rajpoots, and Mahrattas, who were gradually formed during the disorders which followed the breaking up of the Mahratta empire; and who under various leaders went on increasing in number and extending their incursions, which were executed with great rapidity, until their power became too formidable to be withstood by any Native state. The Mahratta chiefs showing that they were unwilling, as well as unable, to put a stop to the ravages of these blood thirsty robbers, the British Government was compelled to interfere. Dowlut rao Sindia, who had encouraged the Pindarees to invade the British territories, and who was also known to be engaged in intrigues with the Peshwa for the subversion of the British power, was in consequence compelled to submit to a treaty which effectually deprived him of the power of doing further mischief, and he has since remained at peace, under the control of the British Government. Dowlut rao died in 1827, and, having no son, was succeeded by a distant relation, adopted by his widow Baiza Bhye, who mounted the throne under the title of Muha raja Junkojee rao Sindia. The capital of this state is Gualior, to which Dowlut rao removed from Oojein soon after the former place was made over to him by the British Government in 1805.

The founder of the Holkar dynasty, Mulhar rao Holkar, was the son of a Mahratta shepherd; at an early age he was taken into the service of the Peshwa, and rapidly rose to distinction as a

History. military leader. He died about 1769, leaving no male descendants, and the government was assumed by Ahlia Bhye, the widow of his son, one of the most remarkable women who have ever lived. Her success in the administration of her dominions was extraordinary, and her memory is still revered throughout the country for the justice and wisdom of her rule. She associated with herself in the government, a relation of Mulhar rao, named Tukojee Holkar, whom she made her commander-in-chief, and nominated as her successor. Ahlia Bhye died in 1795, and Tukojee Holkar in 1797. Tukojee left four sons, two legitimate, Kasee rao and Mulhar rao, and two illegitimate, Wittul rao and Juswunt rao Holkar. These disputed the succession, and Dowlut rao Sindia, who was called in by Kasee rao after putting Mulhar rao to death, seized upon the greater part of the territory for himself. A long conflict ensued between Dowlut rao and Juswunt rao, in which the latter was at first defeated, and in 1801, Dowlut rao took possession of Indoor. Juswunt rao, however, soon afterwards collected another army, and commenced operations against the Peshwa. In a battle which he fought in 1802, he completely defeated the Peshwa's forces and captured Poona, which he was immediately after compelled to abandon by the advance of the British troops under General Wellesley. Juswunt rao took no part in the war which then broke out between Dowlut rao and the English, but his plundering habits, from which he

History. could not be brought to desist, subsequently involved him in hostilities with the British Government, which lasted during the years 1804 and 1805. His troops were completely defeated in several battles, and he was at last obliged to sue for peace which was granted. Juswunt rao not long afterwards became deranged, and dying in 1811, was succeeded by his son Mulhar rao Holkar, whose mother Toolsee Bhye acted as regent during his minority. Toolsee Bhye was unable to control the Pathan and other chiefs of the bands of Pindarees, who had formed a main part of Juswunt rao's forces; and in 1817, their aggressions brought on a second war with the English. Toolsee Bhye, who foresaw the consequences, and would gladly have made peace, was murdered by the Pathan chiefs, who the next day, 17th December, 1817, were attacked by the British army under General Hislop, at Mahidpoor, and totally routed. A treaty was soon afterwards concluded with Mulhar rao, who has since continued in peaceable possession of his principality, under the protection of the British Government. His capital is Indoor.

Bhopal is a Mahomedan principality, founded in the latter part of the 17th century by a Pathan chief, to whom the district was assigned as a reward for his services by Aurungzeb. His family still continue to hold the government, having succeeded in maintaining their independence against all the attacks of the neighbouring Mahratta chiefs, without any aid from the English until 1816,

History. when, in consequence of the widely increasing power of the Pindarees, the British Government found it necessary to yield to the entreaties of the nabob, and to take his state under its protection. Bhopal has ever since remained in peace.

Religion. Generally Hindooism, and in Bhopal, Mahomedanism.

Language. Mahratee, and a mixed dialect called the Rungkee, formed chiefly from the Hindee.

§ 11.

Allahabad.

Boundaries. North, Agra and Oude; east, Bahar; south, Bahar and Gondwana; west, Malwa and Agra.

Divisions. Cawnpoor, Allahabad, Manikpoor, Juwanpoor, Benares, Mirzapoor, Bundulkhund, Rewa.

Rivers. Goomtee, Ganges, Jumna, Tonse or Tunsa, Betwa, and numerous others. The Gogra flows along part of the northern frontier of the province, dividing it from Oude.

General Description. This province is one of the richest and most productive in India. The surface of the districts adjacent to the Ganges and Jumna is level and very fertile. In

General Description. Bundulkhund and Rewa, the country forms an elevated table land, occasionally mountainous and jungly, and diversified with high hills; but for the greater part open and capable of being made very fruitful. The northern frontier of the Rewa country consists of an abrupt front of sandstone rock, rising perpendicularly from two to three hundred feet from a sloping base. A large proportion of the water that falls during the rainy season on the table land of Rewa is precipitated over this rocky margin in numerous cataracts; amongst which those of the Beyhar and Tonsa rivers are of remarkable grandeur. The Beyhar cataract is one of the highest in the world, forming a single unbroken fall of 360 feet.

Productions. Wheat, barley, rice, maize, and other grains; opium, sugar, indigo, cotton, flax, and in the hilly districts, dyeing drugs and gums; chironja nut, catechu, and iron-diamonds, sometimes of large size, are found in the Punna district of Bundulkhund; and, in the district of Benares, there are extensive stone quarries. A good deal of alkali is also supplied from the country between the Goomtee and Ganges, from Kurra to Benares. The province has long been noted for its cotton fabrics, particularly muslins and brocades. Carpets also are manufactured, and coarse cumlies.

Towns. Rusoolabad, Cawnpoor, Akberpoor, Futihpoor, Kurra, Shahzadabad, Allahabad, Manikpoor, Mahowl, Azimgur,

Towns. Mow, Juwanpoor, Benares, Chunar, Ghazipoor, Mirzapoor, Dittea, Jhansee, Keeta, Banda, Kallinjer, Chutturpoor, Punna, Maltown, Hutta, Mow, Douree, and Rewa.

Cawnpoor (or *Khanpoor*) is situated on the west side of the Ganges, which is here more than a mile broad, in lat. 26° 30′ N. long. 80° 13′ E. It is a modern town, and one of the principal military stations in the province, to which circumstance it owes its rise. The neighbouring gardens produce abundance of grapes, peaches, and other European fruits and vegetables.

Travelling distance from Delhi 273 miles, from Allahabad 129.

Allahabad, the capital of the province, is situated at the confluence of the Jumna and Ganges, in lat. 25° 27′ N. long. 81° 50′ E. This was one of the favorite places of residence of the Emperor Akber, who founded the modern city. The fort is large and very strongly built, and is maintained by the British Government as the chief military depôt of the upper provinces. By the Hindoos, Allahabad is named Bhat Prayaga, or, by way of distinction as the largest and principal, simply Prayaga, and it is much resorted to by pilgrims; amongst whom suicide, by drowning themselves at the spot where the rivers unite, is a frequent practice. The word Prayaga means the confluence of any two or more sacred rivers.

Travelling distance from Benares 75 miles, from Delhi 400.

Juwanpoor is situated on the banks of

Towns. the Goomtee, about 40 miles north-westward of Benares. This was formerly a place of considerable importance, and for a short time the capital of an independent sovereignty founded by Khaja Juhan, wuzeer to Sooltan Mahmood Shah of Delhi, who assumed the title of Sooltan Shirkee, and taking possession of Bahar, fixed his residence at Juwanpoor.

There is here a bridge, remarkable for the skill and solidity of its architecture, which was constructed in the reign of the Emperor Akber, and still remains perfectly firm.

Travelling distance from Lucknow 147 miles, from Benares 38.

Benares is situated on the northern bank of the Ganges, in lat. 25° 30′ N. long. 83° 1′ E. This is considered to be the largest and most populous city in Hindoostan, its population (consisting of all classes, including Natives of all parts of India, with considerable numbers of Turks, Tartars, Persians, and Armenians,) being estimated at not less than 700,000 persons. It is, however, very badly built, the streets being extremely narrow, and the whole town remarkably dirty. By the Hindoos it is usually styled *Kusee*, or the splendid, and according to the Brahminical legends, it was originally constructed of gold; which in consequence of the wickedness of the people became stone, and latterly has degenerated into mud and thatch. The city with the surrounding country for ten miles distance, is held by the Hindoos to be sacred, and it is resorted to by great numbers of pilgrims. Many chiefs of

Towns. distant provinces, who cannot visit it in person, are accustomed to send deputies thither to wash away their sins for them by proxy. It is a place of considerable commerce, and a noted mart for diamonds procured chiefly from Bundulkhund.

Travelling distance from Calcutta 460 miles, from Allahabad 75.

Ghazipoor is situated on the north side of the Ganges, in lat. 25° 35′ N. long. 83° 33′ E. This is a large and populous town, and is noted for the manufacture of rose water. Numbers of superior horses are bred here in the Government stud; and there are cantonments for three regiments of cavalry.

Travelling distance from Benares 46 miles.

Mirzapoor, situated on the south side of the Ganges, in lat. 25° 10′ N. long. 83° 35′ E. is a large and flourishing town, well built and populous, containing about 70,000 inhabitants, of a remarkably active and industrious character. It is a place of extensive inland trade, and the principal cotton mart of the province. It is noted for its manufactures of carpets and various cotton fabrics.

Travelling distance from Benares 30 miles, from Calcutta, by Moorshedabad, 754.

Banda is situated in lat. 25° 30′ N. long. 80° 20′ E. This is the modern capital of Bundulkhund, and the residence of the principal British authorities of the district. The cotton of the neighbouring country is of a superior quality.

Kallinjer is situated in lat. 25° 6′ N.

Towns. long. 80° 25′ E. in a large open town, with an extensive and strongly built hill fort. The latter, however, is now dismantled, having been taken by the British in 1812, after a bloody siege, and subsequently destroyed.

Rewa stands in lat. 24° 34′ N. long. 81° 19′ E. about 70 miles southerly and westerly from Allahabad. It is the capital of the district, and the residence of the raja.

Name. The present name of this province was given to it by the Emperor Akber, on its being constituted by him a distinct sooba of the Mooghul empire. Originally there does not appear to have been any one general appellation applicable to the whole. The Hindoo division, answering to the modern district of Allahabad, was denominated Bhat Prayaga.

Inhabitants. Hindoos and Mahomedans. Amongst the former are some tribes of Rajkoomars, who were formerly in the habit of putting their female children to death. This practice, however, has now become infrequent, being punished under the British Government as murder. The people of the Bundulkhund district are generally called Boondelas.

History. In early times the northern districts of this province were included in the dominions of the Hindoo empire of Oude, and subsequently of Karroje. It was invaded and plundered as early as 1017 by Sooltan Mahmood of Ghuznee, and towards the close of the 12th century,

History. or about 1190, it was permanently subdued by the Pathan emperor of Delhi. It subsequently became for a short period an independent kingdom, the capital of which was Juwanpoor. Along with the rest of the Pathan possessions it afterwards fell under the power of the Mooghuls, and was formed into a distinct sooba by Akber, who new named the whole Allahabad. On the dismemberment of the Mooghul empire, the northern districts were appropriated by the nabobs of Oude; but in 1764, the district of Allahabad was ceded to Shah Alum, the then fugitive sovereign of Delhi, for his residence and support, reverting, however, to the nabob on the return of Shah Alum to Delhi in 1772. In 1775 the British Government acquired the districts of Benares, Juwanpoor, and Mirzapoor, from the nabob of Oude by treaty, and at subsequent periods the districts of Allahabad and Cawnpoor. Manikpoor still belongs to the Nabob. Bundulkhund and Rewa, though nominally included in the Mooghul province, appear always to have remained under their Native chiefs or rajas, composing a number of petty principalities. They were partially subdued by the Mahrattas who retained permanent possession of some of the western and southern districts, which with the rest were subsequently annexed to the British dominions. The northern parts are now under the immediate jurisdiction of the British Government, and the remainder is occupied by a number of petty chiefs under British protection and control.

Language. The general language of the province is Hindoostanee. The Bundulkhundee, or Boondelee dialect is spoken principally in the country westward of Allahabad, as far as Kalpee.

§ 12.

Bahar.

Boundaries. North, the Hills of Nepal; east, Bengal; south, Orissa and Gondwana; west, Gondwana, Allahabad, and Oude.

Divisions. Sarun, including Bettia, Tirhoot, Shahabad, Bahar, Boglipoor, Ramgurh, including Chhota-Nagpoor.

Rivers. Ganges, Gunduk, Kurumnasa, and Sone, all three flowing into the Ganges, and many others.

The Kurumnasa, though but an insignificant stream, is noticed on account of the singular character it bears amongst the Hindoos. They consider its waters to be so impure, that if a pilgrim, crossing it on his return from Benares, do but touch them, all the sins which the Ganges had washed away, will return upon him doubled.

General Description. From its northern frontier southward, including Sarun, Tirhoot, Shahabad, and Bahar, the country in general presents a level open surface, copiously watered and remarkably fertile. There are, however, some low sterile hills scattered through

General Description.

the district of Bahar. Boglipoor is occasionally hilly, and towards its eastern frontier mountainous and woody. Ramgurh is mountainous throughout, very rocky, and much covered with jungle. There are hot springs in various parts, and the climate of the northern and central districts is temperate and healthful.

Productions.

Agriculture, manufactures, and commerce have always flourished in this province; opium may be considered its staple commodity. Its other chief articles of produce are rice of the finest kind, excellent wheat and other grains, sugar, indigo, tobacco, cotton, hemp, pan, castor and seed oils, and a great variety of flower essences, particularly *utr*, usually called otto of roses, and rose-water. Sarun abounds in large timber, much used for shipbuilding, and produces a superior breed of cattle. Very good horses are bred in Tirhoot; amongst the wild animals a species of baboon is found in Boglipoor, named the Hunooman, which is held by the Hindoos as sacred as the cow. Bears also are numerous, and in the hilly parts, tigers, wolves, and hyenas. Large quantities of nitre are supplied from Sarun and Tirhoot, and iron, lead, antimony, and mica are found in Ramgurh. The manufactures are principally of cotton goods, and earthen-ware in imitation of English crockery. Opium, which has been mentioned as the staple of this province, is produced from a species of the poppy. When ripe, a small incision is made in the pod of the flower towards evening, from which the

Productions. juice distils during the night. In the morning this is scraped off, and afterwards being dried in the sun becomes opium.

Towns. Bettia or Chumparun, Chupra, Cheerun, Moozuffurpoor, Hajeepoor, Buxar, Arra, Rotasgurh, Dinapoor, Patna, Bar, Bahar, Daoodnuggur, ' Gaya, Monghir, Chumpranuggur, Boglipoor, Rajmahal, Sheergotti, Palamow, Ramgurh, and Burwa.

Hajeepoor is situated at the confluence of the Gunduh and Ganges, nearly opposite to Patna, in lat. 25° 41′ N. long. 85° 21′ E. It is noted for its annual horse fair.

Buxar is situated on the east side of the Ganges, seventy miles below Benares. A celebrated battle was fought here in 1764 between the British and the united armies of Shajaood Dowlut and Kasim Alikhan.

Travelling distance from Calcutta, by Moorshedabad, 485 miles.

Dinapoor stands on the south side of the Ganges, ten miles to the westward of Patna. It is one of the principal military stations of the province. Potatoes are produced here in great abundance.

Patna, the capital of the province, is situated on the south side of the Ganges, which is here, during the rainy season, five miles wide, lat. 25° 37′ N. long. 85° 15′ E. It is a large but irregularly built city, and contains about 300,000 inhabitants. It has always been a place of considerable trade, and was resorted to at an early period by the English, Dutch,

Towns. French, and Danes, who all had factories here.

Travelling distance from Moorshedabad 400 miles, from Benares 155.

Gaya is situated in lat. 24° 49′ N. long. 85° E. about 55 miles to the southward of Patna. The town consists of two parts. One the residence of the Brahmins and others connected with them, which is Gaya Proper, and the other called Sahibgunj, inhabited by merchants, tradesmen, &c.

This is one of the most noted places of pilgrimage in India, both for Booddhists and for followers of the Brahminical system. By the former it is considered to have been either the birth-place or the residence of the founder of their sect. The neighbourhood abounds with excavations.

Travelling distance from Calcutta 309 miles.

Monghir is situated on the south side of the Ganges, in lat. 25° 23′ N. long. 86° 26′ E. This was formerly a place of considerable importance. It is now noted principally for its iron and leather manufactures, including in the former guns, pistols, &c. The gardeners of Monghir are considered, the best in this part of India.

Travelling distance from Calcutta by water 301 miles. About five miles from Monghir is a hot spring named Seetakoond.

Name. The present name of this province is derived from that of the town of Bahar, or Vihar, which is supposed to have been

Name.

its capital at some former period. In Hindoo writings, the districts north of the Ganges were called *Maithila*, and Bahar and Shahabad were included under the name of *Moogadha*.

Inhabitants.

Hindoos, including a great number of Brahmins, and a large proportion of Mahomedans; this province having been conquered by them at an early period.

The hills of Boglipoor are inhabited by a number of original tribes, living in a very uncivilised state, and in the southern parts of Ramgurh are the Lurkakoles and other wild mountaineers.

History.

According to Hindoo legends Bahar appears to have been in ancient times the seat of two independent sovereignties, that of Maithila, or north Bahar, and Moogadha, or south Bahar. It was subsequently divided under different chiefs until conquered in the beginning of the 13th century by the Mahomedans, when it was annexed to the dominions of Delhi, and afterwards incorporated with Bengal as a sooba of the empire. Many parts, however, of the hilly districts were never perfectly subdued. Several of the original tribes preserving their independence both under the Hindoo and Mahomedan governments, not being converted or subjugated by either; and it appears that even in the most flourishing period of the Mooghul empire, there were still many petty chiefs, who did not acknowledge the authority of the Mahomedan vice-roy. With Bengal this province came under the government

History. of the British, in 1765, when the deewanee of the sooba was granted to them by the emperor of Delhi.

Religion. Amongst the Hindoos of this province there are a considerable number of the Sikh sect, and some Jains. The Boglipoor, and other hill tribes in general, have not adopted the Brahminical system, but still follow their original practices.

Language. Hindoostanee and Moogadhee. The latter, which is the vernacular language of the Hindoos of the province, does not greatly differ from Hindoostanee.

§ 13.

Bengal and its Dependencies.

Boundaries. Including the various minor states or principalities dependent upon this province, its boundaries are, north, Nepal and Bootan; east, Assam and Arracan; south, Arracan, the Bay of Bengal, and Orissa; west, Bahar.

Divisions. Exclusive of the dependent states, which will be separately noticed, the principal divisions of this extensive province are the following:—

Purnea, Rungpoor, Dinajpoor, Mymoonsing, Silhet, Beerbhoom, Moorshedabad, Rajshahee, Dacca-Julalpoor, Burdwan, Jungul-Mahals, Midnapoor, Hoogly, Twenty-four Purgunnas, Nud-

Divisions. dea, Jessoor, Bakergunj, Tippera, and Chittagong.

Rivers. Ganges, Hoogly, Teesta, Brahmapootra, and numerous others.

General Description. Along the whole northern frontier of this province there runs a belt of low land from 10 to 20 miles in breadth, covered with the most exuberant vegetation, particularly aujiya grass, which sometimes grows to the height of thirty feet, and is as thick as a man's wrist, mixed with tall forest trees. Beyond this belt rise the lofty mountains of Northern Hindoostan. Eastward of the Brahmapootra are other ranges of mountains, and along the westward and southwestward of Beerbhoom and Midnapoor, the country becomes hilly and broken. The whole remainder of the province may be described as one immense open plain, intersected in every direction by rivers and jheels, or small lakes, and having large tracts subject to annual inundation, forming one of the most fertile countries in the world. The whole extent of the southern coast, between the Hoogly on the west, and the Megna on the east, forming the delta of the Ganges, is broken into numberless small marshy islands, called the Sunderbunds, covered with forest, and swarming with tigers of the largest description, and alligators. These are uninhabited, but are resorted to, during the dry season, by woodcutters and salt makers, who carry on their trade at the constant hazard of their lives. Latterly attempts have been

General Description.

made to clear one of the principal of these islands, named Sagur, occupying the south-western corner, but, as yet, little has been accomplished. There are hot sulphurous springs in some parts of this province, and the vicinity of Calcutta is occasionally subject to slight earthquakes.

Productions.

Rice in the greatest abundance, wheat, barley, chenna, and other grains; indigo, cotton, silk, hemp, tobacco, opium, sugar, mustard, ginger, madder, lac, dyeing and medicinal drugs and gums, various seed oils, betel, wax, ivory, iron, saltpetre, limestone, shell lime, coal, and salt. Its manufactures of silk, and of muslins, calicoes, and other descriptions of cotton goods have long been the most celebrated in India. Amongst its fruits are oranges of the finest kind, which are produced in Silhet in such quantities that they have been sold at the rate of 1,000 for a rupee. The sheep and cattle are small, as are also the horses, of which there are some breeds of a remarkably diminutive size. Elephants abound, with tigers, bears, apes, monkeys, and other wild animals, and snakes of all descriptions. The rhinoceros is likewise found in this province, chiefly in the northern and north-western parts, and otters are numerous.

The silk, of which mention has been made above, comes from a small worm which feeds upon the leaves of the mulberry tree. The worm, when full grown, spins from its body, like the spider, a fine thread, which it winds round itself

Productions. so as to form a ball. This ball, which is called a cocoon, is thrown into hot water to kill the worm inside, and then the silk is wound off on a wheel. If the worm be not killed in this way, it changes into a moth, and eating its way out of the cocoon spoils the silk.

Towns. Purnea, Rangamatty, Goalpara, Chelmaree, Dinajpoor, Nussurabad, Silhet, Chera Poonjee, Moorshedabad, Burhampoor, Cossimbazar, Nattoor, Dacca, Fureedpoor, Narraingunj, Burdwan, Bankoora, Midnapoor, Jellasore, Chundernagore, Serampore, Calcutta, Kishenagur, Moorlee, Burrishol, Lukhipoor, Komilla, Chittagong, and Cox's Bazar.

Goalpara is chiefly noticed as a frontier town, and the principal trading mart between Bengal and Assam. Lat. 26° 8′ N. long. 90° 38′ E.

Chera Poonjee is a small English station in the Cassiya hills, about 20 miles to the north of Silhet.

Moorshedabad is situated on both sides of the most sacred branch of the Ganges, named the Bhageratty or Cossimbazar river, about 120 miles above Calcutta, in lat. 24° 11′ N. long. 88° 15′ E. It is a large but very meanly built city, and contains about 160,000 inhabitants. In 1704, it became the capital of Bengal, and continued so until superseded by Calcutta. It is now the principal civil station of the district, and a place of extensive inland traffic.

About 30 miles south of Moorshedabad is the town or village of Plassey, celebrated on account of a battle fought

Towns.

there in 1757, between the English, under the command of Clive, and the Nabob Serajood Dowlut, which decided the fate of Bengal, and, eventually, of all Hindoostan.

Cossimbazar, or *Kasimbazar*, is situated about a mile south from Moorshedabad, of which city it may be considered the port. It is particularly noted for its silk manufactures, this district being perhaps, next to China, the most productive silk country in the world.

Dacca is situated on a branch of the Ganges in lat. 23° 42′ N. long. 90° 17′ E. This was formerly one of the largest and richest cities in India, and was the capital of the eastern division of the Mahomedan government of Bengal. It is a large but irregularly built town, containing about 180,000 inhabitants, and is now probably the second in the province with respect to size and population. It is a place of extensive trade, and has long been celebrated throughout Europe as well as Asia, for its beautiful muslins and other fine cotton fabrics. As a proof of the fertility of this part of the province, it is related that, during the government of the viceroy Shaista Khan, in 1689, rice was so cheap at Dacca, that 320 seers were sold for a rupee. Travelling distance from Calcutta, by land, 180 miles.

Calcutta, the capital of India, and the "emporium of the east," is situated on the east side of the western branch of the Ganges, called, by Europeans, the Hoogly, but by the Natives, the Bhagiratty, about 100 miles from the sea, the

Towns.

whole of which distance is navigable for ships, the river at Calcutta itself being more than a mile in breadth. Calcutta owes its origin entirely to the English. In 1717 it was a petty village of mud huts, it is now a city of palaces. In 1756 Calcutta was beseiged and taken from the English by Surajood Dowlut, the nabob of Bengal, on which occasion the English prisoners, to the number of 146, were confined by him in a small room, called the Black Hole, about 20 feet square; where in one night all, except 23, perished from suffocation. The fort, named Fort William, stands about a quarter of a mile below the city. It was commenced by Lord Clive, shortly after the battle of Plassey, and is considered the strongest in India. The total population of Calcutta, amongst which are to be found Natives of every part of Asia, is estimated at about 550,000 persons.

A few miles distant from Calcutta, higher up the river, are the towns of Serampore and Chundernagore.

Serampore is an exceedingly neat town, and beautifully clean, on the west side of the Hoogly. It belongs to the Danes. This place has long been celebrated as a missionary station.

Chundernagore, distant 16 miles from Calcutta, on the west bank of the Hoogly, belongs to the French. It contains about 45,000 inhabitants.

Chittagong, or, properly, *Islamabad*, is a seaport, situated in lat. 22° 22′ N. long. 91° 42′ E. It is a place of considerable trade, particularly for teak and

Towns. other woods, and numbers of large ships are constructed in its dockyards.

Travelling distance from Calcutta 320 miles.

About 20 miles to the northward of Islamabad is a hot spring, called Seetakoond, and about eight miles from Seetakoond there is a small volcano.

Name. In Hindoo books this province is generally designated as the Gour or Bunya Desa. The lower part of the province was anciently called Bung, from which, probably, has been derived its present general appellation of Bungalee or Bengal. The upper parts of the province, not liable to inundation, were distinguished by the term *Barindra.*

Inhabitants. Hindoos of various classes, and Mahomedans. The Hindoos of the central parts of the province are styled Bengallies or Bengalese, and are distinguished for their effeminate and timid character, though, in words, forward and litigious. There are also connected with this province several savage tribes, probably the original inhabitants, dwelling in the woods and hills. The principal of these are the Garrows, Cosseahs or Khasiyas, and Kookees.

The Garrows occupy the mountainous tracts along the borders of Mymoon Singh and Silhet, spreading eastward towards Assam and Gentia. In person they are quite distinct from the Bengalese, being strong limbed active people, with broad flat features like the Chinese. They are in an exceedingly savage state,

Inhabitants.

and among other brutal practices, they are accustomed to eat the heads of their enemies, keeping the skulls, which, afterwards, are used by them as money, their value depending upon the rank of the individual to whom they belonged. They are divided into a number of tribes or classes, each having a distinct name, but none acknowledging that of Garrow, which appears to have been given them by the Bengalese.

The Khasiyas, or, as they style themselves, *Khyrs*, inhabit the mountainous tracts along the east of Silhet, southward of the Garrows, towards Assam and Kachar. They differ in appearance from the Garrows and others, not having the peculiar Tartar features by which those tribes are distinguished, and they are, on the whole, somewhat more civilized. They are under the government of a number of petty chiefs, amongst the principal of whom is the raja of Gentia. They are partially followers of the Brahminical system of religion, but mixed with many other superstitions of their own. Their language differs from that of the neighbouring tribes, and has no written character. For purposes of correspondence, however, they use the Bengalee.

The Kookees occupy the mountainous districts on the confines of Tipera and Chittagong, whence they spread over an extensive space northward and eastward. They are divided into numerous distinct tribes constantly at feud amongst themselves, living in an exceedingly savage state, many of the tribes going quite naked and dwelling in hollow trees.

Inhabitants. They are of a remarkably vindictive disposition, and think that nothing is more pleasing to their Creator than destroying the greatest possible number of their enemies. In person they are stout, and generally fairer than the Bengalese, with Tartar features.

It appears probable that these tribes are all of them aboriginal, that is, the first inhabitants of the country.

In the jungles of Midnapoor there is a poor, miserable, proscribed race of men, called Sontals, despised by the other Hindoos as outcasts, and not allowed to abide in any village; yet they are a mild, sober, industrious people, and remarkable for sincerity and good faith, in which respect they are greatly superior to those who think themselves their betters.

A large proportion of the inhabitants of Chittagong are Mugs,—for information concerning whom the student is referred to the description of Arracan.

History. There is no record of the existence, at any former period, of the present province of Bengal as a separate Hindoo kingdom. In the Mahabharat it is noticed as forming part of the empire of Moogadha or Bahar, and it appears subsequently to have been divided under different rajas. It was twice entered and plundered, in 1017 and 1018, by Sooltan Mahmood of Ghuznee. In 1203 it was invaded by a Mahomedan army from Delhi. The capital was surprised, and the greater part of the province subdued, the raja Lukhyaman making his escape

History. to Jugganat, where he died. From this era Bengal was ruled by governors delegated from Delhi until 1340, when a revolt took place, and it became an independent sovereignty. The history of Bengal, from 1340 to 1538, presents nothing but one continued series of assassination and bloodshed. In 1538 Mahmood Shah was expelled by Sher Shah, the Afghan, with whose family the province remained until 1576, when it was conquered by the armies of the Emperor Akbar, and once more annexed to the dominions of Delhi. In the early part of the eighteenth century, Bengal again became independent under its soobadar—usually styled in English writings the nabob—Jaffeer Khan. In 1576, the nabob, Sura jood Dowlut, attacked the English and captured Calcutta, and the war which ensued terminated in the eventual establishment of the British authority over the whole province.

Religion. Hindooism and Mahomedanism.

Language. The prevailing language of the province is called Bengalee, and is written in the Deva-Nagree character. Hindoostanee or Hindee is also general.

BENGAL DEPENDENCIES.

Included in the province of Bengal, and lying along its northern and eastern frontiers, are the following petty districts, before referred to, and which will now be separately noticed: Sikkim, Kooch Bahar, Bijnee, Gentia, and Kachar.

SIKKIM

is bounded on the north by the Himalaya mountains, which separate it from the Chinese dominions in Tibet; east by Bhootan, from which it is divided by the river Teesta and Kooch Bahar; south by Rungpoor and part of Morung; and west by Morung. In length it may be estimated at 60 miles, from west to east, by an average breadth of 40 miles from north to south.

Description and Productions. It is a mountainous district, but fertile and well cultivated. Its principal productions are rice, madder or munjeet, bees wax, and timber of various kinds.

Towns. Its towns are few, and none of any importance. The principal are Sikkim, Tasiding, and Bilsee. Sikkim is the capital, and stands in lat. 27° 16′ N. long. 88° 3′ E. about 110 miles northerly from the town of Purnea.

A short distance to the south-eastward of Sikkim, and about 350 miles from Calcutta, is Darjeling, a station in the hills, which is resorted to by the English from the low country for change of air, the climate being cold and healthful.

Name. This district is called Sikkim, or Sikkim Bhoot, from the name of its capital, and from its being subject to a Bhootiya chief.

Inhabitants. Its inhabitants are composed principally of a hill tribe, called Lapchas. There are also some Bhootiyas, and the hills are said to contain many of the Limboo tribe.

History. This state was formerly much more extensive than it now is, and is said to have included a great part of the northern division of Rungpoor. In 1788, it was invaded and conquered by the Goorkhas, the raja taking refuge in Tibet, after vainly attempting, with the help of a force sent to his assistance from Bhootan, to recover his dominions.

In 1814, on the breaking out of a war between the Goorkhas and British, the dethroned raja gave all the aid in his power to the latter, who, in consequence, rewarded him, at the conclusion of peace in 1816, by the restoration of his territory, which he has since held as their ally. The rajas of Sikkim are of Bhootiya origin, and trace their descent from a chief family of Lassa.

Religion. The system of religion most prevalent in Sikkim is that of Tibet, or Lama Booddhism.

Language. The prevailing dialect is believed to be the Bhootiya.

KOOCH BAHAR

is situated between Bhootan on the north, Bijeen on the east, Rungpoor on the south, and Sikkim on the west.

Description and Productions.

The southern portion of this district is fertile and well cultivated, but to the north of Bahar, approaching to the mountains, the land becomes marshy, covered with thick jungle, intersected by numerous nullahs, and completely choaked up with rank grass, reeds, and ferns. Its principal article of produce is opium.

Towns.

Its chief town is Bahar, (or Vihar,) situated in lat. 26° 18′ N. long. 89° 22′ E. about thirty miles north-easterly from Rungpoor.

Name.

It derived its name from that of its capital Bahar, with the addition of Kooch, to distinguish it from the Indian province of Bahar.

Inhabitants.

The inhabitants of this country are generally styled Kooch, or Koochee, and the Bengalese generally look upon them as a low and impure race. This opinion, however, is very disagreeable to their chiefs, who reject the name of Kooch, and assert that they are of divine origin. The people style themselves Rajbungsees.

History.

Very little is known of the early history of this state. In 1582, Abool Fazil describes the chief of Kooch as a powerful sovereign, having Assam and Kamroop under subjection. In 1661 it was conquered by Meer Joomla, Aurungzeb's general, and thenceforward became a dependency of the province of Bengal.

Religion. The Brahminical system appears to have been introduced at an early period, and is now nearly general; some, however, of the original Kooch tribes, who still remain in a very rude state, follow their ancient practices.

Language. The prevailing dialect is believed to be the Bengalee.

BIJNEE

adjoins Kooch Bahar, having on the north, Bhootan; east, Assam and the Garrows; and, on the south, the Rungpoor district of Bengal. This district is separated by the Brahmapootra into two divisions, the northern called Khuntaghat, and the southern Howraghat.

Description and Productions. It is fertile, and, if well cultivated, would be a very valuable district, being well watered and open, and having an excellent soil. The chief productions are rice, wheat, barley, betel, and sugar. It also possesses the mulberry tree, which, however, has not as yet been made use of for the rearing of silk worms.

Towns. The principal town is Bijnee, situated in lat. 26° 29′ N. long. 89° 47′ E.

Name. It has its name from that of its principal town.

Inhabitants. The inhabitants are of the Kooch tribe, and take the general name of Rajbungsees.

History. As far as is known of this principality, it has always been under the rule of its own chief, or, as he is at present styled, zumeendar; but always tributary to the government of Bengal, and sometimes, also, to that of Bhootan. The right of nomination to the succession, on the death of a zumeendar, is exercised by the British.

Religion. Their religion consists of a mixture of the Brahminical system, with various other superstitions of their own.

Language. Bengalee.

GENTIA OR GENTIAPOOR

lies between Assam on the north, Kachar on the east, Silhet on the south, and the Garrows on the west. Its extreme length, from east to west, is estimated at 100 miles; and its extreme breadth, from north to south, at about 80.

Description. For some miles from its borders, north and south, this territory consists partly of thickly wooded hills, and partly of low land; but the intermediate country, about 50 miles in extent, is an undulating plain, free from jungle, and well adapted for pasturage, but very thinly inhabited and not cultivated.

Productions. Chiefly cotton, rice, and a coarse kind of silk, called *tussur*, from the wild silkworm. Elephants and ivory also are exported, and amongst the minerals are iron, limestone, and coal.

Towns. The only town is Gentiapoor, the residence of the raja, situated about 30 miles to the northward of Silhet.

Name. It is called Gentia or *Juntiya* from its capital.

Inhabitants. The inhabitants of this district appear to be of the same class as those of Kachar.

History. This territory, although of such limited extent, is ruled by a number of petty chiefs, nominally subject to the raja of Gentiapoor, but paying very little real deference to his authority. The people are, in consequence, harassed with incessant feuds, and remain in a very wretched and barbarous condition.

Religion. Their present religion is that of the Hindoos, which has been introduced among them from Bengal.

Language. Their language very much resembles the Chinese, but has no written character. The Bengalee, however, has latterly been adopted by their chiefs, and will probably soon become their general language.

KACHAR

is bounded on the north by Assam; east, by Cassey; south, by Tippera and Silhet; and west, by Gentia. It extends about 140 miles from north to south, and 100 from east to west.

Divisions. It is composed of two divisions, the northern called Dhurmapoor, and the southern Kachar, separated from each other by a ridge of mountains.

Rivers. Its principal rivers are the Kapili and Boorak, both of which rise in the eastern mountains, and flow south-westerly into the Megna.

General Description. This country is, for the greater part, mountainous and much overrun with jungle and swamps. In the level parts the soil is fertile, but not well cultivated.

Productions. Cotton, coarse silk, wax, timber, limestone, iron ore, and salt, with rice and other grains.

Towns. Dhurmapoor, Doodputtee, and Kospoor.

Dhurmapoor is situated in an extensive valley on the banks of the Kapili, about 60 miles northerly from Kospoor.

Doodputtee stands on the banks of the Boorak, in lat. 25° 3′ N. long. 92° 42′ E. Since 1811 it has been the residence of the raja, and, consequently, the capital of the country. It is also noted as the scene of an action which took place in 1824, between the Burmese and a British detachment, in which the latter was defeated with much loss.

Kospoor, the former capital, is situated in lat. 24° 45′ N. long. 92° 45′ E. about 60 miles easterly from the town of Silhet. Previous to the raja's removal to Doodputtee, it was a flourishing town, but has since greatly decayed.

Name. The original and correct name of this country was Hairumbo. It has acquired its present denomination of Kachar from the tribe composing its inhabitants.

Inhabitants. The inhabitants are called Kacharees, and are part of a numerous tribe scattered over this quarter of Asia, though the name is usually limited to the Kachar principality. They are a robust race, of fairer complexion than the Bengalese, and of Tartar features.

History. There are no distinct accounts of the early state of this country. In 1774 it was invaded by the Burmese, who, however, were compelled to abandon their design, their troops being seized with the jungle fever, and the greater number perishing. They subsequently sent another expedition, which had better success, and Kachar thenceforward became tributary to Ava. In 1810, Marjeet, the raja of Cassay, being driven out of his country by the Burmese, retired with his followers into Kachar, and expelled the raja, Govind Chandra, who took refuge in the British territories. The country now remained, for several years, in a state of extreme disorder; Murjeet and his two brothers, Gumbheer Sing and Choorjeet, contesting possession amongst themselves, and each in turn expelling the other. In 1823, Kachar was again invaded by the Burmese, and Gumbheer Sing, the last in possession, fled into Silhet. The British government now determined to restore the legitimate raja, Govind Chandra. Their troops accordingly entered Kachar

History. and drove out the Burmese, who, on the conclusion of peace in 1826, finally relinquished all claim to its possession, and it has since remained under its own raja, tributary to the British.

Religion. The present religion of Kachar is that of the Hindoos, which was introduced in 1780.

Language. The Bengalee recently introduced. The original Hairumbian dialect has now become extinct.

CHAP. VII.

DEKKAN.

§ 1.

Khandesh.

Boundaries. North, Guzerat and Malwa; east, Gondwana and Berar; south, Berar and Aurungabad; west, Aurungabad and Guzerat.

Divisions. This province may be considered as consisting of three divisions: British Khandesh, Holkar, and Sindia. The British portion comprises the whole of

Divisions. Khandesh Proper, and occupies the western part of the province from north to south. Holkar's portion occupies a small space in the centre, and Sindia's, a tract along the eastern side.

Rivers. Nurbudda, Tuptee, Poorna, and others.

General Description. This province in general is hilly, and traversed centrally and along its eastern, southern, and western sides, by ranges of mountains. It is, however, for the greater part remarkably fertile and copiously watered, and, until the commencement of the present century, well cultivated and thickly peopled. In 1802 it was ravaged by the Holkar Mahrattas, and the year following it was nearly depopulated by a severe famine. From this period it rapidly declined. Oppressed by a rapacious government, and continually devastated by Bheels and Pindarees, it was rendered almost a desert, and when entered by the British in 1818, the larger portion of the province was found to be overspread with jungle and abandoned without inhabitants to the wild beasts. A long period of time will probably be required ere this territory can be restored to its original prosperity.

Productions. This province is capable of producing in abundance every thing found in the adjoining countries. Its fruits and vegetables are excellent, particularly grapes, which are considered the finest in India. Amongst the wild animals, tigers and wolves are very numerous and troublesome.

Towns. In British Khandesh, Nunderbar, Sindwa, Dowlea, Chopra, Jamneer, Malligaum, and Chundoor.

In Holkar's .districts, Kurgoon and Bejagur.

In Sindia's, Hoshungabad, Hindia, Hurdwa, Charwa, Asseergurh, and Boorhanpoor.

Nunderbar is situated in lat. 21° 25′ N. long. 74° 15′ E.

Sindwa is a fortress situated in lat. 21° 34′ N. long. 75° 7′ E. which commands one of the principal passes through the Satpoora mountains communicating with Malwa.

Doolea is a large town, situated in lat. 21° 1′ N. long. 74° 47′ E.

Chopra, lat. 21° 41′ N. long. 75° 23′ E.

Jamneer, lat. 20° 54′ N. long. 75° 52′ E.

Mulligaum, lat. 21° 31′ N. long. 74° 36′ E.

Chandoor, a fortified town commanding the principal pass into Aurungabad, and situated in lat. 20° 19′ N. long. 74° 19′ E.

Kurgoon is situated in lat. 21° 50′ N. long. 75° 40′ E. It is considered the capital of the Holkar districts in Khandesh, and the usual residence of the Mahratta governor.

Bejagur is a large hill fort, situated in the Satpoora mountains, in lat. 21° 36′ N. long. 75° 30′ E. This was the capital of the old Hindoo province of Neemar, and was subsequently that of the Mooghul province of Khandesh, until supplanted by Boorhanpoor.

Hoshungabad, or, as it is sometimes

Towns. called by the English, *Hussingabád*, is situated on the south bank of the Nurbudda, in lat. 22° 40′ N. long. 77° 51′ E. It is a large town, and of considerable importance on account of its position, as it commands the principal fords in this direction. In 1827 a vein of blind coal was discovered here. The town with its dependent district belongs to the British, and may be considered as annexed to the Gurra-Mundla division of Gondwana.

Travelling distance from Nagpore 187 miles.

Hindia is situated on the Nurbudda, in lat. 22° 56′ N. long. 77° 5′ E. It is the head of a district of the same name, occupying the north easternmost part of the Sindia division.

Asseergurh is a strong hill fortress, situated about 12 miles northerly and easterly from Boorhanpoor. It is noted on account of its siege in 1819 by the British troops, by whom it was captured after an obstinate resistance.

Boorhanpoor, formerly the capital of the province, is situated in a fine plain on the bank of the Tuptee in lat. 21° 19′ N. long. 76° 18′ E. This is one of the largest and best built cities in the Dekkan, and abundantly supplied with water brought into the town by aqueducts, and distributed through every street, the stream being conveyed at a certain depth below the pavement, and the water drawn up through apertures by means of leather buckets. The grapes grown in the vicinity of this town and Asseergurh are considered the finest in India.

Travelling distance from Poona 288

Towns. miles, from Nagpore 256, from Oojein 154. Boorhanpoor is the principal residence of the class of Mahomedans called Boras.

Name. The origin of the name of this province is not correctly known.

Inhabitants. Mahrattas, a small proportion of Mahomedans, including those of the Bora class, and Bheels, of which tribe this province may be considered the original country. The Bheels are found in all the hilly and wooded districts, from Malwa to Bejapoor, and from the eastern parts of Guzerat to Gondwana. They are a distinct people from the Hindoos, and are supposed to form part of the original inhabitants of central India. In person they are generally small and black, of wild appearance, going nearly naked, and constantly armed with bow and arrow. They are divided into a number of tribes, each under its own naik or chief. They are generally averse to agriculture, and addicted to hunting and plunder, but being now subject to a more regular control, they will probably acquire more civilized habits.

History. Prior to the Mahomedan invasion this province formed part of the Hindoo sovereignty of Deogurh. After the dissolution of the Bhamenee empire of the Dekkan, Khandesh appears to have constituted an independent state under a Mahomedan family claiming descent from Oomr Khalif, and having their capital at Asseergurh. Towards the close of the

History. 15th century, it was subdued and added to the Mooghul dominions, from which it was wrested in the early part of the 18th century by the Mahrattas. It was subsequently partitioned among three chiefs, Holkar, Sindia, and the Peshwa, and suffered severely from the disputes in which those rival powers were constantly engaged, particularly from the savages of Holkar's troops, in 1802 and 1803. It remained under these rulers until 1818, when in consequence of the war which then took place between Holkar and the British, the principal portion of the province was transferred to the latter. When entered by the British, the greater part of Khandesh, though nominally subject to the Mahrattas, was found to be actually under the authority of a number of Arab leaders, whom the English were compelled to remove by force, as they refused the offer, which was made to them, of being conveyed back to their own country. These Arabs had originally engaged in the service of the Mahratta chiefs as mercenaries, and, having gradually acquired possession of the principal fortresses, were in a fair way to become the independent rulers of the whole province.

Religion. Hindooism and Mahomedanism.

Language. The prevailing language is the Mahrattee. In the Hoshungabad district the Gondee is commonly spoken.

§ 2.

Gondwana.

Boundaries. North, Allahabad and Bahar; east, Bahar and Orissa; south, Orissa, the northern Circars, and Hyderabad; west, Beder, Berar, Khandesh, Malwa, and Allahabad.

Divisions. Of the numerous districts into which this extensive province is divided, the following may be considered the principal. Baghela or Baghulkhund, Singrowla, Gurra-Mundla, Sohajpoor, Sirgooja, and Sumbhulpoor, belonging to the British dominions, and Deogur, Nagpore, Chanda, Chouteesgur, Wynegunga and Bustar, belonging to the raja of Nagpore.

Rivers. Sone, Nurbudda, Gunga or Wyne-Gunga, Wurda, and Mahanudee; all, excepting the Wurda, having their sources in this province. The Gunga flows southerly, and joining the Wurda, falls with it into the Godavery.

General Description. The greatest portion of this province presents a very wild appearance, abounding with rugged mountains, and covered with forests. The eastern and southern districts, particularly, are in an exceedingly savage state. Westward, though traversed by ranges of hills, and in many parts thickly wooded, the country is more open; and in Chunteesgur and the

General Description.

northern districts there are large tracts of clear and fertile ground. The province in general is poorly cultivated and thinly inhabited. The climate of the hilly and wooded districts is remarkably unhealthy, and usually fatal to the natives of other parts.

Productions.

Rice, wheat, chenna, jowaree, and other dry grains; sugar, hemp, cotton, opium, tobacco, arrow-root, pan, and bees wax; dyeing drugs, oils, gum, and coarse silk, of the description called *tussur*, obtained from the cocoon of a large species of caterpillar. The forests yield a plentiful supply of teak, saul, and other large timber, and the lac insect abounds. Diamonds of a large size, and gold, are to be found in the vicinity of the rivers, particularly of the Mahanudee; but the unhealthiness of the climate prevents their being much sought after. Iron, talc, limestone, coal, red-ochre, and marble are also procured in different parts. The district of Singrowla contains the largest quarry of corundum in India. Wild beasts are numerous, particularly tigers and bears of a large size, with the gaour, mirjee, a peculiar species of wild dog, and some others very little known to Europeans. The gaour is a very powerful and fierce animal of the ox kind, resembling the bison. The mirjee, or mouse deer, so called from its head resembling that of a mouse in form, is the smallest of the deer species, being about the size of a jackal. Among the snakes which abound in this province is the *boa-constrictor*.

Towns. Bandoogur, Saipoor, Gurra, Jubbulpoor, Mahadeo, Chouragur, Choupara. and Mundla, Sohajpoor, Kurgomma and Oomerkuntuk, Sirnadoo, Jushpoor, Gangpoor, Sumbhulpoor, and Patna, Deogur, Babye, Baitool, Jilpee-Amneer, Nagpore, Chanda, Ruttunpoor, Konkeer, and Byrgur, Wynegunga, Wyragur, and Bustar.

Jubbulpoor is situated in lat. 23° 11′ N. long. 80° 16′ E. It is the modern capital of the district, and is better built than the majority of the towns in this part of India. Coal is found in its neighbourhood.

Travelling distance from Nagpore 160 miles.

Mahadeo is situated in the Mahadeo hills, in lat. 22° 22′ N. long. 78° 35′ E. This is one of the wildest tracts in the Dekkan, and was almost unknown to Europeans until 1818, when it was entered by the British troops in pursuit of Appa Sahib, the ex-raja of Nagpore. It is a place of pilgrimage for the Hindoos, but it is chiefly noticed here on account of its hot sulphurous springs, of which there are two in the vicinity.

Oomerkuntuk is situated at the sources of the Sone and Nurbudda, in lat. 22° 55′ N. long. 82° 7′ E. on which account alone it is noticed, being otherwise merely a place of resort for pilgrims.

Nagpore, the capital of the province, and of the Bhonsla Mahratta state, is situated in lat. 21° 9′ N. long. 79° 11′ E. It is a large town, but meanly built, and its site is low and swampy. It contains about 115,000 inhabitants of various classes.

Towns.

Travelling distance from Calcutta 740 miles, from Hyderabad 300, from Bombay 550, from Madras 700.

A short distance from the city of Nagpore is an English Military cantonment, which has the name of Kamptee.

Chanda, situated 80 miles southward from Nagpore, is a populous and strongly fortified town, equal in size to Nagpore, and has generally been the principal depôt of the Mahratta government in this province.

Name.

This province has received its general name of Gondwana, as being the country of the Gond tribe.

Inhabitants.

Gonds, Hindoos of various classes, principally Mahrattas and Telingas, from different parts of Hindoostan Proper and the Dekkan, and a small proportion of Mahomedans.

The Gonds are mentioned in the historical poems of the Hindoos, as being a powerful nation or tribe in early times; and there seems no doubt that they are an original people, the first possessors of the land, and quite distinct from the Hindoos, by whom at different periods they have been partially conquered and driven from the plains to the hills and jungles. They are divided into a number of tribes or clans, the majority of which are in an exceedingly ignorant and savage state, many of them living like wild beasts in the woods, perfectly naked, and subsisting upon roots and vegetables. According to native accounts these tribes are addicted to cannibalism. Their re-

Inhabitants. ligion is of a very rude character, and is occasionally attended with human sacrifices, especially amongst the Bustar tribes. There is, however, a great difference, as well in habits as in size and appearance, between the domesticated Gonds of the plains and the wild tribes, the former being generally tall and well made, and frequently fair and handsome, and in many respects superior to their Hindoo and Mahomedan neighbours. In the districts eastward of Nagpore there are two tribes, named the Golur and Holur, who speak the Canarese language. They are all thieves, but perfectly under the control of their naiks or chiefs, and never troublesome when the latter are conciliated. Nothing has been ascertained regarding their origin.

History. The country over which the Gonds are now scattered seems, at an early period, to have been partially subdued by the Hindoo rajas of the adjacent provinces; and when the Mahomedans first invaded the Dekkan, Gondwana was under the general rule of the three Hindoo monarchs of Gurra, Deogur (in Aurungabad) and Telingana. After the overthrow of the Deogur and Telingana kingdoms, the greater portion of the province appears to have been divided into a number of independent states, some under Hindoo, some under Gond rajas, but all, however, generally styled Gond chiefs, the most powerful of whom was the raja of Deogur. During the reign of Akber, the Gurra raja was conquered, and his territory annexed to the Moo-

History. ghul empire, in which, subsequently, the whole province was nominally included, though never really subject to any Mahomedan government. In 1738, Ragojee Bhonsla taking advantage of internal dissensions and disputed claims to the sovereignty, obtained possession of the Deogur territories, and fixed his capital at Nagpore. Under his successors the remainder of the province was subdued and added to the eastern or Bhonsla Mahratta empire. In 1803 the raja of Nagpore having joined the Sindia Mahrattas, in a confederacy against the English, was compelled to purchase peace by the cession of a large portion of his territories, eastward in Orissa, to the English, and westward in Berar, to the Nizam of Hyderabad; and in 1818 a second war with the English was followed by the further loss of the several districts in the province of Gondwana itself, which have been already enumerated as belonging to the British dominions.

Language. Gondee, Mahratee, and Teloogoo. The Gondee is spoken more or less throughout the province. It contains many words resembling the Teloogoo and Tamil, but has no peculiar written character. The Mahratee is the language of the court and of all government functionaries, and is most common in the districts of Deogur, Nagpore, Chanda, and Wyne Gunga. Teloogoo is spoken in Chanda. Many other dialects and mixtures of dialects are spoken by the various mountain and wild tribes.

§ 3.

Berar.

Boundaries. North, Khandesh and Gondwana; east, Gondwana; south, Beder and Aurungabad; west, Aurungabad and Khandesh.

Divisions. The province is divided into a number of small districts, but which are not sufficiently well defined to be correctly enumerated.

Rivers. Tuptee, Wurda, Paeen Gunga, and two Poornas. The Wurda and Paeen Gunga both have their sources in this province. The Paeen Gunga flows easterly into the Wurda, and the Wurda south-easterly, joining the Wyne Gunga in Gondwana; one Poorna flows westerly into the Tuptee, and the other south-easterly into the Godavery.

General Description. The principal portion of this province consists of an elevated valley shut in on the south by ranges of hills extending from Ajuntee to the Wurda, other ranges of hills traverse the province further northward, but the country in general is open. The soil is chiefly of the description designated black cotton and is naturally fertile, though, owing to the very disturbed state in which the province has long been, it is poorly cultivated.

Productions. Wheat, maize, gram, and other grains; cotton, and flax.

The bullocks of this province are noted for their size and strength.

Towns. Gawilgurh, Narnulla, Ellichpoor, Mulkapoor, Balapoor, Akola, Oomrawutti, Ajuntee, Jaffurabad, Maikher, and Mahoor.

Gawilgurh is a fortress, situated on a rocky hill, in the midst of a range of mountains, lying between the Tuptee and Poorna in lat. 21° 22′ N. and long. 77° 24′ E. fifteen miles north-westerly from Ellichpoor. This was considered by the Natives of India as impregnable, but it was taken by assault in 1803 by the British troops after a siege of not more than a few days.

Narnulla is a fortified town, situated about 40 miles N. W. of Ellichpoor, lat. 21° 40′ N. long. 77° 30′ E. It is an ancient town, and has always been a place of note in the province.

Ellichpoor is situated in lat. 21° 14′ N. long. 77° 36′ E. It is a large open town, the capital of the province, and the usual residence of the Nizam's governor in this part of his dominions.

Travelling distance from Hyderabad 340 miles, from Nagpore 120.

Oomrawutti is situated thirty-four miles south-easterly from Ellichpoor, in lat. 20° 54′ N. long. 77° 57′ E. It is a large and populous town, and a place of considerable inland traffic.

Ajuntee is noticed on account of its situation near the ghat or pass of the

Towns. same name, in lat. 20° 34′ N. long. 75° 56′ E. It is a large town but not populous. In the neighbourhood are some excavations resembling those of Ellora.

In this province are the villages of Assaye and Argaum, where two celebrated battles were fought in 1803 between the British troops, under General Wellesly, and the Mahratta armies of Sindia and the Bhonsla raja.

Name. The derivation of the name of this province is not known.

Inhabitants. Principally Hindoos of the Telinga and Mahratta races.

History. Prior to the Mahomedan invasion in 1294, this province was partly dependent upon the Hindoo sovereignty of Telingana, and partly under different petty Gond chiefs. After its conquest by the Mahomedans, it became part of the Bahmenee empire of the Dekkan, on the dissolution of which, the principal portion of the province was formed into an independent state styled the Oommed Shahee, from its founder, Oommed Ool Moolk. This, however, lasted only from 1510 to 1574, when Berar fell under the dominion of Ahmednuggur, and subsequently of Delhi. In the early part of the 18th century it was overrun by the Mahrattas, and for several years was divided between the peshwa and the raja of Nagpore. The latter having joined Dowlut rao Sindia in hostilities against the British, his share of Berar was transferred to the Nizam of Hy-

History. derabad, with whom the greater part of the province now remains.

Religion. Hindooism and Mahomedanism.

Language. Mahratee and Teloogoo.

§ 4.

Orissa.

Boundaries. North, the river Subunreeka, separating it from Bengal; east, the sea; south, the Ganjam district of the Northern Circars; west, Gondwana.

Divisions. Singhbhoom, Mohurbunj, Balasore, Kunjoor, Boad, and Kuttack, with several smaller zumeendaries.

Rivers. Subunreeka, Solundee, Bytoornee, Bahmunee, Mahanudee, and others.

General Description. This province may be considered as consisting of three distinct regions, the maritime, the central, called the Mooghulbundee, and the western, or Rajwara. The maritime, from the Subunreeka on the north to the Chilka Lake on the south, and, from the sea to about twenty miles inland, is a low, flat, swampy tract, covered with wood, and frequently inundated, and intersected in all directions by numerous rivers. Twenty miles inland the country rises considerably, with an open, dry, and fertile surface, forming the second or Mooghulbundee division,

General Description.

which, about twenty miles further inland, swells into wooded hills; and beyond these is the third, or Rajwara, occupying the western portion of the province, and consisting entirely of ranges of hills. The greater part of the interior of this province is in a very savage state, particularly the Rajwara division, being composed of rugged hills, thick jungles, and deep nullas, and pervaded by a remarkably pestilential atmosphere.

Productions.

Rice, maize, wheat, gram, and other grains; aromatic roots, spices, dyeing drugs, sugar, cotton, tobacco, honey, wax, and dammer. The woods of the maritime districts are chiefly of Soondree, from which wood oil is extracted, and *Janool;* those of the Mooghulbundee abound with resinous trees, and others valuable for cabinet work and for dyeing; and from the Rajwara forests teak of good quality is procured. Iron is abundant; many valuable and curious minerals are found in Rajwara, and, from the mountain streams, gold dust is collected. Diamonds, also, of a large size, are to be found, but the extreme unhealthiness of the climate, in the districts in which they are met with, prevents their being properly sought after. Abundance of salt, of a remarkably white and pure description, is manufactured on the coast. The rivers abound with fish, and the whole province swarms with wild beasts, particularly leopards of a large size, and it is much infested by snakes, alligators, and reptiles of all kinds.

Towns. Singhbhoom, Hurioorpoor, Balasore, Kunjoor, Jajpoor, Kuttack, and Juggernaut.

Singhbhoom is in the Rajwara, in lat. 22° 31′ N. long. 85° 40′ E. and is the residence of the zumeendar of the district.

Hurioorpoor is the principal town or village in the zumeendaree of Mohurbunj. It is in lat. 21° 51′ N. long. 86° 42′ E.

Kunjoor, the chief town of the zumeendaree of the same name, is situated in lat. 21° 31′ N. long. 85° 32′ E.

Balasore, (Balishwar,) the principal seaport of the province, is situated near the mouth of a small river called the Boori-Balang, in lat. 21° 32′ N. long. 86° 56′ E. This was formerly a flourishing town, and at an early period of their intercourse with India, the Portuguese, Dutch, and English had factories here. It is still the principal trading place of the province, and is the regular resort of the Maldive vessels. It has dry docks capable of receiving small vessels, not drawing more than fourteen feet.

Travelling distance from Calcutta 141 miles, from Kuttack 103.

Jajpoor is situated on the south bank of the Bytoornee, in lat. 20° 52′ N. long. 86° 24′ E. This was the ancient capital of the kings of Orissa, and was also a place of importance under the Mooghul government, and was the usual residence of the Mahomedan governor of the province. At present it is little more than a large straggling village of mud huts, but it contains some remarkable ruins of

Towns. Hindoo temples, and it is considered by the Hindoos as a holy place, being frequently styled the first gate of Juggernaut. A good deal of cloth is manufactured here.

Kuttack is situated inland, between two branches of the Mahanudee, in lat. 20° 27′ N. long. 86° 5′ E. It is the capital of the province, and is a large well built town, containing about 40,000 inhabitants. During the rainy season the Mahanudee, near the city, is two miles from bank to bank, but, during the dry season, it is fordable with less than three feet of water. The surrounding country is low, and frequently under water for a circuit of more than ten miles.

Travelling distance from Calcutta 248 miles, from Nagpore 482, from Madras 780.

Juggernaut, or *Jugga-nat*, is on the coast, in lat. 19° 49′ N. long. 85° 54′ E. This is one of the most celebrated places of Hindoo pilgrimage in India, and great numbers of persons annually resort thither to be present at the bathing and car festivals. The idols are three in number, and are formed of rudely carved blocks of wood, painted white, black, and yellow, and having exceedingly hideous and grotesque countenances. The ceremony of the procession is too obscene and disgusting to describe. The present pagoda of Juggernaut was completed in the year 1198, during the reign of the Hindoo rajas of Orissa. The town is named Pooree, and is inhabited chiefly by Brahmins, and others connected with the

Towns. pagoda. The town is usually called *Pooree*.

Travelling distance from Calcutta 297 miles, from Madras 766.

On the sea-shore, eighteen miles to the northward of Juggernaut, are the remains of an ancient temple of the sun, called, in English charts, the black pagoda. The greater part of the temple is in ruins, having been thrown down, apparently, by lightning or earthquake; but, from what remains, it appears to have been one of the most singular edifices ever constructed in India. Part of the tower, 120 feet high, is still standing, and the antechamber, or *jungmohun*, about 100 feet high. They are built of immense blocks of stone and massive beams of iron, some of which are nearly a foot square, and from twelve to eighteen feet long. This temple, which has been long deserted, was built by a raja of Orissa in 1241.

Name. The name "Orissa" appears to be derived from Ooresa or Oor-desa, the country of the Oor or Oorda tribe.

Inhabitants. The inhabitants of the province are Hindoos, with the distinguishing name of Ooreas, but there are also in the woods and hills three distinct tribes, called Koles, Khonds, and Soors, all differing in language and appearance from the Hindoos, and generally supposed to have been the original natives of the province. The Koles, who are subdivided into a number of small tribes, are a hardy athletic race, of black complexions and

Inhabitants. exceedingly ignorant, without any regular system of religion, worshipping the dog, the sahajna tree, paddy, mustard seed and oil. They are, however, generally industrious cultivators, and have their houses tolerably well built of wood. Their original country, which they style *Kolat Desum*, is described by them as the north-western districts of Orissa, between Singhbhoom and Mohurbunj.

The Khoonds resemble the Gonds, and are believed to be of the same origin.

The Soors are found chiefly in the jungles southward and westward of Kuttack, and in the woods which skirt the base of the hills. They are of diminutive stature, of jet black complexion, and of a mean appearance, and in a most barbarous state of ignorance. They worship rocks and stumps of trees, and appear to be entirely destitute of moral feeling.

History. The early history of Orissa consists entirely of ridiculous fables, copied from the Pooranas, mixed with local traditions. No dependence can be placed upon any of the records prior to the commencement of the sixth century, when the accounts begin to assume an appearance of authenticity. According to these, Orissa was governed by a race of Hindoo kings, who successively extended their dominions, by conquest and otherwise, until they included part of Bengal on the north, of Gondwana on the west, and of Telingana southward, as far as the Godavery. It continued to form an independent Hindoo state until

History. 1558, when it was invaded by the Pathan ruler of Bengal, who defeated Mukhum Deo, the raja, and finally overthrew the Orissa sovereignty. In 1578 the Pathans being conquered by Akber, Orissa was annexed to the Mooghul empire, at which period, according to the institutes of Akber, it comprehended the whole extent of country between Midnapoor in Bengal on the north, and Rajamundry on the south. On the dissolution of the Mooghul empire, Orissa formed part of the sovereignty established by the subadar of Bengal. In 1743, it was invaded and plundered by a large army of Mahrattas, and it was afterwards subjected to the predatory incursions of that people every year until 1750, when Aliverdi Khan, the soobadar of Bengal, agreed to pay them a regular *chout*, and, in 1756, he ceded the province to them altogether. From that period Orissa continued in a most wretched state of anarchy and distress, until conquered from the Mahrattas in 1803 by the British. At present the most fertile and best inhabited portion of the province is under the jurisdiction of the British Government divided into a number of zumeendaries, and the remainder is possessed by tributary zumeendars, called *ghurjats* or hill chiefs, but usually styling themselves rajas, who pay an annual rent to the British Government, and are protected by it; and about half of their number being also subject to the British laws.

Religion. The Ooreeas are all followers of the

Religion. Brahminical system, but the wild tribes of Koles, Khonds, and Soors, as has been already mentioned, have no intelligible system of religion, and are entirely strangers to the institution of caste or other Hindoo observances. There are also Jains in this province.

Language. The language of the Ooreea nation is a dialect of the Sanscrit, much resembling the Bengalee, and called the Ooreea. The dialects of the wild tribes are distinct.

§ 5.

Aurungabad.

Boundaries. North, Guzerat, Khandesh, and Berar; east, Berar and Beder; south, Bejapoor and Beder; west, the sea.

Divisions. The following are the principal districts:—Jowar, Kallianee, Bombay, below the mountains; Sumgumneer, Jooneer, Ahmednuggur, Perrainda, above the mountains, belonging to the British dominions, and Aurungabad; Bheer, occupying its eastern side, and belonging to the Nizam of Hyderabad.

Rivers. Godavery, Seena, Beema, all of which have their sources in this province, Moota, Moola, and many smaller.

General Description. This province is traversed, from north to south, by the great range of Western

General Description. Mountains, and its surface throughout is very irregular and broken, abounding with rocky jungly hills. It is in general fertile, and its climate, above the mountains, temperate. There are some remarkable caves or excavations in different parts which will be noticed in connexion with the towns near which they are situated.

On the coast, in about 19° N. lat. and separated from the main land by a narrow strait, are several small islands, of which the principal are Salsette and Bombay.

Productions. Rice and other grains and cotton. Horses of a small but very active and hardy breed are reared in great numbers on the banks of the Beema. Fruits of different kinds are abundant and fine, particularly grapes, melons, oranges, and figs.

Towns. Jowar, Basseen, Kallianee, and Bombay, below the mountains; Nassuck, Sungumneer, Jooneer, Ahmednuggur, Perrainda, Aurungabad, Jalna, and Peytun.

Basseen is a seaport, separated by a narrow strait from the island of Salsette, and distant about thirty miles from Bombay. This place was obtained by treaty, from the sooltan of Cambay in 1531, by the Portuguese, who lost it about 1750 to the Mahrattas, from whom it was subsequently taken by the English.

Kallianee is a populous town, situated inland about thirty miles to the north-eastward of Bombay.

Towns.

Bombay is the third principal English town in India. It is situated in lat. 18° 56′ N. long. 72° 57′ E. on a small island, about ten miles in length and three in breadth, lying south of Salsette, from which it was formerly separated by an arm of the sea about 200 yards across, but now communicating with it by a causeway, which was completed in 1805.

The first European settlement here was formed by the Portuguese, who acquired possession of the island in 1530, from the chief of Tanna, in Salsette. In 1661 the Portuguese ceded it to the English. It is a place of very extensive commerce with every part of the world. Its harbour is the best in India, and its dockyards large and good. Vessels of the largest size, as well for the British navy, as for the merchant service, are built here by Parsee shipwrights, perfectly equal to those constructed in the dockyards of England. The population of the town of Bombay is estimated at 200,000 persons, comprising a mixed multitude of Hindoos, Parsees, Mahomedans, Portuguese, Jews, and a few Armenians.

Travelling distance from Calcutta, about 1400 miles, from Delhi 868, from Madras about 800.

About five miles eastward from Bombay is a small island, named Elephanta, in which is a remarkable cave, formerly used as an idol temple. It is 18 feet high, 55 feet long, and as many broad, and is filled with large idols, of which the principal is a colossal Trimoorti, or three formed figure, combining Bramha,

Towns.

Vishnoo, and Siva. The cavern is not now used as a place of worship. Near the landing place, leading to the cavern, is a large elephant hewn out of the rock, from which the Portuguese gave the island its present name. There are also other remarkable excavations at Kanneri in Salsette.

Nassuck is situated on the Godavery, in lat. 19° 56′ N. long. 73° 56′ E. It is a large town containing about 30,000 inhabitants, principally Brahmins, and is much resorted to as a place of pilgrimage. In the neighbourhood are some extensive Booddhist excavations.

Sungumneer is situated in lat. 19° 21′ N. long. 74° 24′ E.

Jooneer is situated in lat. 19° 12′ N. long. 74° 10′ E. It is a large town, with a strong fortress, and was formerly the capital of the province. There are numerous excavations and cave temples at this place of Jain origin.

Ahmednuggur is situated in lat. 19° 5′ N. long. 74° 55′ E. It was built in 1493 by Ahmed Nizam Shah, who made it his capital. At present it is one of the principal civil stations of the British Government in this province. It contains about 20,000 inhabitants, and has a strongly built fort.

Travelling distance from Bombay 180 miles, from Poona 83, from Hyderabad, 335.

Perrainda is in lat. 18° 18′ N. long. 75° 44′ E.

Aurungabad is situated in lat. 19° 54′ N. long. 75° 33′ E. This city was originally named Goorkha, but, having

Towns.

become the capital of the province, and the favorite residence of Aurungzeb, when viceroy of the Dekkan, it received from him the appellation of Aurungabad. It is a large well built town, abundantly supplied with water brought in stone conduits from the neighbouring hills, and distributed through pipes, into numerous stone reservoirs in every quarter. It has a large and handsome bazar named the Shah-ginj, particularly noted for silks and shawls. Aurungabad is the usual residence of the governor of the northern division of the nizam's dominions.

Travelling distance from Hyderabad 295 miles, from Poona 186, from Delhi 750.

Seven miles to the north-westward of Aurungabad, stands the celebrated fortress of Dowlutabad. Prior to the conquest of this province by the Mahomedans, this place was the capital of an independent Hindoo state, and was then called Deogurh or Tagara. In the early part of the 14th century, the emperor Sooltan Mahomed, endeavoured to make Deogurh the capital of his kingdom, on which occasion he changed its name to Dowlutabad; but he was obliged to desist from his project, after nearly ruining the city of Delhi, by driving away the inhabitants, in order to make them settle at the new seat of government. In a mountain, about a mile to the eastward of Dowlutabad, are the caves of Ellora, or, as the place is called by the Natives, Verrool. In magnitude and execution these excavations excel everything of the kind in India. They compose several temples,

Towns.

and are filled with figures,—some are dedicated to Siva, and others are Booddhist. According to the Brahmins they were formed by Eeloo, raja of Ellichpoor, about 8,000 years ago, but, on investigation, they appear to have been executed about 2,500 years since, and not more.

Jalna, or *Jalnapoor*, is situated in lat. 19° 52′ N. long. 76° 8′ E. It consists of two towns separated by a small river and a fort, and is an English military station.

Travelling distance from Hyderabad 265 miles.

Peytun, properly *Puttun*, is situated on the Godavery, in lat. 19° 26′ N. long. 75° 35′ E. This place was formerly noted for the manufacture of cloths, with beautiful gold, silver, and silk borders.

Name.

In ancient Hindoo geography, this province, with some others, was included under the general name of Mahrashtra. After its subjugation by the Mahomedans, it received successively the names of Dowlutabad, Ahmednuggur, and Aurungabad.

Inhabitants.

The inhabitants of this province are principally Mahrattas, this being the original country of that people.

History.

In early times this province was divided into a number of little principalities and chiefships, which do not appear to have been, at any period, completely subjugated, though frequently invaded by the Mahomedans, and, in the early part of the fourteenth century, considered as

History. part of the Delhi dominions. It was afterwards annexed to the Bhamanee empire of the Dekkan, on the dissolution of which the town and district of Ahmednuggur became an independent sovereignty, known as the Nizam Shahee, existing as such from 1489 until 1634, when, with the other provinces of the Dekkan, this also was subdued and added to the Mooghul empire. The first Mahratta leader who succeeded in uniting the different chiefs and tribes under one head, and in inducing them to combine their efforts for the expulsion of their foreign rulers and the re-establishment of their independence, was the celebrated Sevajee. This chief, the founder of the great federal empire of the Mahrattas, was born in 1628. He successfully opposed Aurungzeb, and, at the time of his death, in 1680, had firmly established his authority over the whole of the country below the mountains from Surat to Goa. He was succeeded by his son Sambajee, who still further extended the boundaries of his dominions, but, in 1689, falling into Aurungzeb's hands, that monarch put him to death. Sambajee's successor was his son, Sahoo raja, who reigned for more than fifty years, though only in name, as he indolently delegated the whole of his authority to his peshwa or prime minister, a Konkan Brahmin, named Balajee Bishun-nat. In this period, however, the Mahratta empire extended itself with astonishing rapidity, until the whole of the Dekkan, and several provinces of Hindoostan Proper, and South-

History. ern India, were either subdued or made to pay an annual tribute, known long subsequently as the Mahratta chout, *(fourth part.)* Sahoo raja died in 1740, and was succeeded by his son, Ram raja, a weak prince, who entirely lost even the shadow of power which his father had retained. The peshwa and the bukhshee, who were the two chief officers of the empire, conspiring together, confined the raja in the fortress of Suttara, and divided the kingdom, though still leaving the title to the raja. The peshwa, Balajee Bajee rao, a son of Balajee Bishun-nat, took possession of the western part of the empire, and made Poona his capital. The bukhshee, named Ragojee Bhonsla, seized the eastern part, and made Nagpore, in Gondwana, the seat of his government. On this, other chiefs, in different provinces, also declared themselves independent, and, eventually, the Mahratta empire ceased to exist as one federal state, and became divided into the several governments of the Peshwa or Poona Mahrattas, the Nagpore raja, or Berar Mahrattas, Sindia, Holkar, and the Gaikowar, with a number of minor chiefships. The province of Aurungabad was one of the earliest conquests of the Mahrattas from the Mooghul empire, their authority over it being fully established in 1707. From that period, with the exception of part of the maritime districts possessed by the British, and the eastern districts of Aurungabad and Bheer, possessed by the Nizam of Hyderabad, it remained under the Poona Mahratta

History. government until 1817, when the peshwa, Bajee rao, urged by extreme hatred towards the English, commenced a war, entirely unprovoked by them, which terminated, in 1818, in the complete annihilation of his power. Bajee rao, after being for many months a fugitive, was compelled to surrender himself a prisoner, and to abdicate his authority. He was allowed to take up his residence at Bittoor, a place of pilgrimage on the banks of the Ganges, near Cawnpoor, with an annual pension of eight lacs of rupees, and the whole of his territories were annexed to the British dominions, with the exception of the district of Suttara, which was assigned to the raja of Suttara, a number of jageers being also reserved for the support of different chiefs and members of the former government.

Religion. Principally Hindooism.

Language. The prevailing language of the province is the Mahrattee. Goojrattee, and Hindoostanee are also spoken.

§ 6.

Beder.

Boundaries. North, Aurungabad and Berar; east, Hyderabad and Gondwana; south, the Kistna; west, Bejapoor and Aurungabad.

Divisions. Puthree, Nandair, Calliany, Beder, Akulcotta, and Kulburga.

Rivers. Godavery, Munjera, Beema, Kistna, and several smaller rivers.

General Description. The surface of this province is broken, and hilly, but not mountainous, generally open, and very productive, but thinly peopled, and consequently not well cultivated; though under its ancient Hindoo government it is said to have been exceedingly populous and fruitful.

Productions. Wheat, cholum, and other dry grains, and cotton.

Towns. Nandair, Neermul, Calliany, Beder, Akulcotta, and Kulburga.

Nandair is situated on the north bank of the Godavery, 135 miles northerly and westerly from Hyderabad, in lat. 19° 3′ N. long. 77° 38′ E. It is a large and populous town, and was the capital of Nandair when it was a distinct province of the Mooghul empire. At this place there is a Sikh college erected on the spot where Gooroo Govind is supposed to have been assassinated, and many of the inhabitants are of that sect.

Neermul is situated to the eastward of Nandair in lat. 19° 19′ N. long. 78° 40′ E.

Calliany is in lat. 17° 50′ N. long. 77° 5′ E.

Beder, the capital of the province, and formerly of the Bhamenee empire, is situated in lat. 17° 49′ N. long. 77° 46′ E. The present town of Beder was built near the ruins of the old Hindoo city of the same name, by Ahmed Shah Bhamenee about the year 1440, and was

Towns. called by him Ahmedabad. It was noted for works of tutenague inlaid with silver. such as hookka bottoms and similar articles, which are still denominated Beder-ware.

Travelling distance from Hyderabad 76 miles.

Akulcotta stands in lat. 17° 30′ N. long. 76° 18′ E.

Kulburga is situated in lat. 17° 19′ N. long. 76° 56′ E. This is now a place of little note, but was of considerable celebrity in ancient times, having been the capital both of a Hindoo and a Mahomedan sovereignty. Rajas of Kulburga are mentioned by Ferishta as independent princes in 1295, and when the founder of the Bhamenee dynasty erected the standard of rebellion in 1347, he made this his capital.

Travelling distance from Hyderabad 107 miles.

Name. The name of this province is derived from that of the old Hindoo city so called.

Inhabitants. Notwithstanding its having so long been under a Moosulman government, this province contains few Mahomedans, the inhabitants being chiefly Hindoos.

History. Previous to the invasion of the Dekkan by the Mahomedans in 1295, this province belonged principally to the Hindoo rajas of Nandair and Kulburga. In 1347 it became part of the celebrated Mahomedan kingdom, known in history as the Bhamenee empire of the Dekkan;

History. after the dismemberment of which it passed through various changes of government, until in the reign of Aurungzeb it was annexed, with the rest of the Dekkan, to the empire of Delhi. In 1717 it became part of the independent sovereignty established by Nizam Ali, with whose successors it has since remained.

Language. The junction of three languages takes place in this province. Northward and westward of Beder, the prevailing language is the Mahratee,—northward and eastward the Teloogoo,—southward and eastward the Teloogoo,—and southward and westward the Kanarese.

§ 7.

Hyderabad.

Boundaries. North, the Godavery, separating it from Beder and Gondwana; east, the Godavery and ranges of hills, separating it from Gondwana and the Northern Circars; south, the Kistna and Toombudra, (dividing it from the Ceded Districts,) and part of the Dooab, and west, Beder.

Divisions. It is divided into several small districts or collectorates for revenue purposes, named after the principal town of each, but which need not be enumerated, as they are liable to occasional alteration.

Rivers. Godavery, Munjera, Moosa, and Kistna. The Munjera flows northerly into

Rivers. the Godavery, the Moosa easterly and southerly into the Kistna.

General Description. The surface of this province is an elevated table land, hilly but not mountainous, and generally open. Southward of the city of Hyderabad, the country is much covered with jungle and thinly peopled. The climate is temperate, and the soil naturally fertile, but it is indifferently cultivated. In former times this province was thickly populated, and prosperous, but from being very badly governed, it has long been in a declining state.

Productions. Wheat, cholum, and other dry grains, and a little opium.

Towns. Maiduk, Warungol, Hyderabad, Neelcoonda, and Kummum-nait.

Warungol was the ancient capital of the Hindoo sovereignty of Telingana, and is situated about 80 miles north-easterly from Hyderabad, in lat. 17° 54′ N. long. 79° 34′ E. It was built about the year 1067. In 1324 it was taken by the Mahomedans, and some time after retaken by the Hindoos. In 1421 it was again finally captured by the Mahomedans.

Hyderabad, also styled in former times Bag-nuggur, stands on the south side of the Moosa in lat. 17° 15′ N. long. 78° 35′ E. It is a large but meanly built town, containing about 200,000 inhabitants, and having been for a long time the capital of a Moosulman government, is now the chief resort of the principal

Towns. Mahomedan families of the Dekkan. It was founded about the year 1585 by Kootb Shah.

Travelling distance from Madras 394 miles, from Calcutta 940, from Bombay 450, from Delhi 967.

Three miles west of the city of Hyderabad stands the fortress of Golconda, formerly the capital, first of a Hindoo, and afterwards of a Mahomedan kingdom. Under the empire of Delhi, this fortress was frequently used as a prison for the Mooghul princes.

Three miles to the north of the city is Secunderabad, the cantonment of the English troops.

Name. The present name of this province is of modern origin, and was given to it under its Mahomedan rulers from its capital.

Inhabitants. There is a large proportion of Mahomedans in this province, but the Hindoos still form the most numerous class.

History. This province was originally part of the old Hindoo country of Telingana, which, while it existed as an independent state, comprehended the greater portion of the districts lying between the Godavery and Kistna. It was first invaded by the Mahomedans in 1295, and after its final subjugation by them, became part of the Bhamenee sovereignty of Beder. On the dissolution of the Bhamenee empire, about the year 1500, Telingana was again formed into an independent government, called the kingdom

History. of Golconda, or by Mahomedan writers, Kootb Shahee of Golconda. In 1690, Golconda was captured by Aurungzeb, and the province annexed to the dominions of Delhi. On the breaking up of the Mooghul empire, after Aurungzeb's death, Nizam-ool-moolk, then soobadar of the Dekkan, established himself in the independent possession of his sooba, comprehending all the Mahomedan provinces in the Dekkan and southern India. He died in 1748, aged, it is said, 104 years, and was succeeded by his second son, Nazir Jung, who in 1750 proceeded with a large army to the Carnatic, to settle the government of that province, and was there assassinated by the three Pathan nabobs of Savanoor, Kurnool, and Cuddapa. His murderers then proclaimed, as soobadar, Moozuffur Jung, a grandson of Nizam-ool-moolk, at that time a prisoner in Nazir Jung's camp, but almost immediately afterwards conspired against him also. In the conflict which ensued, Moozuffer Jung and the three nabobs were all killed; and Sulabut Jung, another son of Nizam-ool-moolk, then succeeded. He was murdered in 1763 by his own brother, Nizam Ali, who took possession of the musnud. During nearly the whole of his reign, Nizam Ali was engaged in disputes with the Mahrattas, who, in 1795, entirely defeated him, and but for the protection and assistance of the British, would soon have conquered his whole dominions. Nizam Ali died in 1803, from which period the government has continued without interruption in his family, with the title of "Nizam."

Religion. Mahomedanism and Hindooism.

Language. Teloogoo and Hindoostanee.

§ 8.

Northern Circars.

Boundaries. North, Orissa; east, the Sea; south, the Northern Carnatic; west, the Ceded Districts, Hyderabad, Gondwana, and Orissa, from which provinces it is separated by ranges of hills.

Divisions. Ganjam, Chicacole, Rajamundry, Ellore, Kondapilly, and Guntoor.

Rivers. Godavery and Kistna, besides many smaller rivers and streams.

General Description. This province consists of a long and narrow tract on the sea coast, shut in throughout the whole length of its western boundary by ranges of wooded hills. The soil along the coast is chiefly sandy, but inland it improves, and is fertile. The climate is hot, and the air of the hills remarkably unhealthy.

Productions. Rice, gram, wheat, and other grains in abundance; sugar, cotton, and excellent tobacco. Large quantities of salt are manufactured and exported, and the forests produce teak of a large size.

The different circars, and their principal towns, will now be separately noticed.

GANJAM.

This is the most northern of the circars. Its north-western part bordering upon Orissa, forms a hilly district, called Goomsur, covered with thick bamboo forests, and inhabited by a rude mountain tribe. The remainder of the circar, towards the sea, is flat and open. It is separated from Orissa by a chain of hills and a large sheet of water, about 35 miles long and 8 broad, called the Chilka Lake.

Towns. Aska, Ganjam, Burhampoor, Munsoorcotta, Ichapoor, and Barwa.

Ganjam, situated in lat. 19° 21′ N. long. 85° 10′ E. is a seaport, and was formerly a place of considerable trade, and one of the principal stations of the English; but for some years past it has been abandoned, on account of the great unhealthiness of its climate.

Travelling distance from Madras 700 miles, from Kuttack 117.

Burhampoor is an inland town, situated 20 miles south-westerly from Ganjam. It is noted for its silk manufactures. The silk is imported from Bengal and China.

CHICACOLE.

This district was anciently designated the *Kalinga Desum*. It is the largest of the circars. It is generally hilly, well watered, having four rivers flowing into the sea at Kalingapatam, Chicacole, Bimlipatam, and Vizagapatam, besides some smaller streams, and very fertile.

Towns. Kalingapatam, Chicacole, Vizianagram, Bimlipatam, and Vizagapatam.

Chicacole is situated a little distance inland on the northern bank of a river of the same name. By the Mahomedans it was named Mafooz Bundur. It is noted for the manufacture of muslins.

Travelling distance from Madras 567 miles, from Ganjam 132.

Bimlipatam and Vizagapatam are both seaports, and places of considerable coast trade. The chief articles of export are cotton cloths, commonly called "piece goods," which are manufactured in various parts of the district.

RAJAMUNDRY.

This district lies along both sides of the Godavery, and from its being so well watered, is the most fruitful of all the circars. About 35 miles from the sea, the Godavery divides into two branches, and forms a triangular or three cornered island, called Nagur, or Nagrum, containing about 500 square miles of ground, and very fertile. The Rajamundry forests in the hills, along the southern bank of the Godavery, abound with teak. The other principal productions of this district are sugar and rice.

Towns. Samulcottah, Rajamundry, Coringa, Injeram, Bundur Mulunka, and Nursapoor.

Rajamundry, (Raja-muhundree,) is situated on the northern bank of the Godavery, in lat. 16° 59′ N. long. 81° 53′ E. about 50 miles from the sea. It is a large town, and the capital of the district.

Towns. During the rainy season, the Godavery is here about a mile broad. Below the town it separates into several branches, forming a number of fertile deltas and large islands.

Travelling distance from Madras 373 miles.

Coringa, about 30 miles south-east from Rajamundry, is a seaport, and has a wet dock, which is the only one of the kind on the coast of India, between Calcutta and Bombay.

Six miles from Coringa, on the bank of the Godavery, is a small French settlement, named Yanam.

ELLORE.

This is a small inland district, lying between Rajamundry on the north, and Kondapilly on the south.

Towns. Ellore, usually called Ooppoo-Ellore, to distinguish it from Ra-Elloor, or Vellore. This is an inland town, situated about 50 miles from the coast, in lat. 16° 43′ N. long. 81° 15′ E. It is noted for carpets, and for leather manufactures.

Travelling distance from Madras 315 miles, from Rajamundry 58.

About 5 miles from Ellore is a large fresh water lake, called the Lake of Kolair, formed chiefly by the overflowings of the Godavery and Kistna. Its breadth varies from seven to twelve miles, and its extreme length is about twenty-two miles. It contains a number of islets, which produce abundant crops of rice. This lake communicates with the sea, by a small

Towns. river, called the Ooputnair, navigable for boats.

KONDAPILLY, OR MOOSTUFFA-NUGGUR.

This district, which now more commonly bears the name of Masulipatam, is separated from Ellore on the north by the Lake of Kolair, and the river Ooputnair, and from Guntoor on the south by the Kistna. It is a very fruitful district, being well watered by the Kistna and other rivers.

There are diamond mines in this circar, but for many years past they have been unproductive.

Towns. Kondapilly and Masulipatam.

Kondapilly, formerly styled by the Mahomedans Moostuffa-Nuggur, is situated inland, a few miles north of the Kistna, in lat. 16° 37′ N. long. 80° 33′ E. This was formerly a hill fort, and the ancient capital of the district, under both its Hindoo and Mahomedan rulers.

Travelling distance from Madras 285 miles, from Masulipatam 55.

Masulipatam, commonly called "Bundur," and also Muchlee-bundur, is a seaport, situated in lat. 16° 10′ N. long. 81° 14′ E. This has been a place of considerable commerce for many centuries, being mentioned as such by European travellers, so far back as A. D. 1295. The French established a factory here in 1669, and after it fell into the possession of the English in 1765, it became the principal station of the latter on the Coromandel Coast. The surf here is less

Towns. violent than on other parts of the coast, and the roads are therefore more convenient for shipping. Masulipatam is noted for chintzes, and other cotton manufactures, large quantities of which are exported to Persia; and also for snuff.

Travelling distance from Madras 285 miles, from Hyderabad 221.

GUNTOOR, OR MOORTIZABAD.

This is the most southern of the circars, and lies between the Kistna on the north, and the Gundigama on the south, separating it from the northern Carnatic. Its principal article of produce is maize, which forms the chief subsistence of the natives of the district; rice is not plentiful, and cotton is only partially cultivated. There are diamond mines in the district, but they have for many years produced nothing.

Towns. Bellumconda, Guntoor, Kondaveer, Nizampatam, and Innakoonda.

About 12 miles east of Innakoonda is a hill, called Buggulkoonda, which is supposed to be an extinct volcano. At present it does not possess the least appearance of the kind, but is subject to frequent earthquakes, which are sometimes of sufficient violence to move the houses of the adjacent villages.

Name. The present name of this province is of modern origin, and was first applied to it by Europeans, on account of its consisting of several distinct circars, or districts, originally five in number, namely, Ka-

Name. linga, Rajamundry, Elloor, Moostuffabad, and Moortizabad.

Inhabitants. Exclusive of a few thousand Mahomedans dispersed in the different towns, the inhabitants of this province are wholly Hindoos, composed chiefly of two classes, originally forming distinct nations, Ooreeas, and the Telingas.

The Ooreeas, or people of Orissa, were formerly separated from the Telingas by the Godavery. Of this tribe are the Rachewars and Woriars, the former the descendants of a Rajpoot colony from the upper provinces of Hindostan, the latter of the ancient race of the Hindoo kings of Orissa.

The Telingas, or Teloogoos, are the original inhabitants of the district south of the Godavery, and bordering upon the Telingana Desum. Of this class are the Vulmas.

By Europeans the Teloogoo people are frequently called "Gentoos," from a Portuguese word, signifying Gentiles, or Heathens.

Total population of the circars, about three millions.

History. At an early period of Hindoo history, this province comprised a number of principalities, some of which are noticed by Ferishta as independent states in 1295; but latterly subordinate or tributary to the kings of Orissa and Telingana. They were first invaded by the Mahomedans of the Dekkan towards the latter part of the 16th century, but were not permanently conquered until 1571, when they were

History. subdued by the Mahomedan king of Golconda, and annexed to his dominions. On the conquest of Golconda by Aurungzeb in 1690, the circars became a part of the empire of Delhi. In 1724 they were taken possession of by Nizam-ool-moolk, and were subsequently ceded by his successor, Sulabut Jung, to the French, as a reward for the services they had rendered him; but the French being afterwards expelled by the English, the circars reverted to the Nizam, with the exception of the town of Masulipatam, which the English retained. In 1765, Lord Clive obtained a grant of the whole province, Guntoor excepted, from the emperor of Delhi, which grant was confirmed by the Nizam; who also a few years afterwards ceded the circar of Guntoor, receiving from the British Government an annual peshkush of 630,630 rupees, which continued to be paid till 1823, when it was redeemed for a final sum of about one hundred and forty lacks of rupees. Some of the descendants of the former Hindoo princes still exist in this province, retaining the title of raja, and the hilly districts along the western borders are filled with petty polygars and zumeendars.

Religion. Hindooism and Mahomedanism.

Language. Ooreea and Teloogoo,—the former language principally in the north-western and northern parts.

§ 9.

Bejapoor, including the Konkan.

Boundaries. North, Aurungabad; east, Aurungabad and Beder; south, the Dooab; and west, the sea.

Divisions. Its principal divisions are Suttara and Kolapoor, the former composing the present dominions of the Mahratta raja, the latter belonging to a petty chief, styled the Kolapoor raja; and on the coast, the northern and southern Konkan.

Rivers. Beema, Kistna, Gutpurba, and some others.

General Description. In the vicinity of the mountains along its western boundary, this province is very hilly, and thickly wooded; eastward it becomes more level and open.

Productions. Cholum, maize, gram, and other dry grains, with a small proportion of rice, cotton, and sugar.

Towns. The principal towns are Colaba, Poona, Severudroog, Suttara, Sholapoor, Rutnagherry, Kolapoor, Merrich, Bejapoor, Vingorla, and Goa.

Poona is situated about 30 miles to the eastward of the Western Mountains in lat. 18° 30′ N. long. 74° 2′ E. It stands on an extensive open plain, and is considered one of the best built native cities in Hindoostan. The small rivers

Towns.

Moota and Moola unite at this place, and form the Moota Moola, which flows into the Beema; and it is thus possible, during the rainy season, to effect a journey by water in a light canoe, from within 75 miles of the west coast of India, to the Bay of Bengal. Under the peshwa's government, Poona was the capital of the western Mahratta empire, and it was here that the chiefs were accustomed to assemble every year with their followers, for the celebration of the Dushura, before setting out upon their plundering excursions into the neighbouring countries. It is now the principal English military station of the province, and contains about 100,000 inhabitants.

Travelling distance from Bombay 100 miles, from Hyderabad 387, from Delhi 913, from Calcutta 1208, and from Madras 690.

About 30 miles north-westerly from Poona, are some Booddhist excavations, called the caves of Karlee. The principal excavation consists of a hall and temple, about 126 feet long, and 46 broad. There is no idol in the temple, but the sides of the hall are covered with carvings of elephants, and various human figures, amongst which is that of Boodh.

Severudroog is a small rocky island on the coast, in lat. 17° 46′ N. long. 73° 15′ E., formerly the strong-hold of a celebrated Mahratta pirate, named Conajee Angria. It was captured by the English in 1756.

Suttara is a strong hill fort and town, situated 56 miles south of Poona, in lat. 17° 42′ N. long. 74° 12′ E. This place

Towns.

was taken from the Mahomedan sovereign of Bejapoor, in 1651, by Sevajee. Subsequently on the usurpation of the government of the Poona Mahratta empire by the peshwa, Suttara was converted into a royal prison, in which Sevajee's successors were confined. Since the restoration of the raja, Suttara has become the capital of his present dominions.

Travelling distance from Bombay 146 miles.

Solapoor, or *Sholapoor*, is a large and flourishing town, with a strongly built fort, in lat. 17° 40′ N. long. 76° 3′ E. It is an important English military station, and is also a place of considerable inland commerce.

Kolapoor is situated about 70 miles south of Suttara, a short distance to the westward of Merrich. It is a neat town, and the capital of the district.

Merrich, or *Mirch*, is situated on the eastern bank of the Kistna, about 70 miles south-easterly from Suttara. This was formerly the capital of a Hindoo principality of the same name, and is now the residençe of a Mahratta jageerdar, subordinate to the raja of Suttara. It is a large walled town, populous and flourishing.

Bejapoor, called by old European writers "Viziapour," is situated in about 17° N. lat. and 76° E. long. This was in former times one of the largest cities in Asia, the fort measuring not less than eight miles round the outside. At present it is almost entirely in ruins, but there remains enough to show that the place was originally of great magnitude. It

Towns. contained numerous handsome edifices, many of which are still in good order. Of these the principal are the mausoleum and musjid of Ibraheem Adil Shah, and the mausoleum of Mahomed Shah. The latter is a plain square building, surmounted by a dome of 350 feet in circumference, the largest in India, and visible from the village of Kunnoo, fourteen miles distant.

Bejapoor was the capital of the Mahomedan kingdom of that name.

Goa is situated upon a small island on the coast, in lat. 15° 30′ N. long. 74° 2′ E.

It consists of two towns, Old Goa, and New Goa, or Panjim. Old Goa, formerly the most splendid city in India, is now generally in ruins; the seat of government having been removed to Panjim, which is a handsome and well built town upon the island of Goa, five miles nearer the entrance of the harbour than Old Goa.

Goa was taken from the Hindoo rajas of Bijanagur by the Mahomedans, about 1469, and in 1510 it was besieged and taken by the celebrated Portuguese Admiral Albuquerque, by whom it was made the capital of the Portuguese dominions in the east. As the Portuguese power declined, Goa gradually lost its former consequence, and though still the residence of the Portuguese vice-roy, it is now a place of no importance. Including Goa and some small island connected with it, the Portuguese possess a small territory of about forty miles in length by twenty in breadth.

Travelling distance from Bombay 318 miles, from Madras 574.

Towns. On the bank of the Toombudra, in lat. 15° 14′ N. long. 76° 37′ E., about 30 miles north-westerly from Bellary, are the ruins of the ancient Hindoo city of Bijanagur, (Vijaya-nuggur, *the city of victory.)* Though long uninhabited, except by a few Brahmins, the numerous pagodas, choultries, and other buildings, composed of massive blocks of granite, still in excellent preservation, bear witness to its former grandeur. Amongst other remarkable buildings, there is at a part of the town, called "Humpee," a magnificent temple dedicated to Mahadeva; the gobrum of which is of ten stories, about 160 feet in height. Including Anagoondy on the opposite bank, this celebrated city is said to have been twenty-four miles in circumference.

It was founded in the year 1336.

Name. This province derives its name from that of its capital, Bejapoor, properly "Vijaya Poorum," "*the city of victory.*" Its usual Hindoo name was *Bijanagur*.

Inhabitants. Principally Mahrattas, and in the southern parts Kanarese. In the hilly parts, along its western boundary, there is a tribe of mountaineers, called Ramoosees. In their habits they resemble the Bheels, being like them professed thieves, but they are not in quite so savage a state.

History. In early times this province was the seat of the Hindoo kingdom of Bijanagur, often called by European writers, *Nursinga*. The kings of Bijanagur successively extended their dominions, until they inclu-

History. ded all the principal provinces of southern India. As the Mahomedans established themselves in the Dekkan, their progress brought them into contact with Bijanagur, and involved them in constant war. The northern and western parts of the province being conquered by the Mahomedans, were added to the Bahmenee empire; and on its dissolution in 1518, it became an independent principality, known as the Adil Shahee kingdom of Bejapoor. In 1564, the four Mahomedan sovereigns of Bejapoor, Ahmednuggur, Golconda, and Beder, combined against Ram-raja, the Hindoo king of Bijanagur, and having totally defeated him, took and plundered his capital. From this time the Hindoo sovereignty rapidly declined, and ultimately became extinct.

The Adil Shahee kingdom lasted till 1689, when the city of Bejapoor was taken by Aurungzeb, and the province was added to the Mooghul empire. It can, however, hardly be said ever to have been really subject to the throne of Delhi, as it was very soon after abandoned to the Mahrattas, who retained possession of it till 1818, when consequent upon the war with the peshwa, Bajee rao, it was transferred to the British.

Religion. Principally Hindooism.

Language. Mahratee and Kanarese.

CHAP. VIII.

SOUTHERN INDIA.

§ 1.

Dooab, or Southern Mahratta Country.

Boundaries. North, the rivers Gutpurba and Kistna, separating it from Bejapoor; east, Hyderabad and the Ceded Districts; south, Mysore and Kanara; west, the mountains dividing it from the southern Konkan.

Rivers. Gutpurba and Malpurba, both flowing into the Kistna; Wurda, flowing into the Toombudra, and the Toombudra.

General Description. The western districts of the province are mountainous and woody; eastward, it is open and generally level. The soil is good, and the climate favourable.

Productions. Principally cotton, and dry grains.

Towns. The chief towns are Belgaum, Kittoor, Dharwar, Gujunderger, Hooblee, and Savanore.

Belgaum, or *Shapoor Belgaum*, is a large flourishing town, well situated in an elevated plain in lat. 15° 52′ N. long. 74° 42′ E. It consists of two distinct

Towns. towns, Belgaum, which has a strong well built fort, and Shapoor. Amongst the inhabitants of Belgaum are many of the Jain sect.

Travelling distance from Bombay 318 miles, from Dharwar 43.

Kittoor is a fortified town, 30 miles south-easterly from Belgaum. It is the residence of a Mahratta jageerdar, usually styled the Jessaye of Kittoor.

Dharwar, called in Mahomedan geography *Nussurabad*, is situated in lat. 15° 28′ N. long. 75° 8′ E. It consists of a large fort and open town, and is the principal station of the civil authorities of the province.

Hooblee, 13 miles S. E. from Dharwar, is a large and populous town, and has long been celebrated as one of the principal places of trade in this part of India. The English had a factory here in 1660.

Savanore, properly *Shanoor*, is only noticed as having been the capital of a small Pathan state; the chief of which was known as the nabob of Savanore, and whose descendants still reside here.

Name. The term "Dooab" is applied to this province from its position between the two rivers Kistna and Toombudra, which flow along its northern and southern boundaries. It is of modern origin, this district having formerly been included in Bejapoor.

Inhabitants. Principally Mahratta and Kanarese, the Mahomedans in this province being very few.

History. In early times this province formed part of the Hindoo sovereignty of Bijanagur. It subsequently fell under the power partly of Béjapoor and partly of Mysore. Latterly the whole was conquered by the Mahrattas, from whom it was taken in 1818 by the British.

Religion. Principally Hindooism. There are also a good many Jains.

Language. Chiefly Kanarese.

§ 2.

Balaghat, Ceded Districts.

Boundaries. North, the rivers Toombudra and Kistna, separating it from Bejapoor and Hyderabad; east, the mountains dividing it from the northern Circars and northern Carnatic; south, Mysore; and west, the Dooab.

Divisions. Its principal districts are Doopad, Kurnool, Adoni, Cummum, Bellary, Gooty, Gundicotta, Cuddapa, Sidout, Raidroog, Gurrumconda, and Punganoor.

Rivers. The Vedavutti, also named the Hajnee or Pajnee, flowing northerly into the Toombudra, twenty miles from Adoni, the Pennar, Toombudra, Kistna, and several smaller streams.

General Description. This province consists for the greater part of an elevated open plain, intersected in different directions by ranges of low hills, and generally very barren of trees.

General Description.

The southern portion of the province consists of valleys lying between the Eastern Mountains which extend from Colar to Gurrumconda, and thence stretch inland to the vicinity of Sera. The soil is remarkably good. The scarcity of trees is not natural, but has been occasioned by the continual passage and encampments of the large armies, by which this province was desolated, during the constant wars of which it was formerly the seat. The climate of this province is intensely hot, and it is much subject to drought, and consequently to famine.

Productions.

Cotton, indigo, sugar, rice, and various dry grains. Diamond mines are found chiefly in the Cuddapa district ; all the diamond mines in this part of India, with a few exceptions, lie between the Kistna and Pennar rivers, from which tract the Golconda diamonds were procured ; the district of Golconda itself not producing any. The district of Bellary is noted for the manufacture of cumlies.

Towns.

The principal towns are of the same names as the districts.

Kurnool, called also *Kumeer-nuggur*, is situated on the south side of the Toombudra, a few miles from its junction with the Kistna, in lat. 15° 44′ N. long. 78° 2′ E. It is strongly fortified, and until 1839, was the residence of a petty Pathan chief, the descendant of the former nabob of Kurnool. This has been for several centuries the principal station of the Dekkan Pathans.

Towns.

Travelling distance from Madras 280 miles.

Bellary, the capital of the province, is situated in about 15° N. lat., and 77° E. long. It has a small hill fort, and a fortified petta.

Travelling distance from Madras 316 miles, from Bangalore 190.

About 30 miles N. W. from Bellary are the ruins of the ancient Hindoo city of Anagoondee, or Bijanagur, (Vijayanuggur,) formerly the capital of the Hindoo empire of Kurnata, already noticed in the account of Bejapoor.

Gooty is a strong hill fort, about 45 miles east of Bellary. The highest part of the rock is 1000 feet above the surrounding plain.

Cuddapa, called by the natives *Kurpa*, stands on the bank of a small river, in about 14° 30′ N. lat., and 79° E. long. This was for many years the capital of an independent Pathan state, the chief of which was termed the nabob of Cuddapa, and many old Pathan families still remain here, who are considered to speak the Hindoostanee language with remarkable purity. Large quantities of sugar and jaggery are made in the neighbourhood. The diamond mines are about 7 miles north-east of the town, upon the bank of the Pennar.

Travelling distance from Madras 166 miles, from Bangalore 154.

Punganoor is a fortified town, situated about 50 miles N. W. from Vellore, in lat. 13° 21′ N., and long. 78° 3′ E. It is the residence of a Polygar, generally styled the Punganoor raja, who holds the

Towns. town and a small adjoining district, under tribute to the British.

Name. The word Balaghat means "above the passes," and was first used by the Mahomedans to distinguish the whole of the upper country, extending from the Kistna to the southern extremity of Mysore, from the *Paeen Ghat*, or country "below the passes." The term "Ceded Districts" was given to the province in 1800, when it was ceded or given up by the nizam of Hyderabad to the British. The original name of this province was "Karnatuk, or Karnata Desum," subsequently misapplied by both Mahomedans and Europeans to the Paeenghat country, to which it is now exclusively appropriated, although no part of the ancient "Kurnata" was below the mountains.

Inhabitants. With the exception of a few thousand Pathans, the inhabitants of this province are all Hindoos ; generally they are more robust and active than the people of the Paeenghat countries, and of a bolder character. The total population is estimated at 2,200,000.

History. This province formed the principal portion of the ancient Hindoo kingdom of the Kurnatuk, a name which was subsequently misapplied by the Mahomedans and Europeans to the country below the ghats, now known as the Carnatic. It was afterwards conquered by the raja of Bijanagur, after whose overthrow, it continued for a long series of years in great disorder ; its central situation causing it

History. to become the common battle field of the successive Mahomedan and Mahratta rulers of the adjacent provinces. Ultimately on the conquest of Mysore by the English, a treaty was concluded with the nizam of Hyderabad and the Mahrattas, by which these districts were transferred to the British Government.

Religion. Principally Hindooism.

Language. Kanarese in the western districts, and in the northern and eastern, Teloogoo.

§ 3.

Northern Carnatic.

Boundaries. North, the small river Gundigama, which separates it from the Guntoor district of the northern Circars; east, the sea; south, the Pennar, dividing it from Central Carnatic; and west, the eastern mountains, separating it from the Ceded Districts.

Divisions. It is divided into the districts of Ongole, and part of Nellore.

Rivers. The Gundigama, which flows into the sea near Moodapilly; the Pennar, and several small streams.

General Description. Towards its western boundary this province is hilly, but for the greater part it is level and open, and tolerably fertile.

Productions. Rice and other grains are cultivated, but the chief article of product is salt; which is manufactured in large quantities on the coast, for exportation. There are also copper mines.

Towns. The principal towns are Ongole and Nellore.

Ongole is situated near the coast, about 150 miles northward from Madras. It is a small irregularly built town.

Nellore is situated on the south side of the Pennar, a few miles from the coast, about 100 miles north of Madras. It is a populous town, and the capital of the province.

In 1787, a peasant, while ploughing near this town, discovered beneath the remains of a small Hindoo temple, under ground, a little pot, containing various Roman coins and medals of the second century. They were all of pure gold, and many of them fresh and beautiful, although nearly sixteen hundred years old.

Name. In Hindoo geography this province formed part of what was denominated the *Undra-desum*. Its present name of Carnatic has been given to it by the English, on account of its being included in the dominions of the nabob of the Carnatic, though properly not applicable to it.

Inhabitants. Hindoos and Mahomedans.

History. This province originally formed part of the Hindoo sovereignty of the Undra-desum, the rajas of which, about the beginning of the Christian era, were possessed

History. of considerable powers. It was first invaded by the Mahomedans during the 14th century. It afterwards became dependent upon the principality of Cuddapa, from which it was transferred to the dominions of the nabob of the Carnatic, by whom it was ceded to the British with the rest of his territories in 1801.

Religion. Hindooism and Mahomedanism.

Language. Teloogoo.

§ 4.

Kanara.

Boundaries. North, the Portuguese territories of Goa, and the Dooab; east, the Ceded Districts and Mysore; south, Malabar; and west, the sea.

Divisions. This province is divided into two parts, called north and south Kanara. North Kanara is divided into the districts of Soonda and Biljee, above the mountains; and Unkola, Honawur, or Oonnoor, and Koondapoor, below the mountains.

Soonda was formerly an independent principality under a Hindoo raja, and was a populous and well cultivated district; but being for many years the principal seat of war between the Mahrattas and Mysoreans, it became completely ruined.

The districts of Unkola and Honawur are commonly designated by the natives the *Haiga country*.

South Kanara occupies the remaining part of the province, southward from

Divisions. Koondapoor. It is called by the natives the *Toolva country*.

General Description. With the exception of the open plains of Soonda above the ghats, the whole of Kanara may be described as a rocky mountainous country, intersected by numerous small rivers running from the mountains to the sea; exceedingly fertile, and abounding with lofty forests. The rains generally commence in May, and last until October.

Productions. Its chief productions are rice, in great abundance, large quantities being constantly exported to other parts of India, and to Arabia. Teak and other woods, pepper and spices, sandal and sugar. The cattle are very small, and are little employed, the cultivation being chiefly done by hand. There are no manufactures.

Towns. There are few towns or villages in any part of the interior, the natives generally residing on their farms. On the coast, however, there are several. The principal of these are Sedashegur, Honawur, or Oonnoor, and Koondapoor, in north Kanara, and Mangalore in south Kanara.

Honawur was formerly a place of considerable trade, Hyder Ali having established a dock-yard for building ships of war there; but it was afterwards entirely destroyed by Tippoo Sooltan. The Portuguese erected a fort at this place as early as 1505. There is a lake here of great extent, reaching nearly to the mountains, and abounding with fish.

Mangalore, called also *Kowrial Bun-*

Towns.

dur, is a flourishing town, situated in lat. 12° 53′ N. long. 74° 57′ E. It stands on a small peninsula, formed by a lake or backwater, which is separated from the sea by a beach of sand. The town is large, and built round the sides of the peninsula, in the centre of which was the fort. This place is celebrated on account of its long siege in 1783, by Tippoo Sooltan, who, though he had a large army, and was assisted by the French, was repulsed in every attempt, and completely defeated by a weak garrison under Colonel Campbell. On the peace in 1784, the town was given back to Tippoo, who then destroyed all that remained of the fort.

Travelling distance from Madras 440 miles, from Bangalore 230.

Above the ghats is the town of Soonda, formerly populous and flourishing, and the capital of the district, but now nearly a ruin.

Name.

The name Kanara, which is a corruption of *Kurnata*, was first given to this part of India by the Mahomedans. It does not properly belong to it, and has never been known by the natives, who do not use it.

Inhabitants.

The inhabitants of this province, called by the English the Kanarese, are composed of several distinct classes. The first is that of the Brahmins, amounting to about one-sixth of the whole population. The next principal class, in the interior, is that of the Nairs, who are the chief farmers. Slavery is common throughout the province, most of the cultivators

Inhabitants. being slaves, either by caste, as the Bakadoora, and Batadoora castes in the Toolva district, or by purchase. The inhabitants of the coast are principally Maplays. These are Mahomedans, descendants of Arab settlers, and are the chief traders of the province. Their first arrival from the Red Sea is supposed to have taken place as far back as the time of Alexander the Great, or B. C. 327. The total population is estimated at about 800,000.

History. According to Hindoo tradition, this province was formerly under the government of Ravana, the king of Lunka, (or Ceylon.) It continued undisturbed under a Hindoo dynasty, until 1763, when it was subdued by Hyder Ali; and on the conquest of the Mysore dominions in 1799, it was transferred to the British.

Religion. Hindooism and Mahomedanism are the prevailing systems of religion, though there are also several thousand called Christians, of the Romish Church, the descendants of settlers invited into the province from the Konkan, in the time of the Hindoo rajas, by whom they were much favoured. The Jain sect of Hindoos is also numerous; this and the adjacent province of Malabar being now the only part of India in which the Jains are found in a collected state, though individuals of the sect are scattered throughout the country.

Language. The language of this province is a branch of the Karnata or Kanarese, intermixed with Teloogoo and Mahratee.

§ 5.

Mysore.

Boundaries. This province is bounded on the north by the Dooab and Ceded Districts; east, by the mountains separating it from the Carnatic, Baramahal, and Salem; south, by Coimbatoor; and west, by Koorg, Malabar, and Kanara.

Divisions. It is divided into three great districts, namely, Chutrkul or Chittledroog, Nuggur or Beduore, and Puttun or Seringapatam, the largest of the three.

Chittledroog, which occupies the northern part of the province, consists of an extensive open plain. It is not very fertile, not being well supplied with water, but it abounds with sheep.

Nuggur is situated in the midst of the western mountains, and is for the greater part covered with forest, producing abundance of sandal wood, pepper, betel, and cardamoms. This district was formerly an independent principality under a Hindoo raja. In 1762 it was conquered by Hyder Ali, who annexed it to Mysore, with which it has since remained.

The Puttun district is partly mountainous, and partly plain, and abounds with rocky hills and forest.

Rivers. The principal rivers are the Toombudra, Vedavutti, Pennar, Panar, Palar,

Rivers. and Cavery, all of which, except the Cavery, have their sources in this province.

General Description. This province presents every variety of appearance in its different districts. It is enclosed on two sides by the Eastern and Western mountains, or ghats, and thus forms an elevated table-land, from which rise clusters of lofty hills, containing the sources of nearly all the rivers which water the low countries adjacent. The altitude of the level land varies from 1800 to 3,000 feet above the sea. Sivagunga, which is the highest hill in the province, is 4,600 feet above the sea.

Productions. Mysore produces rice, raggy, wheat, and other grains; sugar, betel, opium, castor-oil, and various other articles. Raggy, or ragee, is the grain principally cultivated, as it forms the food of all the poorer classes. The western forests yield rich supplies of sandal, and other valuable woods. Sheep are very numerous, red, white, and black, and there is also an inferior breed of horses. Mysore abounds in iron ore, which is worked by the natives, but in a very imperfect manner. Its principal manufactures are black and white cumlies and woollen carpets, and shawls. Cotton manufactures are few, and of inferior quality.

Towns. The principal towns are Hurryhur, Chittledroog, Nuggur, Simooga, Sera, Colar, Bangalore, Seringapatam, and Mysore.

Chittledroog is a fortified town and strong hill fort, the capital of the district,

Towns. situated in lat. 14° 4′ N. long. 76° 30′ E. By the natives it is called "Seetla Doorg," which signifies "*the spotted fortress*," and also "Chuttra kul," "*the umbrella rock*." The fort stands on a cluster of rocky hills, the highest peak of which is about 800 feet above the plain. The ascent is partly by steps, and partly by notches cut in the steep and smooth surface of the rock. There are in the fort two fine tanks of water, several pagodas, and a deep well sunk in the rock, as a magazine for ghee. Chittledroog is famous for the variety and excellence of its fruits.

Travelling distance from Madras 350 miles, from Bangalore 140.

In a dell among the mountains, a short distance to the west of Chittledroog, there is a curious suite of dark subterranean apartments, which probably were formerly the habitations of devotees.

Nuggur, or *Bednore*, is the capital of the district so called, and was formerly a large and very rich city. In 1763 it was taken and plundered by Hyder Ali, who then changed its name from Bednore to Hyder Nuggur. In 1783 it was captured, and again plundered by an English detachment under General Matthews. Soon after which it was besieged by Tippoo Sooltan, assisted by the French, and forced to surrender. General Matthews and many of the officers were afterwards poisoned by the Sooltan's order, and most of the soldiers put to death in their prisons. It is now in ruins, and almost depopulated.

Travelling distance from Bangalore 214 miles.

Simooga is situated on the western

Towns. bank of the river Toonga, about 50 miles easterly from Nuggur. This was formerly a large and populous town, but has fallen into decay, having been twice completely devastated by the Mahrattas in 1790 and 1798. In 1790 a battle was fought close to this town, between a detachment of Bombay troops, consisting of not more than 800 men, under Captain Little, and a Mysore force of 10,000, under Mahomed Ruza, one of Tippoo's best generals. The English were completely victorious, after an obstinate contest. The Mahratta army, under Purseram Bhow, looked on at a distance, taking no part whatever in the engagement, but employed themselves very actively, as soon as it was over, in plundering the town, and slaughtering the defenceless inhabitants.

Sera is situated about 90 miles northerly from Seringapatam. In 1644 it was conquered by the Bejapoor Mahomedans, and became for a time the capital of a Mahomedan principality, until subdued by Hyder Ali, since which period it suffered so much from the constant wars between the Mysoreans and the Mahrattas, that it gradually fell into ruins, and is now a place of little consequence. It is still inhabited principally by Mahomedans, and contains a large stone musjid.

Bangalore is a large fortified town, situated about 200 miles nearly due west from Madras. It is one of the principal military stations of the English, and much resorted to by them on account of its climate, which is much more temperate and healthful, than that of the low country.

Towns. The cantonment, which is extensive and well arranged, stands about two miles from the Petta. The fort is weak, and only calculated for defence against a native enemy. There are coarse cloth and silk manufactories at this place. Bangalore is famous for its gardens, which produce a great variety of fruits, and excellent vegetables.

Travelling distance from Mysore 85 miles.

Seringapatam is situated on a small island in the Cavery, in lat. 12° 25′ N. long. 76° 45′ E. The island is about four miles in length, and one and a half in breadth; the town occupying about a mile at one end of it. The town was first built in about 1630, and became the capital of Mysore under Hyder Ali. The fort was constructed chiefly by Tippoo Sooltan, assisted by French engineers, but with little skill; the works being faulty, and not strong. On an eminence in the centre of the island, at some distance from the fort, stands a large and well built village or town, called Shuhr-Gunjam. In a garden adjoining, amidst some choultries and a musjid, is the mausoleum of Hyder, in which are the remains of Hyder himself, his wife, and Tippoo Sooltan. The proper name of this place is *Sree-runga-puttunum*, but in Mysore it is generally called merely *Puttunum*. After the restoration of the Hindoo raja, and during the administration of the deewan Purnea, a bridge was built across the northern branch of the Cavery; which, although unskilfully constructed, is an extraordinary work, and very much to Purnea's credit.

Towns.

In 1792 Seringapatam was besieged by the English under Lord Cornwallis. On the night of the 6th February of that year, Lord Cornwallis attacked Tippoo's camp, which was under the walls of the fort, within a strong bound hedge, furnished with redoubts, and defended by about 40,000 infantry, besides a body of cavalry. For this attack Lord Cornwallis selected 2,800 Europeans, and 6,000 Natives, without any artillery. It was completely successful. The camp was stormed, 80 guns were captured, and the Mysoreans driven inside the fort with great loss. Preparations were then made to attack the fort, when Tippoo submitted, and made peace, with the cession of half his dominions. In 1799, war again breaking out, Seringapatam was besieged by the English a second time, under General Harris. On the 4th May, at about 2 o'clock in the afternoon, the place was carried by storm, in the course of which, Tippoo was killed. The island was afterwards annexed to the English territories, but being remarkably unhealthy, has since been abandoned.

Travelling distance from Bangalore 80 miles, from Madras 296.

Mysore, the ancient and present capital of the province, is situated about 9 miles south from Seringapatam. The town is large and populous, and the fort, which is separated from it, is built in imitation of the European style. The raja's palace is inside the fort, and the British residency, on a rising ground, a short distance outside. A large tank extends from near the fort, towards the foot of Mysore

Towns.

hill, which is a conical mountain, about 1,000 feet high, rising from the plain at 5 miles distance from the city. On the summit is a house belonging to the British residency, and on the south-western declivity, in the midst of a Brahmin village, there are two pagodas of great repute, to which the raja is accustomed to make an annual visit. Lower down, on the same part of the hill, is a figure of a bull, 16 feet high, cut out of the rock.

The name Mysore, or as it is termed by the natives *Mysoor*, is a corruption of *Mahesh Usoora*, a fabulous monster of Hindoo mythology.

Inhabitants.

The inhabitants of the province, or Mysoreans, are chiefly Hindoos, and they are generally stouter and taller than the people of the Carnatic. There are also considerable numbers of Mahomedans dispersed through different parts. The total population is estimated at about 3,000,000.

History.

This province was under the dominion of a succession of Hindoo rajas, until 1760, when the government was seized by the celebrated Hyder Ali. This individual was the son of a poor adventurer, and first entered the service of the raja of Mysore as a private soldier, about the year 1749. He soon distinguished himself by his bravery and skill, and obtained great influence with Nunseraj, the dalawai or prime minister, who promoted him to the command of the whole army. In 1760, finding himself sufficiently powerful, Hyder deposed and banished his patron Nunseraj, and confining the nomi-

History. nal raja, assumed the sovereignty of Mysore. In 1780 he invaded the Carnatic, which he desolated with fire and sword, up to the very gates of Madras. The English collected an army under Sir Eyre Coote, who stopped Hyder's further progress, and defeated him in several battles; but being greatly assisted by the French, Hyder was enabled to carry on the war until the 9th December, 1782, when he died, and was succeeded by his son Tippoo Sahib, who assumed the title of Sooltan. Tippoo was born in 1753, and named after a Mahomedan Fukeer of Arcot, for whom Hyder had a particular veneration. Tippoo's elder brother, Kureem Sahib, was set aside, being imbecile. The Sooltan prosecuted the war, which his father had commenced, until 1784, when he made peace; his French allies being obliged to withdraw their aid, hostilities between their nation and the English having ceased. In 1790, he unwisely attacked the raja of Travancore, an ally of the English. A war commenced in consequence with the latter, which terminated in March, 1792, in a peace concluded by Lord Cornwallis, under the walls of Seringapatam, at the cost of half of Tippoo's dominions. This, however, had not the effect of making the Sooltan more prudent, and in 1799 a second war broke out, which proved decisive. Seringapatam was taken on the 4th May of that year, by the English troops under General Harris, and Tippoo was killed in the assault. With Tippoo Sooltan terminated the Mahomedan government, after a duration of only thirty-eight years. In June,

History. 1799, the English placed upon the musnud of Mysore, Krishna Oodiaver, then six years of age, of the family of the ancient rajas, with whom the government remained until 1831, when in consequence of the long continued misrule of the raja, and the cruel and rapacious conduct of the Brahmins in power, a general insurrection of the people broke out, which compelled the British to interfere, and Mysore is now under their rule.

Religion. Hindooism and Mahomedanism.

Language. The general language of the province is the Karnataka, or Kanarese. The official documents of the government are usually written in Mahratee.

§ 6.

Baramahal.

Boundaries. This province is bounded on the north by Mysore, and Central Carnatic; east, by Central Carnatic; south, by Salem; and west, by Mysore.

Rivers. Its principal rivers are the Palar and the Panar.

General Description. This is a small province, situated amongst the Eastern Mountains. It is generally of a wild irregular appearance, and in former times was thickly studded with formidable hill forts.

Productions.

The valleys produce rice, and other grains, but the articles principally cultivated are dry seeds, vegetables, and plantations of cocoanuts and palms. The manufactures are coarse, and consist of little besides inferior cumlies and cotton cloths.

Towns.

The principal towns are Venkatagherry, Satgurh, Oossoor, Sooloogherry, Vaniambaddy, Rutnagherry, Kistnagherry, Ryacotta, Tripatoor, and Allambaddy.

Satgurh is situated at the foot of the mountains, a few miles from the Naikunairy ghat, or pass. There was formerly a hill fort here, to which the name of Satgurh properly belonged; the petta being called Lalpet. This place is now chiefly noted on account of its gardens, which produce abundance of fine fruit, particularly oranges and mangoes.

Kistnagherry is a small town, situated in lat. 12° 32′ N. long. 78° 23′ E. only noticed on account of its fort, built upon a very bare and steep mountain, of 700 feet perpendicular height; several times besieged, but never taken, except by surprise. In 1791 the British troops attempted to storm it, but were repulsed with loss. The fortifications are now in ruins.

Ryacotta is about 15 miles to the east of Kistnagherry. Its fort is built upon a rocky mountain, 1150 feet in perpendicular height, and is a place of some strength; the present fortifications being principally of English construction. It commands one of the passes from the Carnatic into Mysore.

Name. This province derives its name of Baramahal from its having been formerly divided into twelve small districts.

Inhabitants. The inhabitants are principally Hindoos, with very few Mahomedans.

History. This province was originally subject to the Hindoo sovereignty of Kurnatuk, and on the dissolution of that kingdom fell under the rule of a number of polygars, or hill chieftains. Hyder Ali annexed it to the dominions of Mysore, and in 1792 it was ceded by Tippoo Sooltan to the British, with whom it has since remained.

Religion. Hindooism and Mahomedanism.

Language. Teloogoo.

§ 7.

Salem.

Boundaries. North, the Baramahal, and Central Carnatic; east, Central Carnatic; south, Southern Carnatic, and Coimbatoor; west, Coimbatoor, and Mysore.

Rivers. The only river of any note is the Cavery, which flows along the western side of the province.

General Description. This is an elevated district, generally open, with occasional ridges and clusters of hills, and towards its western boundary, mountainous. The Shevaray hills in the

General Description. vicinity of the town of Salem are particularly noted, and have been much resorted to by Europeans for change of climate. These hills consist of three distinct divisions, the Salem Naad, the Moko Naad, and the Moottoo Naad. The last is the loftiest, its elevation above the sea being about 5,000 feet. It has a table-land, seven miles by three, producing coffee of very good quality, wheat, barley, and millet. The inhabitants of these hills are exclusively of the Vullaler caste, and according to their own traditions, emigrated from Conjeveram about the year 1200.

Productions. The chief productions of this province are rice, maize, cotton, coffee, salt-petre, and magnesia. Its cotton manufactures of all kinds are extensive.

Towns. The principal towns are Dhurmpooree, Salem, and Namkool.

Salem, which is the capital, is situated in a plain, six miles south of the Shevaray hills, in lat. 11° 37′ N. long. 78° 13′ E. It is a celebrated mart for cotton goods.

Travelling distance from Madras 210 miles, from Bangalore 114.

Name. This province has its name from its capital.

Inhabitants. The inhabitants are chiefly Hindoos.

History. This province was originally part of the great Hindoo sovereignty of the Carnatic. It was afterwards conquered and annexed to the dominions of Mysore,

History. until 1792, when it was ceded to the English.

Religion. Principally Hindooism.

Language. Tamil and Teloogoo.

§ 8.

Central or Middle Carnatic.

Boundaries. This province is bounded on the north by the Ceded Districts, and the river Pennar; east, by the sea; south, by the Coleroon; west, by Salem, the Baramahal, and Mysore.

Divisions. Its principal districts are part of Nellore, Venkatagherry, Kolastree, Chandgherry, Chittoor, Madras, Arcot, Chinglepet or the Jageer, Cuddalore, and part of Trichinopoly.

Rivers. The chief rivers are the Pennar, Palar, and Panar, besides many smaller streams.

General Description. This province is in general level and open, gradually rising from the coast to the eastern mountains; broken in different directions by ridges and clusters of rocky jungly hills. It is well watered by rivers and large tanks, and is considered fertile.

Productions. Rice, raggy, gram, and other dry grains; indigo, and salt. Iron is abundant, and is manufactured into steel, of very superior

Productions. quality, at Porto Novo. Copper is also found in the neighbourhood of Kolastree.

Towns. The principal towns are Kolastree, Chandgherry, Pulicat, Chittoor, Madras, Amboor, Vellore, Arcot, Congeveram, Chinglepet, Arnee, Vandiwash, Sadras, Trinomally, Ginjee, Pondicherry, Tricaloor, Cuddalore, and Chillumbrum.

Pulicat is situated on the sea coast, about 25 miles north from Madras. It formerly belonged to the Dutch, who established themselves there in 1609. The town stands on the bank of a lake, of about 40 miles in length, and 6 in breadth, which communicates by means of a canal with Madras.

Chittoor is situated in the hills, about 80 miles west from Madras. It was formerly one of several small pollams, or hill districts, and came into the possession of the English in 1801, though the Polygars, or hill chiefs, were not finally subdued till 1804.

Madras, which is the capital of the British government in southern India, is a large and populous town, with a strong fort, situated on the sea-coast, in lat. 13° 5′ N. long. 80° 21′ E. This town was founded in 1936, in which year the English obtained the grant of a piece of ground, for the erection of a town and fort, from the raja of Chandgherry, Sree-rung-Rayeel. The raja desired that the new town should be named after himself, *Sree-runga-raya-Puttun*; but the naik, or governor of the district, ordered the English to give it the name of his own father, Chinnapen, and it was accordingly called

Towns.

"*Chinna-Puttun.*" Madras was the name of the village which existed before the present town was founded, and this name has been continued by the English to the town, the fort being denominated "Fort St. George." Madras soon became a flourishing city, and the chief station of the English on the Coromandel Coast. In 1702 it was besieged by Daood Khan, one of Aurungzeb's generals, who notified that he had orders to take the fort and entirely destroy it. However, he was defeated, though the fort was then a very weak place, with only a few soldiers to defend it. In 1744 it was besieged and taken by the French, who kept it until 1749, when peace was made, and the place was restored to the English. In 1758 it was again besieged by the French, under the celebrated Lally, who was obliged to retreat, after a siege of two months. Since that time, Madras has never been besieged by an enemy; though, in 1769, it was threatened by Hyder Ali, who encamped his army within a few miles from the fort, and forced the English to make a treaty with him.

In the quarter called Triplicane, or Tiroomul-kheree, a little to the south of the fort, is the residence of the nominal nabob of Arcot, the descendant of the former Mahomedan rulers of the Carnatic. Near Triplicane, on the sea side, is the small town of Mylapoor, or St. Thome, the latter being the name given to it by the Portuguese, who captured the place, and formed a settlement there in the year 1547.

Eight miles southward from the fort

Towns.

is the Mount, the principal station of the Madras Artillery. At this place is an old Romanist chapel, built by the Portuguese, upon the summit of a rocky hill, from which it has its name of "St. Thomas' Mount." By the Natives it is usually called "Furingee Konda," or "Furingee Mulye." Two miles from the Mount, towards Madras, is the "Little Mount," a low rocky hill, on which stand the remains of an old Portuguese convent. The road here crosses the Adyar river, over which is a narrow bridge of twenty-nine small arches, 1230 feet long, called the Marmalong Bridge. It was built by an Armenian gentleman of Madras. The total population of Madras is estimated at 450,000, including about 30,000 Mahomedans.

Amboor is situated near the eastern hills of the Baramahal, about 120 miles westerly from Madras. The town is neat and well built, and manufactures large quantities of castor-oil. On a mountain, to one side of the town, there was formerly a strong fort.

Vellore, called by the Natives, *Rae-Elloor*, is situated about 90 miles westerly from Madras. The fort is large, and strongly built, and surrounded by a deep ditch, which was formerly filled with alligators, but it is completely commanded by the neighbouring hills. It is now a place of little importance.

Arcot (Urkat,) is situated on the south side of the river Palar, 70 miles south-westerly from Madras. This was the capital of the Carnatic, under the government of the Mahomedan nabobs, and it is

Towns.

still a favourite place of residence with Mahomedan families. The fort was formerly large and tolerably strong, but it is now in ruins. The celebrated Clive took it in 1751, with a small party of 200 Europeans and 300 Natives, although the garrison then consisted of 1100 men. The place was immediately besieged by raja Sahib, with an army of 10,000 men, assisted by 150 French and artillery; but after a hard struggle of fifty days, Clive, with his handful of men, entirely defeated them. On the north side of the river is an English cavalry cantonment, and a large open town connected with it. This also is named by Europeans Arcot, but by the Natives it is usually termed Raneepet.

Travelling distance from Madras 71 miles.

Congeveram, or *Kanchipoorum*, is a large open town, situated about 45 miles south-westerly from Madras. It stands in a valley, and being built in a straggling manner, covers a space of ground nearly six miles in length. It consists of two divisions, one named Vishnoo Kanchi, and the other Siva Kanchi. The principal street is about two miles and a half in length. This place is noted on account of its being the chief Brahmin station in the Carnatic. The great pagoda in Siva Kanchi has a lofty tower over its entrance, from the summit of which there is a fine view of the surrounding country. Besides Brahmins, Congeveram is inhabited by a considerable number of weavers.

Arnee is situated about 20 miles to the south of Vellore. During the wars with

Towns. Hyder Ali, this was a place of considerable consequence, and its fortress was Hyder's chief magazine. It is noted for its clever workmanship in cloths, which are held in great estimation by the Natives of this part of Hindoostan.

Sadras, or *Sadrungaputtanum*, is situated on the sea-coast, about 40 miles south from Madras. It belongs to the Dutch, who settled there in 1647; and it was formerly a flourishing town, but it now consists of merely a few houses and a native village. About five miles to the northward of Sadras is a Brahmin village, called Mahabalipuram, (*Muha-Buli-poorum*, the city of the great Nuli, one of the titles of Vishnoo,) or, as it is named by the English, the Seven Pagodas, remarkable for various extraordinary remains of Hindoo temples and sculptures of great antiquity. According to the Hindoo legends, there was, at some very remote period, a considerable town at this place, the site of which is now covered by the sea.

Trinomally, (*Tiroona-Mulye*,) is situated about 50 miles from the coast, in lat. 12° 11′ N. long. 79° 7′ E. It is chiefly noted as a place of pilgrimage for the Hindoos. It consists of a large craggy mountain, on which are several pagodas, and at its base, a populous town. The principal pagoda is built at the foot of the mountain, and has a large gateway of twelve stories, 222 feet high.

Pondicherry, (*Phool-cheree*, or *Poodoo-cheree*,) is situated on the coast, about 90 miles south from Madras. It is a handsome well built city, belonging to the

Towns.

French, and was once the most splendid European settlement in India, though now much decayed. The French first came to India in 1601; and in 1672, having purchased the ground from the king of Bejapoor, they built the town and fort of Pondicherry. In 1748 it was besieged by the English, who were defeated, and obliged to retreat. In 1761 it was again besieged by the English under Coote, and taken. It was restored to the French in 1763, but war breaking out again, it was besieged once more, and taken in 1778. At the peace of 1783, it was again transferred to the French, and again taken in 1793; restored to them in 1802, and, for a fourth time, occupied by the English in 1803. At the peace in 1815, it was again given up to the French, with whom it has since remained.

Cuddalore, (*Goodaloor*,) is situated on the coast, 12 miles south from Pondicherry, standing between two arms of the river Panar. It is an extensive and populous town, and was formerly the seat of the English Government. The English factory was first established there in 1691, when a piece of ground was purchased from the raja, and a fort erected, called Fort St. David. After the capture of Madras by the French in 1746, Fort St. David became the head of the English settlements, and continued so until 1758, when it was besieged and taken by the French under Lally, who entirely demolished the fort.

Chillumbrum is a large and populous town, situated on the coast, 36 miles south from Pondicherry, and not far from

Towns. the river Coleroon. There is a large indigo factory at this place, and the islands in the Coleroon are covered with the indigo plant. It is also celebrated on account of its pagodas, which are large and ancient. About a mile to the north of Chillumbrum are the remains of Porto Novo, formerly a large and wealthy town, but destroyed by Hyder Ali, when he invaded the Carnatic in 1782. It is still a place of some trade.

Name. The present name is of English origin.

Inhabitants. The inhabitants of this province are Hindoos and Mahomedans, the latter being found chiefly in the Madras and Arcot districts. At Porto Novo, and along the coast, there is a distinct class of Mahomedans, denominated "Lubbees." They are of Arab origin, and are the principal traders of this part of India.

History. In ancient times this province formed part of the Hindoo sovereignty of the *Karnatuk Desum;* the various petty principalities, which it comprised, being all nominally subject to it. It was first invaded by the Mahomedans in the year 1310, but was not actually taken possession of by them until the early part of the 18th century, when it was annexed to the sooba of the Dekkan, as part of the Mooghul empire. In 1743 the government of the Carnatic was given by Nizam-ool-moolk to Anwarood-Deen, as his deputy or nabob; on whose death, in 1749, the succession to the musnud was actively disputed, the opposing claimants

History. being respectively supported by the English and the French. The contest which ensued continued with intervals, until towards the close of the century, when the authority of Mahomed Ali, son of Anwarood-Deen, whose claim had been supported by the English, was finally established. Mahomed Ali died in 1795, and was succeeded by his son Oomdutool-Oomra, who died in 1801, in which year the whole of the nabob's dominions were transferred by treaty to the British Government, in consideration of a fixed annual pension to be paid to the nabob and his family.

Religion. Hindooism and Mahomedanism.

Language. The prevailing languages of the Hindoo population of this province are, in the northern and western districts, Teloogoo, and in the southern, Tamil.

§ 9.

Malabar.

Boundaries. North, Kanara; east, Mysore, Koorg, and Coimbatoor; south, Travancore; west, the sea.

Divisions. It is divided into three districts, Wynaad, Palghat in and above the mountains, and Malabar below.

General Description. The description already given of Kanara, is equally applicable to Malabar, in all particulars.

Productions.

Black pepper may be considered the staple of this province, which also produces abundance of rice, cocoa-nuts, and jaggery. Gold dust is found in some of the mountain streams, and the forests of the Wynaad and Palghat abound with excellent teak and bamboo.

Towns.

The principal towns are Cannanore, Tellicherry, Mahé, Manantoddy, Calicut, and Palghatcherry.

Cannanore is situated on the coast, in lat. 11° 42′ N. long. 75° 27′ E. This town, with a small surrounding district, was formerly under the government of a bebee or princess, whose descendant still retains the title, and resides in her palace, under the protection of the English. Her ancestor, a chief of the Maplays, purchased the estate from the Dutch. It was subsequently seized by Hyder Ali, and in 1799 annexed to the British dominions; an adequate pension being settled upon the bebee. The Portuguese had a factory at this place in 1505.

Travelling distance from Madras 423 miles, from Mangalore 90, from Bangalore 200.

Tellicherry is a small seaport town, situated in lat. 11° 45′ N. long. 75° 33′ E. It was for many years the principal English settlement on the western coast, a factory having been established there in 1683. It is the principal mart in India for sandal-wood, brought from the forests above the ghats, and for the cardamoms of Wynaad, which are considered the best on the coast.

Travelling distance from Madras 412

Towns. miles, from Cannanore 16, from Bangalore 206.

Mahé, situated on the coast, in lat. 11° 42′ N. long. 75° 36′ E. was formerly the chief French settlement on this side of India, and is still in their possession. The French first settled there in 1722.

Manantoddy is a small inland village, situated in the forest of Wynaad. It is the principal military post of the district, and commands the Peria Pass.

Travelling distance from Madras 365 miles, from Bangalore 160.

Calicut, on the coast, in lat. 11° 15′ N. long. 75° 50′ E. was formerly the capital of the province. It is also celebrated as being the first place in India, at which any European settlement was formed, the Portuguese, under Vasco de Gama, having landed there in 1498.

Travelling distance from Madras 422 miles, from Bangalore 200.

Palghatcherry is situated inland, about 70 miles S. E. from Calicut, in lat. 10° 45′ N. long. 76° 38′ E. Under Hyder Ali, this was a place of considerable importance as a military post. It is still a station for an English garrison. The surrounding forests abound with excellent teak.

Travelling distance from Madras 340 miles, from Bangalore 209.

Name. The name Malabar is a compound of the two words *Mulye*, hill or mountain, and *bar* or *var*, region or district, "the hilly country." In ancient Hindoo geography, this province forms part of a division called "*Kerala*."

Inhabitants.

The inhabitants of this province are principally Hindoos, divided into Numboorees, or Brahmins, Nairs, Tiars, and Maliars, who are all free men; and Poliars, and other lower castes, who are all slaves. There are also several thousand Christians of the Romish and Syrian churches, and on the coasts, Maplays and Jews. The total population is estimated at 1,000,000.

History.

It appears probable that this province originally formed part of the dominions of one of the Hindoo kings above the ghats, by whom it was placed under the government of Brahmins; and that these, for their greater convenience in collecting the revenues, established the Nairs as their deputies, who, in course of time, became independent, forming the country into a number of principalities, the chief of each taking the title of raja. Amongst the number, the Zamooree raja, or raja of Calicut, of whom frequent mention is made in the writings of European voyagers as the Zamorin of Calicut, was the most powerful. The many local difficulties of the country presented such formidable obstacles to invaders, that it escaped subjugation by the Mahomedans until 1760, when it was attacked and partially subdued by Hyder. His successor, Tippoo Sooltan, determined that the whole province should embrace Mahomedanism; to effect which, he entered it in 1788 with a large army, and forcibly circumcised numbers of the Brahmins and Nairs. This caused a general insurrection, which, however, the Sooltan

History. promptly quelled, driving out the rajas, and circumcising all of whom he could get hold. After the first war between the British and Tippoo, the rajas and Nairs who had been leading a predatory life in the jungles, were reinstated in their authority by the former, as tributaries to the English Government. Their mode of ruling, however, was soon found to be such as could not be allowed or supported consistently with humanity; and it became necessary, for the relief of the country, from the confusion into which their misrule had plunged it, to deprive them of their power. The rajas were in consequence deposed, an allowance being settled upon them of one-fifth of the revenues for their support. Dissatisfied with this arrangement, the rajas excited a rebellion, which terminated in the final annexation of the province to the British dominions.

Religion. Hindooism is the prevailing system of the inland districts, and Mahomedanism mixed with many Hindoo usages, that of the maritime parts. Though ruled by a Hindoo government, this province appears to have received the Mahomedan system at a very early period; and when the Portuguese first visited the Zamorin's dominions, they found them filled with Moosulmans. Christians also of the Syrian and Romish churches are numerous. There are likewise many of the Jain sect in the interior.

Language. The languages most generally spoken are the Kanarese and the Malayalim.

§ 10.

Koorg.

Boundaries. North, Mysore; east, Mysore; south, Mysore; west, Malabar, and Kanara.

Rivers. The Cavery and Boodra, both have their sources in Koorg, and there are various other small streams.

General Description. This province, being situated in the midst of the mountains, is composed of a succession of hills and valleys, in some places open, with some scattered trees and shrubs; but the hills, for the greater part, are wild and covered with forest.

Productions. The valleys are exceedingly fertile, yielding a plentiful supply of rice, and cattle are in abundance, the pasturage being excellent. The forests produce sandal, teak, and other valuable woods, and abound with elephants. There are no manufactures.

Towns. There are no towns of any consequence in this province, the Koorgs preferring to live scattered over the valleys and in their woods. The raja's principal residence, and which may therefore be called the capital, was Merkara, situated nearly in the centre of the country, about 50 miles north-easterly from Tellicherry, and 178 from Bangalore.

Name.

The origin of the name of this province is not known.

Inhabitants.

The natives of this province, or as they are usually styled, the Koorgs, are a division of the Nair caste of Hindoos, and have always been considered as a people of martial habits. Some of the tribes inhabiting the hills and forests are of a very wild character. The total population is estimated at 200,000.

History.

The Hindoo principality of Koorg is one of the most ancient in India. Its rajas, named the Beer and Veer rajas, are mentioned by the Mahomedan historian Ferishta, as independent princes, so early as A. D. 1583, and there is an authentic history of the family commencing in 1632. It remained under the government of its hereditary raja until subdued by Hyder Ali. In the year 1779, on the death of the raja Linga, Hyder excluded the next heir, Beer Rajindra, from the succession, and confining him in a Mysore fortress, partitioned the country into jageers among a number of his Mahomedan officers. Tippoo Sooltan caused the young raja to be circumcised, but in 1787 he made his escape, and returning to Koorg, succeeded after a long struggle in expelling the Mysoreans, and recovered possession of his dominions. Under the protection of the British, Koorg continued undisturbed under its own government until 1834, when in consequence of the violent conduct of the raja, Veer Rajindra Woodiyer, nephew of Beer Rajindra, it became necessary to deprive him of his

History. power. He was consequently removed, and placed under restraint, and Koorg now forms part of the British territories.

Religion. Hindooism.

Language. Kanarese.

§ 11.

Coimbatoor.

Boundaries. North, Mysore, Salem; east, Salem, Southern Carnatic; south, Southern Carnatic, Travancore, Malabar; west, Malabar.

Divisions. Its principal divisions are the districts of Suttimunglum, Coimbatoor, Caroor, and Darapoorum.

Rivers. The Cavery, Bhoowani, Amravutti, and smaller streams.

General Description. This is an elevated district, especially towards the north and west, much diversified with hill and dale, forest and open country, generally fertile and well cultivated. The soil for the most part is dry, but in the vicinity of the hills, and also in some of the southern parts, there is much low marshy ground. In the district of Coimbatoor, along the western frontier, are the celebrated Neilgherry mountains.

Productions. The chief articles of produce are cotton, rice, and tobacco. The province also yields abundance of muriatic and common salts, nitre, and iron.

Towns. The principal towns are Suttimunglum, Bhoowani, Coimbatoor, Caroor, and Darapoorum.

Bhoowani, being situated at the conflux of the rivers Bhoowani and Cavery, is considered a sacred place, and is in consequence much resorted to by the Hindoos.

Coimbatoor, the capital of the province, is situated in lat. 10° 52′ N. long. 77° 5′ E. This was formerly one of the principal military stations of Tippoo Sooltan. It has a musjid, which was built by him; and at Penura, two miles distant, is a celebrated Hindoo temple, called Mail-Chittumbra.

Travelling distance from Madras 306 miles, from Bangalore 178.

Sometime since an ancient *tumulus*, or mound, was dug open near this place, which on examination was found to contain various weapons and other articles, such as were formerly used by the Romans.

A short distance to the northward and westward of this town, are the Neilgherries, a range of mountains connecting the eastern and western ghats. They extend from east to west about thirty-four miles, and from north to south fifteen, containing a fertile and well cultivated table-land, entirely free from jungle, and varying in height from 5,000 to 9,000 feet above the level of the sea. Jackanairy being 5,659, Dimhutty 6,041, Ootakamund 6,416, and one of the highest peaks, named Dodabet, about 9,000. The air is exceedingly clear, and the climate cool and healthy, on which account they are much resorted to by European invalids.

Towns.

The inhabitants of these hills are of four classes, Toders, Koters, Burgers, and Kurrumbers. The Toders are the aborigines and lords of the soil, which, however, they do not cultivate, restricting themselves to pasturing cattle. They are quite distinct in language and religion from the Hindoos, and though a fine looking race, often fair, and generally of good size and figure, are in a very rude and ignorant state. They are not numerous, not exceeding more than five or six hundred. The Koters appear to be nearly of the same description as the Toders, but occupy themselves as artisans, chiefly in the manufacture of coarse iron tools. The Burgers are the cultivators of the land, which they hold under tribute to the Toders. They are of Hindoo origin, and speak the Kanarese language. They are estimated at between six and seven thousand. The Kurrumbers are a very wretched race, black and small, inhabiting the jungles upon the skirt of the hills, in number not more than a few hundred.

These hills produce barley, and other dry grains, and very fine vegetables and fruits. The animals are black cattle, and buffaloes, a species of sheep, wild elk, bears, and tigers.

The proper appellation of these hills is the "Neelagiri," from *neela*, blue, and *giri*, hill or mountain.

Caroor is situated on the northern bank of the river Amravutti, not far from the Cavery, and about 50 miles westerly from Trichinopoly. The Amravutti being the ancient boundary between the do-

Towns. minions of Mysore and Trichinopoly. Caroor was formerly a place of considerable commerce, and is still a neat pleasant town.

Darapoorum is situated in a fine open country, about half a mile from the Amravutti, near the south end of the province. It is populous and well built, and the surrounding country produces abundance of rice and tobacco.

Name. In ancient times this province was called "*Kunjum*." The derivation of its present name Coimbatoor is uncertain.

Inhabitants. The inhabitants of this province are chiefly Hindoos, there being few Mahomedan families to be found. The total population is estimated at about 700,000.

History. This province originally formed part of the Hindoo kingdom of Madura, from which it was conquered about the year 1650, by the raja of Mysore, under whose government it remained until 1799, when it was transferred to the British.

Religion. Chiefly Hindooism.

Language. Tamil.

§ 12.

Southern Carnatic.

Boundaries. North, the Cavery and Coleroon, separating it from Salem and Central Carnatic; east, the sea; south, the Gulf of

Boundaries. Manar; west, Travancore, and Coimbatoor.

Divisions. The following are its principal districts, Trichinopoly, Tanjore, Tondiman's Country, Dindigul, Madura, and Tinnevelly.

Rivers. Coleroon, Cavery, Vygaroo, Vyparoo, and several smaller streams.

General Description. This province presents great variety of appearance. The districts of Trichinopoly and Tanjore are level and open, well watered and fertile, particularly Tanjore. Tondiman's Country consists for the greater part of thick jungle. Dindigul and Madura are mountainous and wooded, well watered and fertile. Tinnevelly level and open.

Productions. Rice, tobacco, cotton, and jaggery, the latter two articles principally in Tinnevelly. There are elephants in the southern and western parts of Madura and Dindigul.

Towns. The principal towns are Trichinopoly, Tanjore, Combaconum, Tranquebar, Nagore, Negapatam, Poodoocotta, Dindigul, Sholavandrum, Madura, Shevagunga, Ramnad, Tinnevelly, Palamcottah, and Tuticorin.

Trichinopoly, also called *Trichirapoora*, the capital of the province, is situated on the south side of the Cavery, and is a large and populous town. By the Mahomedans it is commonly called *Nuthur-Nuggur*. Trichinopoly is celebrated for a memorable siege, which it

Towns.

sustained from 1751 to 1755, when it was successfully defended by the English against the French and their Native allies. Within the fortified city is a rock, about 300 feet high, on which are a pagoda and other buildings. In a durgah outside the city, not far from the western wall, under a plain slab, lie the bones of Chunda Sahib; and in a sort of choultry adjoining, are the burial places of Umeer-ool-Oomra and his family. Trichinopoly is one of the principal military stations of the English.

Travelling distance from Madras 207 miles, from Bangalore 206.

Opposite to the town of Trichinopoly, the Cavery separates into two branches, forming an island called Seringam, (*Sreerungum.*) About thirteen miles to the eastward of the point of separation; the branches again approach each other, but the northern one is at this spot twenty feet lower than the southern. The northern branch, which takes the name of Coleroon, is allowed to run waste to the sea; but the southern, which retains the name of Cavery, is led by numerous channels to irrigate Tanjore. Near the east end of Seringam an immense mound, called the annicut, has been formed to prevent the waters of the Cavery from descending into the Coleroon. About a mile from the western extremity of the island, at a short distance from the bank of the Coleroon, stands the celebrated pagoda of Seringam. It is composed of seven square enclosures, 350 feet distant from each other; and each enclosure has four large gates, with high towers, placed one

Towns.

in the centre of each side opposite to the four cardinal points. The outward wall is nearly four miles in circumference.

Tanjore, (Tunjavooroo) the capital of the district so named, is situated in a fertile plain, in lat. 10° 42′ N. long. 79° 11′ E., about 38 miles easterly from Trichinopoly. It consists of two parts, the fortified town, and the fort or citadel, both on the same level, and connected together by a wall. The city is regularly built, and contains many good edifices. In the fort is a celebrated pagoda, one of the finest specimens of the pyramidical temple in India. Its principal tower is 199 feet high. In ancient times Tanjore was one of the chief seats of learning in southern India.

Travelling distance from Madras 205 miles.

Combaconum, in the same district, is situated about 23 miles north-easterly from Tanjore. This was the ancient capital of the Chola rajas. It is still a large and populous town, chiefly inhabited by Brahmins, and possesses a number of fine tanks and pagodas.

Tranquebar, in the same district, is situated on the coast, in lat. 11° N. long. 79° 53′ E. It is a very neat regularly built town, and belongs to the Danes, who settled there in 1616, having purchased the ground from the raja of Tanjore.

Nagore, or *Nagoor*, is also in the same district, and on the coast, 13 miles south of Tranquebar. It is a populous and busy place, and possesses a number of trading vessels, some of them of a consid-

Towns.

erable size. The main branch of the Nagore river forms its harbour. There is here a curious minar, 150 feet high, and several mosques, erected at different times by the nabobs of the Carnatic. Nagore is the principal resort of the Lubbees.

Negapatam, in the same district, is situated on the coast, 20 miles south of Tranquebar, in lat. 10° 45′ N. long. 79° 54′ E. This place, originally a Portuguese settlement, was taken in 1660 by the Dutch, who made it the capital of their possessions on the Coromandel coast. It is now much decayed and depopulated.

Dindigul, the capital of the district so named, is situated in lat. 10° 18′ N. long. 78° 2′ E., near the western entrance of an extensive plain, about 30 miles from east to west, and 25 from north to south, almost surrounded by mountains. It is a clean and neatly built town, and has a strong fort built upon a rock about 400 feet high, on the summit of which is a Hindoo temple. Under the northern ledge of the rock there is a remarkable natural cavern, inhabited by some Mahomedan fukeers.

Travelling distance from Madras 275 miles, from Trichinopoly 60.

Poodoocotta, the capital of Tondiman's Country, situated in lat. 10° 18′ N. long. 78° 58′ E., is a remarkably clean well built town, of modern erection.

Travelling distance from Trichinopoly 34 miles.

Sholavandrum, in the Madura district, is situated 12 miles north of Madura,

Towns.

upon the northern bank of the Vyar or Vygaroo river. It is a large open town, though consisting chiefly of small thatched huts.

Madura, the capital of the district, and formerly the capital of an Hindoo kingdom, is situated in lat. 9° 55′ N. long. 78° 14′ E., upon the south side of the Vygaroo. This is a city of considerable antiquity, and contains the remains of many magnificent edifices, comprising some of the most extraordinary specimens of Hindoo architecture now extant, particularly the ancient palace of the rajas. It has a pagoda covering an extent of ground almost sufficient for the site of a town, in front of which is a celebrated choultry, called Tiroomul Naik's, 312 feet in length, and covered with grotesque sculptures. Near the town is a remarkable eminence, called from its shape the "elephant rock."

Travelling distance from Madras 292 miles, from Trichinopoly 82.

There was formerly at Madura a celebrated college, called by the Natives, "Maha Sunkum."

Shevagunga, in the same district, was formerly the capital of a polygar principality, tributary to Madura, and ruled by a ranee. It is a large open village, agreeably situated, and clean. Lat. 9° 55′ N. long. 78° 32′ E.

Ramnad, in the same district, is situated near the coast, in lat. 9° 23′ N. long. 78° 56′ E. It is the capital of a pollam, generally styled the Ramnad zumeendaree, which was granted to the present zumeendar's family under the Hindoo government of Madura, with the title of

Towns. *Sutti-putti*, for the defence of the road, and protection of the pilgrims resorting to the pagoda of Ramiserum. The town is of an irregular appearance, and contains nothing of note.

In the gulf of Manar, opposite to Ramnad, and about a mile from the coast, is Ramiserum, a small sandy uncultivated island, about eleven miles long, and six broad. This island is celebrated throughout India as a place of pilgrimage for the Hindoos. The pagoda is about 9 miles from Pambum, the port of the island, and is considered a fine building. A line of black rocks stretches across the gulf from Ramiserum to Ceylon, known by the name of Adam's Bridge.

Tinnevelly, the capital of the district so named, is an inland town, situated in lat. 8° 48′ N. long. 78° 1′ E. a little to the westward of the Tumbrapoornee river, about 25 miles distant from the Western Mountains. It is a large and populous place.

Palamcottah is situated on the eastern side of the Tumbrapoornee, which divides it from Tinnevelly. It is a fortified town, and was formerly the principal stronghold of one of the southern polygars.

Travelling distance from Madras 390 miles, from Trichinopoly 180.

Tuticorin, in the same district, is situated on the coast, in lat. 8° 57′ N. long. 76° 36′ E. It is a large town, and is noted for its pearl fishery, which has existed for many centuries, and still continues productive, though the pearls are considered inferior to those found in the bay of Condatchy in Ceylon.

Name. This province has its present general name of Southern Carnatic from the English. There is no native name applicable to it as a whole.

Inhabitants. Hindoos of various castes, and Mahomedans, the latter principally in the district of Trichinopoly, and those of the Lubbee caste along the coast.

History. In ancient times this province was divided into a number of principalities, nearly all of which formed part of, or were dependent upon the two great Hindoo kingdoms of the Chola Desum, and Madura. For the better understanding of their history, we will notice the several districts separately.

Trichinopoly was originally part of the Chola Desum, and remained an independent Hindoo principality until 1736, when Chunda Sahib acquired possession of it. Chunda Sahib lost it in 1741 to the Mahrattas, from whom it was taken in 1743 by Nizam-ool-Moolk; and it thenceforward continued to form part of the dominions of the nabobs of the Carnatic, until the country passed under the government of the British.

Tanjore, the ancient Chola Desum, was conquered in 1675 by Ekhojee, a Mahratta chief, brother of Sevajee, and remained subject to his descendants until 1799, when the territory was transferred to the British—still, however, preserving to the raja his title, and allowing him to retain the city and fort of Tanjore, with several palaces in different places for his residence. Never having been subdued by the Ma-

History. homedans, Tanjore retains more of its original Hindoo character than most other parts of the country; and, until lately, the barbarous practice of suttee was very frequent. It is considered one of the most fertile districts in all India, and is thickly populated.

Tondiman's Country, or the *Tonda-mundalum*, was originally connected with the Chola dominions. It subsequently became a distinct zumeendaree, under the rule of a Hindoo chief called by the English the Tondiman, from Tondi, and the English word *man*, a corruption probably of the old Hindoo name Tonda-mundalum. Although at present nominally a dependent of the British Government, the Tondiman is allowed the full possession of his zumeendaree free from tax or tribute of any kind, as a reward for the remarkable fidelity exhibited by his family in their connection with the English through all changes of fortune, especially during the early wars of the Carnatic. The Natives of this district were long celebrated as most expert thieves, from which circumstance they derived their name of collaries, (*kullurees*, from *kullur*, thief,) but so much is their character improved, that now a theft is seldom known amongst them. The instrument commonly called by Europeans the "Cholera horn," derives its name from this people, and is properly the "kulluree horn."

Dindigul was formerly subordinate to the kingdom of Madura, and continued an independent Hindoo principality until 1755, when it was subdued by the raja of Mysore, and annexed to that country;

History. from which it was separated, and finally transferred to the British in 1792.

Madura was the seat of the ancient kingdom so named. In the remote periods of Hindoo history, this was one of the holy countries of the south of India, and its capital was styled the southern Madura. Its ancient sovereigns were named the Pandian race, and it is supposed to have been the "Pandionic region" of Ptolemy. After the dissolution of the Pandian monarchy, Madura fell under the rule of a number of turbulent polygars, sometimes tributary to the nabobs of the Carnatic, but more frequently refusing to acknowledge their authority. After much conflict, particularly from the middle to the end of the 18th century, the province was finally subjugated by the British, and added to the Carnatic territory, with which it was transferred to them in 1801.

Tinnevelly originally formed part of the Chola sovereignty. Subsequently it was divided amongst a number of independent polygars, under whom it remained for a long time in a state of great anarchy; until, after much conflict, it was finally subdued by the English in the beginning of the present century.

Religion. Hindooism and Mahomedanism.

Language. The general language of the province is Tamil.

§ 13.

Travancore.

Boundaries. North, Malabar; east, the Western Mountains, separating it from Coimbatoor and Southern Carnatic; south and west, the sea.

Divisions. North Travancore, including the small principality of Cochin, and south Travancore.

Rivers. None of any magnitude, but numerous small streams.

General Description. This province consists of a long strip of land, shut in from the main country, by a lofty range of mountains running from its northern to its southern extremity, terminating at Cape Comorin. In length it may be estimated at 140 miles, by an average breadth of about 40. Through the mountains are three passes. The northern, or Chow-ghat, leading into Coimbatoor; the central, or Ariyungol, not practicable for carriages, about 10 miles in length, leading into Tinnevelly; the southern, or Arumboolee, twelve miles from Cape Comorin, a broad level opening between the mountains, into the south of Tinnevelly. Along the coast, separated from the sea by a narrow strip of sandy soil, is a backwater, or brackish lake, communi-

General Description. cating with the sea by creeks at different points, and extending from Chowghat to Quilon, a distance of about 140 miles. Its breadth and depth vary very much, but it is navigable throughout for boats. From Quilon, a canal connects this backwater with another at Anjengo, continuing the water communication as far as Trivanderam. Travancore is one of the richest and most fertile countries in India. Its surface is beautifully varied with hill and dale; and winding streams, flowing down the mountains, preserve the valleys in a constant state of verdure. The mountains are covered with lofty forests.

Productions. The productions of this province are numerous and valuable. Pepper, cardamoms, cassia, betel-nut, cocoa-nut, ginger, mace, nutmegs, bees-wax, ivory, sandal-wood, ebony, &c. Rice is always in the greatest plenty, a scarcity being quite unknown; the country generally yielding three crops in the year. The cattle are of a small breed, and there are no sheep, except such as are procured elsewhere. The forests are filled with teak and other valuable woods, and abound with elephants. Buffaloes and tigers are numerous, as are also monkeys, apes, and other wild animals. The black tiger is a native of this province.

Towns. There are few towns of any consequence, the Natives preferring to live dispersed over the country upon their farms. The principal are Trichoor, Cranganore, Cochin, Aleppic, Qui-

Towns. lon, Trivanderam, Oodagherry, and Nagracoil.

Trichoor is only noted as being situated near the Chow-ghat. It belongs to the Cochin raja.

Cranganore is situated on the coast, 16 miles north from Cochin. It formerly belonged to the Dutch, and was a commercial settlement of some consequence. Its inhabitants are principally Jews, and, according to their statements, Cranganore was possessed by their people as early as A. D. 490.

Cochin, (Koochee,) is also upon the coast, in lat. 9° 51′ N. long. 76° 17′ E. In the year 1503, the celebrated Portuguese Admiral Albuquerque obtained the permission of the raja to erect a fort at this place, which was the first possessed by any European nation in India. In 1663, it was taken by the Dutch, under whose government it became a very flourishing town, having an extensive commerce with Arabia and other countries. It came under the dominion of the English in 1795, and still has a considerable traffic with other parts of India, and also with Arabia, China, and the Eastern Islands. Ship-building is likewise carried on here. About a mile distant from Cochin is a small town, called Muttacherry, inhabited by Jews.

Aleppie is also on the coast, about midway between Cochin and Quilon. It is the chief depôt from which the Travancore government exports its pepper and timber.

Quilon, (Koollum,) is situated on the coast, in lat. 8° 53′ N. long. 76° 39′ E.

Towns. This was formerly the principal town of the province, and is still a place of considerable native trade.

Trivanderam, situated about 3 miles from the coast, and about 50 miles from Cape Comorin, is the modern capital of the province, and the usual residence of the raja, who has here a large palace built in imitation of the European style, and decorated with a variety of coarsely executed paintings, clocks, and other European ornaments. There is also at this place a menagerie, or collection of wild beasts, but it possesses nothing worthy of notice.

Travelling distance from Madras 480 miles.

Oodagherry is a small fortress, 30 miles south of Trivanderam, formerly one of the principal military stations of the province. Adjoining is the town or village of Papanaveram, where the raja has a palace.

Nagracoil, including also *Kotar*, is a small town of little note, except from its situation upon the main road to the Aramboolee pass. Fourteen miles from this place is Cape Comorin, called by the Natives, *Kunya Koomuree*, forming the southern extremity of India.

Name. The present name of this province is derived from that of the principality of Travancore. Its general native name, applicable to the whole territory, is "Malayalim."

Inhabitants. The inhabitants of this province, called in English writings by the general name

Inhabitants. of Travancoreans, may be classed as follows:—Nambeorees or Brahmins, Nairs, and other Hindoo divisions, as in Malabar, forming the bulk of the population—Romanists, that is, followers of the Romish church, consisting chiefly of the fishermen, and others dwelling on the coast, and amounting to about 115,000 persons—Syrians, (called by the Hindoos, Soorianee Maplay, or Nazaranee Maplay,) so named, as being Christians of the Syrian church, and amounting to about 125,000, being principally in the inland parts of north Travancore—Jews in number about 2,000, living at Cochin and Cranganore, and a few thousand Mahomedans. The total population is estimated at about 1,500,000.

History. From the earliest traditions, Travancore has been subject to a Hindoo government. Originally it appears to have been divided into a number of separate principalities, in which state it remained until about the middle of the 18th century, when raja Martandan, of the principality of Attingal or Travancore, succeeded in adding several of them to his own territory. From this time the rajas of Travancore, partly by intrigue, and partly by force, went on extending their conquests until they had subdued the whole province, with the exception of Cochin. In 1799, the purchase of Cranganore from the Dutch brought on a war with Tippoo Sooltan, who denied the power of the Dutch to make the sale, the principality of Cochin being tributary to Mysore. The Travanco-

History. reans were entirely defeated, and but for the interposition of the English, the whole province would have been conquered. The country continued undisturbed under the protection of the British Government until 1809, when in consequence of a conspiracy set on foot against the English by the dewan, or minister of the raja, a war broke out, which speedily terminated in the conquest by the former of the entire kingdom. The raja's territories remained under the immediate direction of the British resident until 1813, when they were restored, and have since remained at peace.

The principality of Cochin was resorted to at an early period by the Europeans; the Portuguese under Albuquerque having obtained leave to build a fort at the town of Cochin in 1503, the first possessed by that nation in India. In 1663 the Portuguese were driven out by the Dutch, with whom the town of Cochin remained until the establishment of the English. The raja of Cochin maintained his independence until the latter part of the 18th century, when he was compelled to pay tribute to Mysore. In 1791, his tribute was transferred to the English, who had restored to him the places conquered by Hyder and Tippoo. The dewan having afterwards confederated with the dewan of Travancore in the war of 1809, and having treacherously attacked the British resident and troops, the raja was for a time deprived of his authority, and his country has since remained chiefly under the

History. control of the English, the raja's government being restricted to about one-half of his original territory.

Religion. Hindooism. There are also in this province, as already noticed, a considerable number of Syrians and Romanists, and a small proportion of Mahomedans and Jews.

Language. The general language of the province is Malayalim. In the southern parts, bordering upon Tinnevelly, Tamil.

CHAP. IX.

Islands connected with India.

The islands which may be classed as connected with India, are the Laccadives, the Maldives, and Ceylon.

THE LACCADIVES.

Situation and Description. The Laccadives are opposite the coast of Malabar, and distant about 75 miles from it. They consist of thirty small low islets, extending from the 10th to the 12th degree of north latitude, being separated from each other by wide channels, and the largest not containing six square miles of land.

Productions. They are all very barren, producing nothing but cocoa-nuts, coir, jaggery, and a little betel-nut, which are exported to India in exchange for grain, cloths, and other articles.

Name. The name Laccadives is a corruption of the Sanskrit words, "Luksha Dwipa," or *hundred thousand islands*, and was given them at a time when, being very little known, they were supposed to be much more numerous than they are now ascertained to be.

Inhabitants. The inhabitants are Mahomedans of the Maplay class; they are very poor, and subsist chiefly upon cocoa-nut and fish.

History. These islands were probably peopled at an early period by colonists from the Malabar coast, but nothing was known of them to Europeans prior to their discovery by the Portuguese navigator, Vasco de Gama, in his passage to India. They subsequently came under the rule of the bebee of Cannanore, by whom they were ceded to Tippoo Sooltan, since whose time they have been independent, though nominally forming part of the British province of Kanara.

THE MALDIVES.

Situation and Description. The Maldives lie between lat. 7° 6′ N. and lat. 0° 46′ S. They consist of numerous circular clusters, separated from each other by narrow passages, and amounting to about 1200 of various sizes;

Situation and Description. the largest not being more than three miles in circumference. The larger islets are inhabited and cultivated, but the greater number are mere rocks and sand banks. The principal island is named "Mull," and is the residence of the chief.

Productions. Their chief articles of produce are coir, cocoa-nut oil, cowries, tortoise-shell, and dried fish, which are exported by the islanders in their own boats, to the coast of Orissa, and to the straits of Malacca, in exchange for rice, sugar, and other necessaries.

Name. The name Maldives is a corruption of the two Sanskrit words, "Muluya Dwipa," the isles of Muluya.

Inhabitants. They are inhabited by Mahomedans, the descendants of Arab colonists.

History. These islands were known at an early period to the ancients, being mentioned by Ptolemy; and are supposed to have been colonised by the Arabs soon after the commencement of their intercourse with Ceylon, some centuries probably prior to the first visit to India of the Portuguese navigators. They are under the government of a chief who takes the title of Sooltan.

Language. It is not accurately known what language is properly that of the Maldives, but the islanders all understand and speak Hindoostanee.

Religion. Mahomedanism mingled with paganism. Like the Biajoos of Borneo, they annually

Religion.

send adrift into the seá a vessel laden with perfumes, gums, and flowers, as an offering to the spirit of the winds, and sometimes a like offering is made to the spirit whom they term the king of the sea.

CEYLON.

Situation and Description.

Ceylon is situated on the south-east of southern India, from which it is separated by a narrow channel, called the gulf of Manar, between lat. 5° 56′ and 9° 46′ N. and long. 79° 36′ and 81° 58′ E. From Point Pedro, the northern extremity, to Dondra Head, at the southern, its greatest length is about 270 miles, and its greatest breadth about 145. The inland districts are mountainous and covered with forest, the highest peaks rising to about 6,000 feet above the sea. There are numerous small rivers and streams running down on all sides from the high land.

Productions.

Its principal productions are cinnamon, cocoa-nut oil, coir, betel-nut, and tobacco; arrack also of a superior quality is distilled from the toddy of the cocoa-nut tree. The island abounds with elephants and other animals, and has numerous kinds of snakes. The forests produce a great variety of the finest sorts of wood, and the mountainous districts are rich in gems of different species, such as the cats'-eye, the amethyst, topaz, ruby, garnet, &c. Ceylon also possesses an extensive pearl fishery in the bay of Condatchy, on its north-

Productions. western coast, and another fishery of chalk shells.

Towns. The principal towns are Jaffnapatam, Calpenty, Chilaw, Negombo, Colombo, Caltura, and Point de Galle, along the western coast, Trincomalee and Batticolo on the eastern coast, and Matura at the southern extremity.

Colombo is the seat of government. It is situated in lat. 6° 55′ N. long. 79° 45′ E.

Trincomalee, in lat. 8° 32′ N. long. 81° 17′ E., is a place of great importance on account of its large and excellent harbour, which is the best in India, and forms the depôt of the British ships of war employed in the eastern seas.

Candy, situated nearly in the centre of the island, was its ancient capital, but was never superior to a village of mud-huts, its population not exceeding 3,000 persons.

Name. The proper name of this island is Singala, from which the English name of Ceylon has probably been derived. By the Hindoos it is called Lunka, or sometimes from its former capital, "Khundi," and by the Arabians, Serindeb (Surundeeb.) By the ancient Romans it was called Taprobane. The name Lunka, though now generally applied to Ceylon, belongs properly to a fabulous island which the Brahmins supposed to be situated on the equator, and through which the Hindoo astronomers were accustomed to draw their first meridian, which they called the meridian of Lunka.

Inhabitants. The great body of the Natives may be divided into three classes, nearly equal in number:—the Singalese, the Candians, and the Tamil people. The Singalese occupy the southern half of the island, the Tamil people the coasts of the northern half, and the Candians the central parts. There are also some Maplays.

The total population of the island is estimated at 900,000.

History. Little is known of the history of Ceylon prior to 1505, when the Portuguese formed settlements upon the coast, where they found that the Arabs had already obtained a footing. In 1603, the Dutch arrived, and in 1656, having succeeded in completely expelling the Portuguese, acquired possession of all the maritime districts, the Native prince being confined to the interior, where he was protected from invasion by the natural obstacles of a mountainous and jungly country. In 1796, the Dutch possessions were conquered by the English, who were subsequently engaged in various wars with the raja until 1819, when their authority was finally established over the whole island.

Religion. The religion of the Singalese and Candians is that of Boodh. The Tamil people follow the Brahminical system. Christians are also numerous and increasing.

Language. The prevailing languages are Singalese, Tamil, and a corrupted Dutch.

CHAP. X.

Beloochistan.

Boundaries. Beloochistan lies to the north-westward of Hindoostan. It is bounded on the north by Persia and Afghanistan; east, by Afghanistan, and the Brahooee Mountains, separating it from Sind; south, by the sea; and west, by Persia.

Divisions. Its chief divisions are Shawl, Kelat, Kuch-Gundava, formerly called Sewistan, and Mukran.

General Description. The general character of this country is mountainous, and its climate in winter, in the northern parts, intensely cold, the snow lying deep, even in the valleys, from the end of November to the beginning of February. The soil is generally sandy, stony, and arid, but there are occasional tracts of great fertility. Kuch-Gundava, in particular, was formerly much celebrated as a very populous and well cultivated district, though now from the prevalence of light drifting sand almost desert.

Productions. Its productions are in general the same as those of Afghanistan and Sind. Wheat, barley, and other grains, but no rice. Fruits of all kinds, both European and Asiatic. Sheep and cattle are nu-

Productions. merous, and camels and horses in abundance. The woods are principally the apoor resembling the teak, tamarind, and the babool. The date also grows in the plains. Minerals of all descriptions are said to be found in different parts, but our information on this subject is as yet defective. The greyhounds of this country are excellent, and are bred with great care by the Beloochees, who hold them in great estimation.

Towns. The principal towns are Kevetta, in Shawl; Kelat, Dadur, Bhag, and Gundava, in Kuch-Gundava; and Kedje, in Mukran.

Kelat, which is the capital, is situated in a well cultivated valley, in lat. 29° 8′ N. long. 65° 50′ E. It is inhabited by a mixed population of Beloochees, Afghans, and Hindoos, the latter principally traders from Mooltan, and speaking the Punjabee dialect. The gardens around Kelat produce every kind of fruit European and Asiatic in great abundance, notwithstanding the severe cold of the winter.

Gundava is the second town in importance, and is the usual winter residence of the Khan, the cold not being so great here as at Kelat. It is situated in lat. 27° 55′ N. long. 67° 38′ E.

Name. The name of this country is of Persian origin, and signifies the land of the Beloochees.

Inhabitants. The inhabitants are called by the general name of Beloochees. They are composed of two great divisions, the one

Inhabitants. named Beloochee, the other Brahooee, and both subdivided into a number of smaller tribes and families. There are also many Hindoo and Afghan settlers, and a tribe called Juts, who appear to be descended from the original Hindoo inhabitants of the country converted to Mahomedanism.

History. Previous to the first invasion of the Mahomedans in 664, this country was possessed by the Hindoos; and, as late as the year 1600, Kelat belonged to a Hindoo raja. It subsequently fell under the dominion of a Beloochee chief, in whose family it now remains. For many years past, however, the country has been in the greatest disorder, and involved in incessant broils and revolutions, so that it can hardly be considered to have been under any regular government.

The title of its chief is "Khan of Kelat." Previous to the war between the English and Afghans, which broke out in 1838, he was nominally feudatory to the chief of Cabul. He may now be considered as dependent upon the British Government.

Religion. In religion, both Beloochees and Brahooees are Mahomedans of the Soonnee sect.

Language. Each division has its own language, neither of which has any written character. The Beloochee partakes very much of the Persian, and the Brahooee of the Punjabee.

CHAP. XI.

Afghanistan.

Boundaries. This kingdom lies upon the north-western frontier of Hindoostan. It is bounded on the north by ranges of mountains separating it from Tartary; east, by Cashmeer and the Indus; south, by Sind and Beloochistan; and west, by Persia.

Divisions. It is divided into a number of districts, corresponding with the divisions of tribes of the inhabitants, but its main portions may be considered as included under the following general heads:—Herat, Kafiristan, Cabul, Peshawur, and Candahar.

Mountains. The principal mountains are the Hindoo Koosh, or Indian Caucasus, which are a continuation of the Himalayas, and run westward, terminating nearly north of the city of Cabul; the Paropamisan, which run from the Hindoo Koosh towards Herat; and the Sooliman Mountains, which run from north to south, from about 34° to 29° north lat. There are several other inferior ranges of hills connected with those above mentioned, which cross the country in various directions.

Rivers. Numerous mountain streams flow through the country; but with the

Rivers.

exception of the Cabul river, the Helmund, and the Urghundab, none are of any size. The Cabul river rises in the Paropamisan mountains, and flows past Cabul easterly into the Indus, a little above Attock. The Helmund also rises in the same mountains, about thirty miles to the westward of Cabul, and flows southerly and westerly into a large lake called the Zoor, on the borders of Persia. The Arghundab rises in the hills, about 80 miles north-east of Candahar, and flows south-westerly into the Helmund.

General Description.

This country possesses great variety of surface, as well as of climate and productions. It may be described generally as consisting of wild bleak mountains and hills, with extensive tracts of waste land, together with fertile plains and vallies, populous and well cultivated. The climate of different parts vary extremely, owing partly to the difference of latitude, but chiefly to the difference of elevation. About Herat the snow lies deep through the winter months, and in the Cabul district the cold is severe. At Ghuznee especially where the snow is often on the ground from October to March, while the rivers are frozen, the cold is quite equal to that of England. The climate of Candahar is mild, snow being rarely seen, and that of Peshawur is oppressively hot during summer, and not colder in winter than that of Hindoostan.

During winter the inhabitants of the cold districts clothe themselves in woollen garments, and in some places in clothes

General Description. of felt, over which they wear a large great coat, called a *posteen*, made of tanned sheep skin, with the wool inside. They have fires in their houses, and often sleep round stoves.

Kafiristan occupies the mountainous country lying along the northern frontier of Cabul. It is composed of snowy mountains covered with deep pine forests, with small but fertile valleys producing abundance of grapes, and furnishing pasture for sheep and cattle.

Cabul is also mountainous, but has extensive plains and forests, though between the city of Cabul and the Indus there is a great scarcity of wood. The part lying between Cabul and the mountains is called the *Kohistan* or highlands.

Candahar is more open, but not so fertile, and large portions are desert. Herat is hilly towards the north and north-east, but generally open, and one of the most fertile countries in the world.

Productions. Wheat, barley, and rice, are the principal grains produced in this country. Wheat is the general food, barley being given to the horses. It also yields abundance of fruits and vegetables, both European and Asiatic; besides tobacco, sugar, assafœtida, alum, rock salt, saltpetre, sulphur, lead, antimony, iron, copper, and a little gold. The wild animals are generally the same as in India, the elephant excepted, which is not an inhabitant of Afghanistan. The common Indian camel is found in all parts of the level country, and wild sheep and goats are numerous. Herat is celebrated for a

Productions. fine breed of horses, and Bameean for a description of poneys, called yaboos, much used for carrying burdens. Mules and asses also abound, and are used for the same purpose. The sheep, of which large flocks are pastured, are generally of the broad fat tailed kind. There are fine dogs, especially greyhounds and pointers, and cats of the long-haired description, known in India as the Persian. Snakes and scorpions are found, but no alligators. Wolves are numerous, and during winter are fierce, sometimes attacking men. The commonest woods are oak, cedar, walnut, and a species of fir.

Wind-mills and water-mills are generally used for grinding the corn. Neither palankeens nor wheeled carriages are used, both sexes being accustomed to travel on horses or camels.

Coal is found about Kohat in the Peshawur district, and naphta, or petroleum, that is, *earth oil.* Silk worms are also reared in this part.

Towns. The principal towns are Herat, Cabul, Julalabad, Peshawur, Ghuznee, Candahar, Khelat-i-Ghilzee, and Dura Ismail Khan.

Herat is situated on the western frontier, in lat. 34° 20′ N. long. 60° 50′ E. in a very beautiful and fertile plain. It is one of the most ancient and celebrated cities in Asia, giving its name to an extensive province at the time of the invasion of Alexander, and subsequently it was for many years the capital of the empire established by Tymoor Lung. It

Towns. was taken from the Persians by the Afghans in 1715, and was retaken by Nadir Shah in 1731. It was again captured by the Afghans in 1749, and has ever since remained in their possession. It usually formed a government for one of the king's family, and on the dissolution of the Dooranee monarchy in 1823, it became a separate principality under Shah Kamran, the son of the king Shah Mahmood, and has since continued under his rule.

Cabul is a very ancient and beautiful city, situated in a fine plain upon the banks of the Cabul river, in lat. 34° 10′ N. long. 69° 15′ E. After the subversion of the dynasty of Ghuznee Cabul became the capital of the country, and is to be considered as such. It has not many buildings of note, the houses being constructed principally of wood, in consequence of the frequency of earthquakes. It had a very fine covered bazar built by Ali Murdan Khan, a celebrated nobleman in the service of the emperor Juhangeer, but which was destroyed by the English on their second capture of the city in 1842. On a neck of land at the eastern side of the city, about 150 feet above the plain, stands the Bala Hissar or upper citadel, the usual residence of the kings. Outside the town is the tomb of the renowned emperor Baber. Cabul enjoys a remarkably fine climate, and is celebrated for its beautiful gardens which produce fruits and flowers of all kinds in the greatest abundance. Fruit indeed is more plentiful than bread, and is considered by the people as one of the

Towns.

necessaries of life. Its population, before the war with the English, was estimated at 60,000.

In the mountains, a short distance to the north-westward of Cabul, in lat. 34° 40′ N. long. 66° 57′ E. is the city of *Bameean*, the capital of a small district of the same name, dependent upon Cabul. It consists for the greater part of a multitude of apartments and recesses cut out of the rock, which are believed to be of great antiquity. Amongst other remarkable objects are two colossal statues cut in the face of the mountain, about 150 feet in height, and supposed to be ancient idols. There are also some large mounds, or, as they are termed by the Natives, *topes*, constructed of blocks of stone, by some considered to have been the work of the Greeks.

Julalabad is situated in lat. 34° 6′ N. long. 69° 46′ E., a short distance to the westward of the Khyber Pass. It was formerly a place of considerable importance, and is still one of the principal towns; but it is chiefly noted on account of its gallant defence by a handful of British troops, under Sir Robert Sale, against the Afghans in 1842.

Peshawur is situated in lat. 34° 6′ N. long. 71° 13′ E. It stands in a well cultivated populous plain, forming a circle of about thirty-five miles across, and nearly surrounded by mountains.

This city was founded by the emperor Akber, and from its convenient situation between western Afghanistan and India, it has become a place of considerable commerce. Its population is estimated

Towns. at 100,000, principally of Indian origin. It was captured in 1825 by Runjeet Sing, and has since remained in possession of the Sikhs.

Ghuznee is situated in lat. 33° 10′ N. long. 66° 57′ E. For nearly two centuries this was the capital of a powerful kingdom, commencing with Subuktageen in 975, to the time of Mahomed Ghourie in 1171, who subdued the empire of Ghuznee and burnt the city. For many years afterwards, however, Ghuznee continued to be one of the principal towns in Afghanistan, and has always been regarded with veneration by the Mahomedans, in consequence of its containing the tombs of numerous distinguished personages of their faith. About three miles from the city is the tomb of the celebrated Sooltan Mahmood. Ghuznee was taken by storm by the British troops in 1839. Upon the insurrection in 1841, it again fell into the hands of the Afghans, from whom it was re-captured in 1842, when the English entirely demolished the fort, and carried off the sandal-wood gates of Mahmood's tomb, which had been taken by him from the Hindoo temple of Somnath in 1024. They also took away the Sooltan's mace as a trophy of their conquest.

Travelling distance from Cabul 80 miles, from Delhi 920.

Candahar is situated in lat. 36° 11′ N. long. 66° 28′ E. This place is believed to have been founded by Alexander the Great, and has always, from its position near the frontiers of Persia, been a place of considerable importance. The origi-

Towns. nal city was destroyed by Nadir Shah, and the present town was built in 1753 by Ahmed Shah, who made it his capital. It contains about 100,000 inhabitants, of whom a large porportion are Dooranee Afghans.

Travelling distance from Delhi, by Cabul, 1070 miles.

Name. By Europeans this country is commonly designated by the general name of Cabul. By the Persians it is styled Afghanistan, meaning the land of the Afghans, by which name also it is usually mentioned in Indian history.

Inhabitants. The inhabitants are known by the general name of Afghans, which is a Persian appellation. Their common national designation, among themselves, is Pooshtanu or Pookhtanu, but they more frequently use the names of the different tribes. In India they are generally denominated Pathans, and in the province of Delhi, Rohillas.

The Afghans assert that they are descended from the Jews, and often style themselves "Bun-i-Israeel," or *children of Israel*, though they consider the term *Yahoodee*, or Jew, as one of reproach. It is certain that they have in many points a strong resemblance to the Jews, and there appears reason to believe that the tradition of their origin is not unfounded.

They are divided into a number of distinct tribes, or *Oolooss*, each consisting of a number of separate clans ; and these last again subdivided into *khails*, which means a band or assemblage.

Inhabitants.

The principal are the following:—First, the Dooranee, formerly called the Abdallee, which includes amongst its clans the Populzye, the head Khail of which is the Suddoozye, the chief division of the whole of the Dooranees and containing the royal family; the Barikzye, the Achikzye, Noorzye, and others. Second, the Ghilzees. Third, the Berdooranees, or eastern Afghans, including the Yoosoofzyes, Khyberees, and others. The termination *Zye*, means *son*, corresponding with the *Mac* prefixed to Scotch names.

There are also in the towns many of mixed descent, from different parts of Asia; amongst whom are the Kuzzilbashes and Tajiks of Persian origin, and the Hindkees, the descendants of settlers from Hindoostan. The inhabitants of Kafiristan, which means *the land of the infidels*, are called the *Syah posh*, or *Syah posh Kafirs*, from their usually wearing dresses of black sheep skin; *syah* signifying *black*, and *posh* a covering. They are a fine handsome race, very fair, many of them having light hair and blue eyes, on which account it has been conjectured that they are the descendants of the Greeks. There seems reason, however, to believe that this is not the case, and that they are the descendants of the original inhabitants of Cabul and Candahar. They are a brave and hospitable people, though in a rude state, and have never been conquered by the Afghans. They have no king, but are divided into a number of independent tribes. Some of the tribes, occupying the

Inhabitants.

borders, are termed Neemchu-Moosulmans, or *half Moosulmans*, from their having partially adopted the Mahomedan faith. They are generally idolaters.

History.

Little is known of the early history of this country, the first mention of it being made by the Greeks, who traversed it under Alexander the Great. In A. D. 664, the Arabs who were then actively engaged in extending their conquests and propagating their faith, invaded Afghanistan; and by the year 700 succeeded in effecting the general subjugation of the country, and making converts of the majority of the inhabitants. It subsequently became the scene of repeated invasions by the Tartars until 977, when a permanent government was established by Subuktageen, under whose son, the celebrated Sooltan Mahmood, the empire of Ghuznee was extended over the whole of Afghanistan and various provinces of India. The Ghuznee monarchy continued, with various alterations, until 1171, when it was subverted by an Afghan chief, named Mahomed Ghourie, who took and destroyed the capital, and expelled the whole of the royal family. The dynasty of Ghor continued until about the year 1208, when on the death of the last king, Mahomed Ghourie, a general civil war ensued; the country was plunged into a state of miserable confusion; and, in 1215, was conquered by the king of Kharizm. It appears, however, again to have recovered its independence, when it was invaded and overrun by Tymoor Lung. Another

History. blank occurs in its history until 1506, when Cabul and Ghuznee were conquered by Sooltan Baber, prior to his invasion of Hindoostan. From that period Afghanistan continued to form part of the Mooghul empire of Delhi, until the death of Aurungzeb, when like many other provinces of that vast kingdom, it resumed its independence.

In 1720 the Afghans invaded Persia, and captured Ispahan, but were not able to retain their conquest; and in 1737 their own country was completely subjugated by Nadir Shah.

Upon the death of Nadir Shah in 1747, Ahmed Shah Abdallee, who had been a distinguished general under the Persian monarch, succeeded in establishing his authority over his countrymen, and founded the Dooranee empire. Under this brave and enterprising leader, the Afghans rapidly extended their power, and made conquests both in India and Persia; in the former of which countries, after capturing Delhi, he compelled the emperor to cede to him the provinces of Lahore, Mooltan, and Sind. Their occupation of these provinces soon brought them into collision with the Mahrattas, and in 1761 one of the most remarkable battles ever fought in India took place between Ahmed Shah and the Mahrattas at Paniput. The Mahrattas were defeated, and their immense army, amounting with its followers and families to nearly five hundred thousand persons, was almost wholly destroyed either in the fight or the pursuit. Ahmed Shah died in 1773, and was succeeded by his

History. son Tymoor Shah. Little of any note occurred during the reign of this prince, who was of an indolent character. On his death in 1793, the throne was seized by his son Zuman Shah. A succession of disorders followed. After frequent rebellions on the part of different members of the royal family, Zuman Shah was dethroned in 1800 by his brother Shah Mahmood, by whose orders he was deprived of his sight. Shah Mahmood's authority was soon contested by Shooja-ool-moolk, the next brother of Zuman Shah, who though at first defeated, succeeded in 1803 in driving out Shah Mahmood, who took refuge with his son Shah Kamran, then in possession of Herat. After repeated conflicts, Shah Mahmood with the powerful aid of Futih Khan, the head of the Barukzyes, obtained in 1809 a final victory over Shooja-ool-moolk, who fled to Hindoostan. Shah Mahmood remained for some years in security, leaving his government chiefly in the hands of the vizier Futih Khan. But his son Kamran, dissatisfied and suspicious, determined to remove this formidable chief, and having succeeded in leading his father to adopt the same views, Futih Khan was seized by Kamran at Herat, and immediately deprived of sight. A few months afterwards Kamran, with the full consent of the king, put the unfortunate vizier to death.

The tragedy which terminated the life of Futih Khan is perhaps without parallel in modern times. Blind and bound, he was led into the court of Mahmood,

History. where he had so lately ruled with absolute power. The king taunted him with his crimes, and required him to use his influence with his brothers then in rebellion. Futih Khan replied, with calm firmness, that he was now but a poor blind man and had no concern with affairs of state. Mahmood irritated by his refusal gave the last order for his death, and the chief was deliberately cut to pieces in the Shah's presence by the nobles around. Joint was separated from joint, limb from limb; his nose and his ears were lopped off, nor was life extinct until the head was separated from the mangled body. Futih Khan endured these cruel tortures without a groan, exhibiting the same reckless contempt for his own life that he had so often shown for the lives of others. This brutal murder was perpetrated in 1818, and drove the whole of Futih Khan's brothers into open rebellion. Shah Mahmood fled to Herat, and after some years of fearful disorder, in the course of which Shooja-ool-moolk and his brother Shah Eyool were successively placed upon the throne and again driven out, the different brothers succeeded in establishing their authority over nearly the whole kingdom. Dost Mahomed Khan obtained possession of Cabul and Ghuznee, and the other brothers of Candahar and Peshawur, leaving Herat as the only relic of the Dooranee sovereignty. Shah Mahmood died in 1829, and was succeeded by his son Kamran, who still retains the province. Their old enemies the Sikhs did not fail to take advantage

History. of these disorders, and Runjeet Singh first succeeded in conquering the valley of Cashmeer, which has ever since formed a province of the Sikh kingdom, and afterwards obtained possession of Peshawur. In 1839 the British Government, apprehensive of the result of an alliance which was supposed to be in progress between Dost Mahomed and the Persians and Russians, came to the determination of restoring the exiled monarch Shooja-ool-moolk, who had for some years been residing in India as a pensioner of the state. A British army accordingly entered Afghanistan, and in the course of a few months Shooja-ool-moolk was replaced upon the throne. Ghuznee having been taken by storm, and his troops having been defeated in repeated actions, Dost Mahomed suddenly made his appearance unattended at Cabul, and surrendered himself a prisoner to the English.

The authority of Shah Shooja appeared to be established throughout the kingdom, and in 1841 the British Government were preparing to withdraw the last division of their troops, when in the month of November, an insurrection, which had long been secretly preparing, broke out simultaneously in all parts of the country. Shut up without supplies, and surrounded on all sides, the envoy and other officers having in the interim been treacherously murdered, the English general agreed to evacuate the place under an oath of protection from Dost Mahomed's son, Akber Khan, the principal leader of the Afghans. The troops

History. were betrayed, and partly overwhelmed by numbers, but chiefly overcome by exposure without cover in the depth of a severe winter, and the want of food, nearly the whole force was miserably slaughtered. In the conflicts which ensued amongst the Afghans, Shah Shooja was murdered; and in 1842, Candahar and Jullalabad having meanwhile been successfully defended by the troops under Generals Nott and Sir Robert Sale, a fresh army was despatched from India. Ghuznee and Cabul were again captured, and the few English prisoners having been recovered, the British finally evacuated the country, and Dost Mahomed, who had from the time of his surrender been residing in India, was permitted to return to Cabul.

Religion. Mahomedanism of the Soonnee sect.

Language. The language of the Afghans is called Pushtoo. It is written in the Persian character. Persian is also used by the chiefs, and the descendants of the Hindoo settlers speak a mixed dialect resembling Hindoostanee, called Hindkee.

CHAP. XII.

Tartary.

Boundaries. Tartary, properly so called, lies between about 34° and 50° north latitude, and 50° and 75° east longitude. It is bounded on the north, by Russian Tartary; east, by Chinese Tartary; south, by Afghanistan and Persia; west, by Persia, the Caspian Sea, and part of Russian Tartary.

Divisions. Toorkistan, Khiva, Kokan, Bokhara, Toorkmania, Koondooz, each of which will be separately noticed.

Rivers. The principal rivers are the Jaxartes, Zur-Ufshan, the Oxus, and the Moorghab.

The Jaxartes, called by Asiatics the Sir or Sihoon, rises in the Beloot Tagh, and flows westerly and northerly through Kokan, Bokhara, and Toorkistan, into the sea of Aral.

The Zur-Ufshan, *(scatterer of gold)* called also the Kohuk, rises in the mountains eastward of Samarcand, and flows westerly and southerly past Samarcand and Bokhara, some distance to the southward of which last city, it forms a small lake.

The Oxus, called by Asiatics the Jihoon, and more commonly the Amoo,

Rivers. has its source on the northern side of the Hindoo Khoosh, and flows westerly and northerly through Koondoor, Bokhara, and Khiva, into the sea of Aral.

The Moorghab, or river of Merue, rises on the northern side of the Paropamisan mountains, and flows north-westerly past Merue, fifty miles beyond which place it falls into a small lake.

Between the northern part of Khiva and Toorkistan is an inland sea, about 200 miles in length from north to south, by 70 in breadth, named the sea of Aral. It is supposed by the common people of the country to flow below ground into the Caspian.

Mountains. The principal mountains are the Beloot Tagh, running from north to south along the eastern frontier; and the Ghour mountains, Hindoo Koosh, and Paropamisan on the south.

General Description. As the several divisions of this country differ a good deal in their general character, each will be separately described.

Productions. The southern and eastern parts of the country produce rice, wheat, barley, and other grains, with fruits of different kinds in great abundance. Horses, camels, and sheep, are very numerous throughout, particularly in the northern and western divisions, where each horde has large herds and flocks of them. The horses of Bokhara called Uzbekees, and of Toorkistan and Toorkmania known as Toorkmanees, are particularly cele-

Productions.

brated for their great strength and power of enduring fatigue. The camel is of a large strong breed with two humps, commonly known as the Bactrian camel; the Indian camel with the single hump, being properly the dromedary. The wild animals are principally tigers, which are found in the Beloot Tagh mountains, wolves, horses, asses, and the chamois goat. There are also numerous smaller animals, such as ermines, and others affording valuable furs. Gold is found in the sand of the Oxus, and to a smaller extent in the Zur-Ufshan, and other rivers; and the mountainous parts contain silver, copper, iron, vitriol, and different kinds of valuable stones and marbles. There are large cotton manufactories at Bokhara, and a considerable trade with the neighbouring countries in silk, wool, and lamb skins. The people of Bokhara make great use of tea, which they obtain from China.

TOORKISTAN.

General Account.

This division occupies the northern part of the country. It is generally open, but not cultivated, and devoted chiefly to pasturage. It is inhabited by wandering tribes of Toorkmans, who have large herds and flocks of horses, camels, cattle, and sheep, with which they move from place to place according to the season. They have no towns, but live in camps formed of tents, made of woollen, like thick black cumlies. Each tribe or horde is independent. No

General Account. estimate can be formed of the total population.

KHIVA,

Description. also called Orgunje, and anciently Kharizm, occupies the western part, between Bokhara and the Caspian Sea. Excepting in the immediate vicinity of the Oxus, this province is almost entirely a sandy desert, its inhabitants depending for their support principally upon their camels, which are bred in great numbers, and upon the sale of slaves captured in the adjoining territories of Russia and Persia.

Towns. The only places of any note in the province are Orgunje and Khiva.

Orgunje, which is situated about six miles from the bank of the Oxus, is the principal place of trade in the country. It contains about 12,000 inhabitants.

Khiva stands about 15 miles to the southward of the Oxus. It is a modern town, and only distinguished on account of its being the residence of the khan. It contains about 6,000 inhabitants.

Inhabitants. The inhabitants of this province are chiefly Toorkmans, consisting principally of wandering tribes, under the immediate control of their several chiefs, but subject to the general government of an Uzbek, who has the title of khan of Khiva. The total population is supposed not to exceed 200,000.

This province is the "country of the Chorasmi" noticed in Arrian.

KOHAN,

General Account.

called also Ferghana, occupies the northeastern part of the country, separated by ranges of mountains from Toorkistan on the north, and Koondooz on the south, and bounded on the east by the Beloot Tagh. It may be described as the valley of the Jaxartes, which flows through the middle from east to west. It is a fertile and well cultivated district, and its productions are similar to those of Bokhara. It is celebrated for its silk. The principal town is Kokan, situated on the Jaxartes, and containing about 150,000 inhabitants.

This province forms an independent principality under an Uzbek chief who bears the title of khan, and claims his descent from Alexander.

BOKHARA

General Description.

forms a part of Toorkistan, or *the land of the Toorks*, and is so denominated by the Natives themselves, though generally known to Europeans by the designation of Bucharia, from the name of the city of Bokhara. It is an open champaign country, and in the vicinity of its rivers rich and fertile, but at a distance from them barren and uncultivated.

The valley of Samarcand especially has always been celebrated for its fruitfulness and beauty.

Included in this province is the country of Balkh, formerly the seat of the Greek kingdom of Bactria. In its general appearance it resembles the rest of

General Description.

Bokhara, the southern parts in the vicinity of the rivers being fertile and well cultivated, while the north are composed chiefly of naked and sterile plains.

The climate of Bokhara is very pleasant and healthful. It is dry, and in the winter very cold, as is usual in elevated sandy countries, the Oxus being frequently frozen and the snow lying for three months at the city of Bokhara.

The climate of Balkh, to the southward of the Oxus, is quite the reverse, being oppressively hot and very unhealthy, owing as is supposed by the Natives, to the bad quality of the water.

Towns.

The principal towns are Bokhara, Samarcand, and Balkh.

Bokhara stands about six miles from the southern or left bank of the Zur-Ufshan, in lat. 39° 43′ N. long. 64° 30′ E.

This is a city of great antiquity, and particularly celebrated amongst the Mahomedans from its having been at an early period conquered and converted to their faith. On this account, as well as because of the number of learned men whom it produced, its Mahomedan rulers gave it the title of *shureef* or holy, by which name it soon became distinguished in the east. It was for many centuries a very rich and populous city, but in common with all other places under Mahomedan rule, it has undergone many changes and has long ceased to be of any importance. The present city is about eight miles in circumference, and is surrounded by a wall having twelve gates. It has a great many mosques

Towns.

with lofty minarets, particularly the Great Mosque, part of which was built by the renowned Tymoor; besides colleges of various kinds, said to be 366 in number, frequented by students from all parts of the country. It has a population of about 150,000, including about 4,000 Jews of a remarkably handsome race, emigrants from Meshid in Persia, and about 300 Hindoos chiefly Shikarpoorees from Sind. In this city may be found Persians, Turks, Russians, Tartars, Chinese, Afghans, and Indians, all assembled together in the same bazars. This city is remarkable for the prevalence of guinea-worm, nearly one-fourth of its population being attacked by it in the course of every year.

Samarcand is situated near the southern bank of the Zur-Ufshan, about 120 miles to the eastward of Bokhara. This was in the early times of the Mahomedan power one of the most renowned cities in the east, and it is still regarded with great veneration by the people of the country; and no king of Bokhara is considered by them to be the lawful sovereign who has not possession of Samarcand. It was the capital of Tymoor, whose tomb still remains. It has now declined to a provincial town of not more than 10,000 inhabitants, and gardens and fields occupy the place of its former streets and mosques. A few colleges and other buildings still exist, some of them of beautiful architecture, particularly one which originally formed the observatory of the celebrated astronomer, Ulug Beg. The manufacture of paper

Towns. was introduced into Europe from this city, on its conquest by the Mahomedans about the year 710.

Balkh is situated in lat. 36° 48′ N. long. 65° 16′ E. It is believed to be one of the most ancient cities in the world. By Asiatics it is commonly designated as the *mother of cities*, and it is said by them to have been built by Kyamoors, the founder of the first empire of Persia. It was long celebrated after the conquest of the country by Alexander, as the capital of the kingdom of Bactria; and it was the residence of the chief of the Magi or fire worshippers of Persia, until conquered by the Mahomedans about the year 710. In the early part of the 13th century, the city was taken and plundered by the celebrated Jungez Khan; and in the course of the many vicissitudes to which it has since been exposed, it has decayed into an insignificant town, of not more than 2,000 inhabitants, though its ruins extend over a circuit of about twenty miles. It is remarkable for a great abundance of fruit of various kinds, apricots for example being commonly sold at the rate of two thousand for a rupee. Snow is brought from the mountains, about twenty miles distant, and sold in the bazar during the summer.

TOORKMANIA

General Account. occupies the southern and western part of the country, from Balkh to the Caspian sea; having Khiva and the Oxus along its northern frontier, and ranges

General Account.

of mountains separating it from Persia and Afghanistan on the southern. In the south-western parts it is mountainous, but for the rest it consists of sandy desert, very scantily supplied with water, in some places quite flat, and in others rising up into mounds, some of which, towards the Caspian, attain a height of from sixty to eighty feet.

There are no towns or villages properly so called, the Toorkmans being all *nomade*, that is wandering tribes, moving from one well to another with their flocks and herds, and taking their conical huts, called *khirgahs*, with them, in search of water and pasture.

The only fixed settlement worth noticing is Shurukhs, situated in lat. 36° 31′ N. It consists of a small fort almost in ruins, and a few mud huts, which have been built by Jews from Meshid in Persia, the Toorkmans living in their khirgahs. These are huts of a conical form, constructed of wood, surrounded by a mat of reeds, and covered on the roof with felts. In lat. 36° N. long. 61° 1′ E. stand the ruins of Merve, formerly the capital of a principality of the same name, and said to have been built by Alexander the Great. It is still styled by the Natives "Merve Shah-i-Juhan," or Merve the king of the world; and a celebrated epitaph on one of its kings is often quoted by eastern writers. "You have witnessed the grandeur of Alp Arslan exalted to the skies: repair to Merve, and see it buried in the dust."

Under the government of the Persians, Merve was long a great and opulent

General Account. city, and the surrounding district was one of the most fertile in the world. But in the latter end of the 18th century the district was conquered by the king of Bokhara, who destroyed the canals, and drove out the inhabitants; and the country soon became as sterile as the rest of Toorkmania, while its former fixed population has been succeeded by the wandering tribes of Toorkmans.

Inhabitants. The inhabitants of this province are Toorkmans, divided into a number of independent hordes or tribes; they have no permanent ruler, and acknowledge only the general direction of their Aksukals or elders. Their life is passed in the most reckless plunder of the neighbouring countries, from which they carry off the men and women as slaves. Their children are brought up from their earliest years in the same habits. They have a proverb, which very aptly illustrates their character, namely, that a Toorkman on horseback knows neither his father nor mother.

They have no science nor literature, nor any mosques, though nominally Mahomedans. Their food consists of the milk and flesh of their herds and flocks, the milk of the camel especially being a favourite drink.

KHOONDOOZ,

General Account. which now includes Budukhshan, is situated in the south-eastern part of the country, between Bokhara and Balkh,

General Account.

and Afghanistan; having the Beloot Tagh along its eastern side, and on the southern the Hindoo Koosh.

The district of Khoondooz consists of a valley among low hills, which extend from east to west for about thirty miles, and from north to south forty. Its climate is very unhealthy, the heat of the summer being excessive, while in winter the snow lies upon the ground for three months. The greater part of the valley is so marshy that the roads across are constructed on piles of wood.

The district of Budukhshan, on the contrary, is celebrated for its climate, and for its abundance of fruits and flowers, though from having been repeatedly ravaged by the neighbouring tribes, it is now almost depopulated.

Productions.

Khoondooz produces abundance of rice, and in the dry parts wheat and barley; silk also is produced on the banks of the Oxus.

Budukhshan is celebrated for its ruby mines. It also yields lapis lazuli, sulphur, salt, and iron.

The chief traffic of the province is in cattle and slaves.

Towns.

The principal towns are Khoondooz and Khooloom.

Khoondooz is the residence of the chief, but is otherwise an insignificant town, and does not contain more than 1500 inhabitants.

Khooloom is situated on the western frontier, and is the principal trading town. It contains about 10,000 inhabitants.

Inhabitants. The inhabitants of Khoondooz are chiefly Tajiks, with a small proportion of Uzbeks; and the province is under the government of an Uzbek chief, who bears the title of Meer of Khoondooz.

Name. The name of Tartary was formerly given by European writers to the whole of northern and central Asia, from Persia, Hindoostan and China to the Northern Ocean, and from the Black Sea and the frontier of Russia to the Pacific. The Tartars, properly *Tatars*, were a tribe who usually led the van of Jungez Khan's armies, and their name was thus carried into Europe by the fugitive inhabitants of the countries they invaded, and gradually came to be employed to designate a great part of Asia as above noticed.

The name of Tartary is not known in eastern geography, the general name given by eastern writers to the country north of the Jaxartes being Toorkistan, and to that part between the Jaxartes and the Oxus, Mawur-ool-Nuhr.

By the Greeks it was divided into *Sogdiana*, now the district of Samarcand and Bokhara, on the north; and *Bactriana*, or the modern Balkh, on the south.

Mawur-ool-Nuhr also is often designated as *Transoxiana*, which names are synonymous; the first meaning *beyond the river*, as the second does *beyond the Oxus*.

The whole of this country in ancient geography formed part of Scythia.

Inhabitants. The inhabitants of the several countries included under the name of Tar-

Inhabitants. tary, are composed of Tajiks or Tats in Mawur-ool-Nuhr, and various tribes of Toork and Tartar origin.

The Tajiks are of Persian origin, and are chiefly occupied in commerce and agriculture.

Of the other tribes the principal are the Toorkmans, the Uzbeks, the Kirghizes, and the Kuzzaks, all of Toorkee origin, and the Kalmuks who are Tartars.

The Toorkmans are entirely a nomade race, divided into a number of tribes or clans. They occupy Toorkistan, Khiva, and Toorkmania. The Uzbeks, partly nomade, but generally living in a settled manner, occupy Bokhara, Kokan, and Khoondooz.

The Kirghizes inhabit the eastern parts of Khoondooz, and the Kuzzaks, (known in Europe as the Cossacks, who appear to be nearly the same people as the Kirghizes,) occupy the northern and north-eastern borders towards Russia.

The Kalmuks, or *Calmuck Tartars*, who for many centuries occupied the eastern shores of the Black Sea, are now chiefly to the north of the Jaxartes, having migrated thither in the latter part of the 18th century.

All these tribes have the same origin as the Scythians and Huns of ancient times, and have always been marked by the same fierceness of character, and the same wandering and predatory habits.

The Toorkmans and other nomade tribes depend for their subsistence entirely upon their flocks and herds. Their chief food is mutton, and as a delicacy, horse-flesh ; and their common

Inhabitants. drink is milk, not only of cows, but also of mares, goats, ewes, and camels. Of mares' milk the northern tribes make a spirituous liquor, called *Koumis*, of which they are exceedingly fond. They carry on some trade with the neighbouring districts, exchanging horses, cattle, wool, and furs, for arms, and other manufactured articles; but their main traffic is in slaves, whom they capture from the Persian and Russian territories.

The Tajiks and Uzbeks are greatly superior to the others in all respects, being industrious and civilized, and they carry on a considerable commerce with Persia, India, Tibet, China, and Russia.

History. This has been one of the most celebrated countries in the east, having been the seat of empire of the famous Jungez Khan and of his successors including Tymoor, until the dissolution of the Tartar government in the 16th century.

Very little, however, is known of its early history. As far as has been ascertained, it appears in all ages to have been occupied by successive hordes of restless plunderers, known under the general appellations of Scythians, Huns, and Tartars, whose devastations have extended on all sides both in Europe and Asia.

In the eastern districts south of the Jaxartes kingdoms of some note have existed, though they none of them appear to have subsisted for more than a few centuries, owing to the constant invasions to which they have been exposed.

The Greeks under Alexander overran

History. the province of Balkh, where they founded the Greek kingdom of Bactriana; and several chiefs in Budukhshan, and to the eastward, still claim a Greek descent, some even affirming themselves to be of the family of Alexander.

In the course of the 6th century, the country was invaded by the Arabs, at which time it appears to have contained several principalities, but of little importance, and in a low state of civilization. The Arabs succeeded in a few years in making converts of the people to the Mahomedan faith; and under its Mahomedan rulers the kingdom of Bokhara soon became one of the most flourishing in Asia.

In 1232 Bokhara was invaded and overrun by the Tartars under Jungez Khan, whose descendants subsequently ruled over the greater part of the country. The Tartar dynasty attained its greatest power under Tymoor, well known in Europe as Tamerlane the Great, who died A. D. 1405.

The successors of Tymoor, after some generations, were driven out by an invasion of the Uzbeks, and proceeding eastward under Sooltan Baber, established themselves A. D. 1525 in India, where their leader founded what has since been styled the Mooghul empire of Delhi.

The Uzbeks maintained their supremacy until the invasion of the Persian monarch Nadir Shah in the early part of the 18th century, which was followed by a long series of disorders and civil wars.

At present the principal states are those of Khiva, Bokhara, and Khoondooz.

History. Under the descendants of Jungez Khan, Kharizm and Bokhara were distinguished above all the countries of the east for learning and magnificence, and from the ruins which may still be seen in places now quite desolate, it is evident that there were formerly many populous and well built cities now unknown. The Persian and Arabic languages were carefully cultivated under the patronage of the Khans, and many of the most learned of the Mahomedan writers are numbered among those of Samarcand. The name of Ulug Beg, the grandson of Tymoor, is well known to astronomers, and that of Abdool Ghazee, the Khan of Kharizm, is celebrated for his history of the Tartars.

Religion. The tribes are generally Mahomedans of the Soonnee sect, with the exception of the Kalmuks, who follow the Lama system of religion.

Language. The prevailing language is the Toorkmanee, and amongst the Tajiks, Persian.

CHAP. XIII.

Chinese Tartary.

Boundaries. Chinese Tartary lies between lat. 35° and 55° N. and long. 70° and 145° E. and is bounded on the north by Siberia ; east, by the Gulf of Tartary, and the Sea of Japan ; south, by the Yellow Sea, China, and Tibet ; and west, by Tartary.

Divisions. This country may be divided into the country of the Eluts, or Kalmuck Tartars, the country of the Mooghuls, and the country of the Manshoors.

The Kalmuks occupy the western parts, including little Bucharia or eastern Toorkistan, the Mooghuls the central, and the Manshoors the eastern. Belonging to the Manshoor country, and separated from it by the gulf of Tartary and a very narrow strait, is the island of Sagalin.

Rivers. It has several rivers, but none of any importance. The principal is the Sagalin, flowing eastward into the gulf of Tartary. There are also several large lakes.

Mountains. Its principal ranges of mountains are the Altaian on the north, and Beloot Tagh, dividing it from Tartary on the west. The Beloot Tagh mountains are named in ancient geography the Imaus.

General Description. The face of this country is much diversified with mountain and plain, though with little forest. The greater part consists of a vast plain, supported like a table by the Tibet mountains on the south, and the Altaian on the north, and considered the most elevated level land on the face of the globe.

Part of this plain is occupied by two large sandy deserts, the Desert of Cobi, and the Desert of Sharno. The rest is devoted to pasturage.

Productions. The productions of this country, as far as they are known, are few; the Tartar tribes in general paying little or no attention to agriculture or manufactures, but depending chiefly upon their flocks and herds, of which they have great numbers. Horses and cattle are very abundant, they have also the bush tailed or grunting ox, and the camel. Wild horses and asses are numerous, and the tiger is also found in different parts. Ginseng root, and sable, and other furs, form the principal part of their trade, and in the Manshoor country pearls are found in some of the rivers.

Towns. The different tribes in general form wandering hordes and live in tents, which they remove from place to place according to the season, or as they find pasturage for their flocks. Except in the western division, inhabited by the Kalmuks, there are consequently few towns. The principal are Kashgar, Turfan, and Yarkhund, in little Bucharia; Hami or Chamil, in the Mooghul country; and

Towns. Sangalin Oula, Tsitchikar, and Chinyang or Moogden, in the Manshoor country.

Name. The general name of Tartary has been applied to this country by Europeans, but it has no distinct native appellation, the different tribes having each different names for their respective lands.

Inhabitants. The inhabitants may be divided into the three principal tribes of Kalmuks, Mooghuls, and Manshoors. The ancient inhabitants of the Kalmuk country were of the race called by the Roman and Greek historians the Scythians; these were driven westward by the Huns, and these again by the Kalmuk tribes. The Huns were, correctly speaking, the original Tartars. Their complexion is generally of a reddish or yellowish brown.

History. From the earliest times this country appears to have been inhabited by various wandering hordes or tribes, addicted to a pastoral life, each horde under its own khan or chief. They were all, however, brought under subjection by the celebrated Jungez Khan in the beginning of the 13th century, and remained under the rule of his family until their empire fell to pieces in the 16th century, and the tribes again became independent. Jungez Khan invaded China, and his Tartars maintained possession for about a hundred years, but were driven out in 1368. In 1644 the Manshoor tribes again entered China, and finally established themselves, and at present the whole of Chinese Tartary is subject to the authority of the Chinese empire.

Religion. The prevailing religion of the tribes is Booddhism of the Lama sect. Many are also followers of what is called Shamanism, that is idolaters who acknowledge a Supreme Being, but worship a multitude of inferior deities. In little Bucharia there are also Mahomedans of the Soonnee sect.

Language. The languages of the tribes are distinct; that of the Manshoors is said to be exceedingly copious, though not written until the 17th century, when the Mooghul character was introduced.

CHAP. XIV.

Tibet.

Boundaries. This country lies on the northern frontier of Hindoostan. It is bounded on the north by Chinese Tartary; east, by China; south, by Assam, Bootan, and Hindoostan; west, by Cashmeer and Tartary. In general terms it may be said to lie between long. 74° and 100° E. slanting southwards along the Himalaya mountains, from lat. 28° to 37° N.

Divisions. Its chief divisions are Lakdack, Undesa, Teshoo-Loomboo, and Lassa.

Rivers. Its principal rivers are the Sanpoo and Mounchoo, and in it are also the sources of several of the principal rivers in Asia. The Indus, Sutluj, Brahmapootra, of the Indian rivers, besides others of China, and of northern Tartary. The Sanpoo is believed to be one of the most considerable rivers in Asia; but as yet the information regarding it is very defective.

Mountains. It has two great ranges of mountains, the Himalayas lying along its southern limits, and the Kailas, nearly parallel to the Himalayas, in about lat. 32° N. and of about the same elevation; some of the villages on them being situated at a height of nearly 20,000 feet above the sea.

General Description. Tibet may be considered as consisting of two portions, the valley between the Himalaya and Kailas mountains, studded with irregular hills, and averaging a height of 10,000 feet above the sea; and an extensive table-land beyond the Kailas of similar elevation, declining towards the north and east.

Of the interior of Tibet, north of the Kailas, little is known; but it is believed to consist of extensive stony and sandy plains, diversified by hills, and by pastures traversed by small streams.

Between the Himalayas and Kailas are two remarkable lakes, the Manaswarora, in lat. 31° N. long. 81° E. and the Rawun Hrood, about ten miles further westward. The former is considered by the Hindoos as the most sacred of all their places of pilgrimage. The

General Description.

Chinese and Tibetians of Undesa call it Choo Mapang, and it is considered by them also a holy place. Rawun Hrood is the source of the river Sutluj.

In consequence of the great elevation of this country its climate is exceedingly cold, particularly in the vicinity of the Himalaya range; where during winter the cold is quite as severe as in the north of Europe; meat and fish being preserved in a frozen state as in Russia.

Productions.

Its vegetable productions are not numerous, its chief riches consisting in its animals and minerals. Barley, coarse peas, and wheat are the grains; rice is not cultivated. Turnips and radishes are the only vegetables, and peaches and bynes the only fruits. Tibet, however, abounds in cattle and sheep and wild fowl and game of every description. Horses and mules are numerous, the latter being commonly used for carriage. The sheep also are used for the same purpose. The horse and the ass are both found wild. The most remarkable animals of Tibet are the yak, or bushy tailed ox, sometimes called the *grunting ox*, the musk-deer, and the shawl goat. The yak is rather larger than the Malwa bullock, and is covered all over with a long thick hair, from which are manufactured ropes and cloths for tents. Their bushy tails are greatly valued, and are much used as fly flaps, (or *chowries*) or as ornaments for horses and elephants, for which purposes they are in much request in India, China, and Turkey. These oxen are never employ-

Productions.

ed in agriculture, but generally for carriage. The musk-deer is about the size of a common hog, which it resembles a good deal in appearance. The musk is found only in the male, in a little bag at its navel. The shawl goat is so named from its yielding the soft silky hair used for the manufacture of the celebrated Cashmeer shawls. This species of goat is found in no other country. All the animals of Tibet are provided with thick coats of hair and fur adapted to the coldness of the climate. The dogs are large and powerful, and the cat of the long-haired kind, known in India by the name of Persian or Lama cats. The minerals are principally gold, quicksilver, nitre, and salt. Firewood is very scarce throughout the country beyond the Kailas, the dried dung of animals being almost the only fuel.

Towns.

The principal towns are Leh, Garoo, Teshoo-Loomboo, and Lassa.

Leh, or *Lah*, the capital of Lahdack, is situated on a branch of the Indus, here called the Lahdack river, in lat. 34° 10′ N. and about long. 78° 20′ E. It is the residence of the raja of Lahdack, and is a place of considerable trade, being a principal mart for the shawl wool of Tibet.

In the neighbouring district is a breed of remarkably small sheep, not larger than lambs in India of six months old, but covered with a very large and fine fleece.

Garoo, or *Gartope*, is situated in lat. 31° 8′ N. long. 80° 23′ E. It is only

Towns. noted as a mart for wool, the town itself being a mere assemblage of woollen tents.

Teshoo-Loomboo is situated in lat. 29° 7′ N. long. 80° 2′ E., 180 miles north from the frontier of the Rungpoor district of Bengal. It is the second town in Tibet, and the residence of the teshoo lama.

Lassa is situated in lat. 29° 30′ N. and long. 91° 6′ E. It is the capital of Tibet, and the residence of the dalai, or grand lama.

Name. The origin of the name Tibet, now generally given to this country, is not known, as it does not appear to have been applied by the Natives. In Hindoo geography, the tract lying along the Himalaya mountains is termed Bhoot, and the people Bhootiyas. The Native name of Tibet is said to be Pue, or Pue-Koachin, signifying "the snowy land." By the Chinese it is called Tsang.

Inhabitants. The inhabitants are called by the English Tibetians. They are considered to belong to the same general race as the Tartars, and are entirely distinct in appearance from the Natives of Hindoostan. They are described as a mild and contented, but indolent people. Their manufactures are chiefly of shawls and woollen cloths, of which they supply large quantities to China, their principal intercourse, both commercial and political, being with that country. The Tibetians have the singular custom of *polyandria*, that is, of one wife belonging to several husbands; the elder brother of a family having the right to

Inhabitants.

select a wife for himself and all his brothers. They do not bury their dead, but burn the bodies of the lamas, and expose those of the other classes to be devoured by the beasts and birds. Their chief food is mutton, which they are fond of eating raw, and barley prepared in various ways. They use plates of china or copper, with knives and forks.

History.

As far as is known of the history of this country, it appears to have been formerly under the government of a Tartar prince, who, in consequence of his refusal to do homage to the dalai lama, was driven from his throne and put to death; from which time, supposed to be between 1600 and 1650, the dalai lama became the sovereign of the whole of Tibet until about 1720, when the emperor of China, taking the opportunity to interfere on occasion of disputes among the lamas, established his authority; and Tibet, though still nominally under the sovereignty of the grand lama, is now actually governed by a Chinese viceroy who resides at the lama's capital, and the country is garrisoned by Chinese troops. Lahdack, however, is independent, and is still governed by its own chief who has the title of raja of Lahdack.

Religion.

The religion of Tibet is that of Booddh, which appears to have been introduced from India, and established throughout this country at an early period. The priests are all styled lamas, and amongst these the dalai lama, or grand lama,

Religion. and the teshoo lama are held to be particularly sacred. The grand lama is considered to be no less than the deity in a human form, on the dissolution of which he enters a new one. The teshoo lama is also looked upon as an incarnation of Booddh, and is honored by the emperor of China as his religious teacher and guide. There are two sects of the lama Booddhists, distinguished from each other by the dress of the lamas, the one wearing a red, and the other a yellow cap. The latter may be considered the principal, being that of the grand and teshoo lamas and of the Chinese emperor. The red division is chiefly established in Bootan. The lama Booddhists entirely reject all distinction of caste, and admit proselytes of any nation. The principal idol in their temples is that of Maha Moonee, *(great saint,)* the Booddh of Hindoostan.

Language. The language appears to be quite distinct from the languages of India, though the alphabet and character are believed to have been derived from the Sanscrit. It has two dialects; one for works of learning and religion, the other for common purposes. The letters run from right to left. Printing with wooden blocks is practised, and is said to have been known to the Tibetians from a very early period, but it has been so limited in its use through their superstition, that not the slightest improvement in it seems to have been made, and it therefore remains in a very imperfect state.

CHAP. XV.

§ 1.

China.

Boundaries.

China, properly so called, exclusive of its territories in Tartary and Tibet, lies between lat. 20° and 42° N. and long. 100° and 123° E. and is bounded on the north by Chinese Tartary; east, by the sea; south, by the sea, Tunquin, and Siam; and west, by Ava, Assam, Tibet, and Chinese Tartary.

The different parts of the sea forming the eastern and southern boundary, are named as follows:

The Yellow Sea, from about lat. 42° to 34° N.; the Eastern Sea, along the remainder of the east coast; the Chinese Sea, along the south; and the Gulf of Tunquin, between Hainan and Tunquin. These different seas all form part of the Pacific Ocean.

Divisions.

This empire is divided into 18 large provinces, each governed by its viceroy.

Rivers.

It has numerous rivers, of which the principal are the Hoang-ho, or yellow river, and the Kian-ku, or blue river; so named from the colour of their water; the first being very muddy, and the other clear.

Rivers.

Both rivers rise in or near Tibet. The Hoang-ho flows through China into the Yellow Sea, after a course of 2,150 miles. The Kian-hu flows into the same sea, about 100 miles to the southward of the Hoang-ho, after a course of about 2,200 miles. These are considered the longest rivers in the world.

The Peiho and Quantung may also be noticed—the former is the Pekin river, and flows into the Gulf of Peehelee at the head of the Yellow Sea; the latter is the Canton river, and flows into the sea below that city.

There are also several extensive lakes, one of which named the Tong-ting, situated in nearly the centre of the country, is about 300 miles in circumference.

General Description.

Along the northern frontier runs what is called by European writers the great Wall of China. This is an immense rampart built to protect the country from the invasions of the Tartars. It is upwards of 1,000 miles in length, and in some parts, is carried over mountains not less than 5,000 feet in height. Since the establishment of the Tartar empire in China, however, this wall has been allowed to go to ruin.

The face of the country is much diversified, in some parts mountainous, in others level, but in all most carefully cultivated; in this respect excelling even the most civilised countries of Europe. Excellent paved roads communicate with all parts, and there are every where inns or choultries, for the accommodation of travellers.

Productions. The productions of this country include all that are known in India, besides some peculiar to itself. Its grand article of export is tea, the prepared leaves of a plant, and the use of which is now general throughout Europe and America. Rice is the chief food of the people. The manufactures are of every description, this country having long been celebrated for its cotton and silk fabrics, and for its earthen ware; which latter was for a long time so peculiar to China that it still bears the name of "China," though now manufactured in Europe of a superior quality. It possesses all the common domestic animals, and a very small breed of camels not larger than horses. The wild animals are the tiger, rhinoceros and bear, with the usual smaller kinds. Metals are abundant, gold, silver, copper, tutenag, lead, tin, and iron; coal is also plentiful.

Towns. The cities and towns are numerous; the principal are Peking, Sinkang, Nanking, and Canton.

Peking, or the Northern Court, is the capital. It is situated in lat. 39° 54′ N. long. 116° 27′ E., about 40 miles from the great wall, and contains two millions of inhabitants.

Sinkang, situated inland towards the western frontier, is reported to be equal to Peking.

Nanking, or the Southern Court, the former capital, situated near the eastern

Towns. coast upon the river Kianku, is the largest city in the empire, though not so populous as Peking. The cloth called nankeen, takes its name from this city.

Canton is the largest seaport town in China, and the only one to which Europeans were formerly permitted to resort. It is situated on the banks of the river Quantung, or Pekiang, in lat. 32° 4′ N. long. 118° 4′ E.; and has, besides the suburbs on shore, a large floating town upon the river, containing altogether nearly a million and a half of inhabitants.

There are factories in the suburbs established by England and America, and by most of the European powers. No foreigners are permitted to enter the city itself, but are restricted to the suburbs. The Russians are excluded from the seaports, because a land trade is carried on with them on the frontiers of Siberia.

About 80 miles below Canton, on a small peninsula near the mouth of the river, the entrance of which is called by Europeans the Bocca Tigris, stands the town of Macao, belonging to the Portuguese, who were permitted to form this settlement in 1586 by the emperor of China, in reward for services rendered by them in expelling some pirates. Until 1842 it was the only European settlement in the Chinese empire, and is under strict supervision, being in reality governed by a mandarin. No foreign females are allowed to pass beyond Macao, where European ships are consequently obliged to land any who may be on board, before they can proceed up the river.

Towns. A short distance from Macao is the small island of Hong-kong, which was finally ceded to the English in 1842, and is now an English settlement.

Name. The English name for this country is derived from the word "Cheen," by which China is generally designated in the east. The Native name is said to be "Tchong kwe," or "the kingdom of the centre." It is also sometimes styled in their public documents, "the celestial empire."

Inhabitants. The Natives of this country, who are by Europeans termed the Chinese, consist of two classes, Tartars and Chinese who are also of Tartar origin. They vary in complexion from a dark and swarthy brown, to a florid white, with broad flat faces, and very small narrow eyes wide apart. In their dress they are entirely distinct from both Europeans and Asiatics in general; and are particularly distinguished by the practice of wearing their hair platted into a long tail hanging down their backs. They are a very ingenious and most industrious people, very skilful artists, and capable of correctly imitating almost any thing given them as a model, yet they are greatly behind European nations in every branch of art and science, which is owing to their pride and their great dread of all innovation, which prevent their adopting any new inventions, especially from foreigners. Thus they remain in the same state to which they appear to have attained many centuries

Inhabitants.

ago, and though far advanced in civilization, while European nations were yet in barbarism, the latter have now passed far beyond them. Though they have European ships of all kinds continually in their sight, they still adhere to their own clumsy and imperfect style of building, and the Chinese junks, as their large vessels are called, are proverbial as the worst adapted to the sea of any that are known. They make use of the compass, but they know nothing of navigation; their astronomy is very imperfect, and so in every other department of knowledge; every thing having long stood still with the Chinese, while other nations, whom they call barbarians, have been continually advancing. The total population of China is said to amount to about 148,000,000.

History.

Like other eastern nations, the Chinese pretend to an antiquity which is beyond all reason, carrying their history to a period of more than fifty thousand years back. They are, however, admitted to be one of the most ancient nations now existing; and they possess apparently credible records reaching as far as about 3,000 years before Christ. According to these, the country was then in a state of complete barbarism, and continued divided into a number of petty states, nominally subject to an emperor, until about 500 years before Christ, when it appears to have been formed into one regular government. From early times China was subject to invasions from the neighbouring Tartar tribes, and was twice

History.

overrun and conquered, though not retained, by Jungez Khan and Tymoor. In 1644, taking advantage of internal rebellions and disorders, the khan of the Manshoor Tartars invaded and subdued the empire, and from that time it has been under the rule of his descendants; the country of the Manshoors having become incorporated as part of the Chinese dominions, under the name which it now bears of Chinese Tartary. The government is purely despotic, all power and honor of every kind emanating solely from the sovereign. The title given him by Europeans is "emperor." His native titles vary, and are usually remarkable for their absurd vanity, such as "sole governor of the earth"—"celestial monarch"—"son of heaven."

Religion.

The prevalent religion of China, being that followed by the emperor, is Booddhism of the yellow lama sect. Booddh is known in this country by the name of Fo, and his system of religion was introduced from India about 65 years before the Christian era. The Chinese priests of this sect are usually called by Europeans Bonzes.

There are two other systems of religion, the one of Confucius, the other of Lao-kien.

Confucius, called by the Chinese Confoo-tsee, was a very eminent philosopher, who was born about the year 550 before Christ. His religion may be briefly described as a system of morals founded upon the acknowledgment of a Supreme Being, rewarding virtue and punishing vice.

Religion. The religion of Lao-kien appears to be a confused system of idolatry, including with the worship of a Supreme Being that of a multitude of spirits, and its priests profess to practise magic.

Mahomedanism also exists among the Tartars.

Language. The Chinese language is considered the most singular in the world. It is monosyllabic, that is, all its words consist of a single syllable, and it is written in a very complicated character, the words being placed in columns from right to left, and reading from top to bottom of each column. For writing, the Chinese use a hair-pencil or brush and the ink generally called by the English "Indian ink," with which they trace the characters upon paper or silk. Printing with wooden blocks has been practised by the Chinese from a very early period.

§ 2.

Islands connected with China.

General Account. There are several islands on different parts of the coast, either tributary to China, or included in its provinces. Of these, the principal are the Chusan, the Loochoo, Formosa, and Hainan.

The Chusan islands form an extensive group, of which the principal one, named Chusan, is situated in lat. 30° N. long. 122° 14′ E., about 10 miles from the mainland. They form part of the adjacent province.

General Account.

The Loochoo islands are situated about 400 miles from the coast, occupying the 27th degree of north latitude, and the 129th degree east longitude. They are tributary to China. The inhabitants are a kindly, intelligent race of people, and have frequently shown great hospitality to shipwrecked crews of European vessels.

Formosa is a large island, about 180 miles in length, and 50 in average breadth, lying off the south-eastern coast of China, distant about 200 miles, between lat. 23° and 24° N. According to Chinese accounts, this island was not known to them until A. D. 1430, when it was accidentally discovered by some of their ships. The Dutch took possession of it during the 16th century, and retained it until 1661, when Kue-sing-kong, called by European writers, *Coxinga*, a governor of a province in China, not being willing to submit to the Tartar conquerors of his country, determined to establish himself in Formosa, which he invaded with a numerous body of followers and conquered. It remained under the rule of his successors until 1683; when it was voluntarily surrendered to the emperor of China, and became part of his dominions. At present it is in an unsettled state, the Ladrones or pirates disputing possession with the imperial governor.

This island was found, when taken possession of by the Dutch, to be inhabited by savage tribes, who still occupy the eastern part, the Chinese having colonised the western.

General Account. Hainan is situated at the southern extremity of China, separated only by a narrow channel from the province of Canton. It is about 190 miles in length, and 70 in breadth, and though so close to the mainland, is in a very rude state, the inhabitants still consisting principally of the original savage tribes.

§ 3.

Corea.

General Account. Corea consists of a remarkable peninsula, bounded on the north by the mountains dividing it from Chinese Tartary; and separated from Japan on the east by the Sea of Japan, also called the Straits of Corea; and from China on the west by the Yellow Sea.

This country, which is 400 miles from north to south, by 150 from east to west, is traversed through its whole length by a chain of mountains, but contains a considerable extent of fertile and well cultivated plains, though in some parts sterile and rugged.

The capital is Kingkitao, an inland town, situated nearly in the centre of the country.

Very little is known of Corea, the inhabitants, called by Europeans Coreans, having always shown great jealousy of all foreigners, never allowing them to proceed into the interior, nor to obtain any information regarding the country. It is under its own sovereign, paying only a nominal tribute to China. The

General Account. written language is the same as the Chinese, but the language spoken by the people is quite distinct. The population is understood to be about 8,000,000.

CHAP. XVI.

Japan.

Boundaries. The empire of Japan consists of four large and several small islands, lying to the east of Chinese Tartary and China, and about 150 miles distant, extending from lat. 46° to 30° N.

The large islands are Jesso, Nipon, Sikoke, and Kinsin, and of these the largest and principal is Nipon, which is about 850 miles in length.

General Description. They are all mountainous and have several volcanoes, some of which are continually in action. They are well watered, and cultivated with remarkable industry and skill. Their principal productions are rice and other grains and vegetables, tea, cotton, silk, varnish, and camphor. The animals are not numerous. There are horses and cattle but no sheep, and the wolf is the largest of their wild beasts. Gold is abundant, and they have also silver, copper, lead, iron, sulphur and coal.

Towns. There are numerous towns, many of them large and populous. The principal are Jeddo, Miako, and Nungasaki.

Jeddo, which is the capital of the empire, is situated upon the southern coast of Nipon, in lat. 36° 29′ N. long. 140° E.

Miako is an inland town in the same island, and is the second capital or residence of the religious ruler of the empire.

Nungasaki is situated on the western coast of Kinsin, in lat. 32° 48′ N. long. 132° 35′ E. It is the only seaport to which Europeans are allowed to resort.

Name. The name of Japan is derived from the Chinese term Sippon or Jippon. By the Natives their country is called Nipon.

Inhabitants. The inhabitants, called by the English Japanese, appear to be of the same general race as the Tartars and Chinese, being distinguished by the same small narrow eyes and flat faces. Their complexion is yellowish, occasionally approaching to white. They are an exceedingly ingenious people, and in point of civilization may be considered on a footing with the Chinese. Their manufactures of all kinds are excellent. In silk and cotton fabrics they are superior to any other eastern country, and in varnished and lacquered wares they are unequalled even by Europeans. So celebrated have they always been for this last art, that "*japan*" has become the common English term for this description of ware. Their acquirements in science, however, are limited, as this nation, like the Chinese, has remained stationary; so

Inhabitants.

that in navigation, mechanics, &c. they are still very far behind. The amount of the population is not known. It probably does not exceed 15 or 20 millions.

History.

The early history of this nation is involved in fable. Their records, as far as they can be trusted, begin about the year 660 before the Christian era; and according to these, the empire was from that period under the regular hereditary government of a single monarch, combining the offices both of king and priest, without interruption, until A. D. 1150; when the succession to the throne being disputed brought on a civil war, which terminated in the establishment of two authorities much on the same footing as in Bootan, the one having the temporal power of government, the other all religious authority. The first, although nominally inferior to the other, is actually the real monarch. His native title is the kubo, and by Europeans he is styled the emperor of Japan.

Religion.

In religion the Japanese are idolaters, some of the Booddhist system, introduced it is understood from China, and others of a more ancient system, recognising a Supreme Being but worshipping a multitude of inferior deities. Japan was visited by Portuguese missionaries in 1549, and they continued to teach their religion with very considerable success until 1638, when the government becoming suspicious of their intentions commenced a fierce persecution, and after massacreing many thousands, entirely rooted out the

Religion. Romish religion; since which time, all attempts to introduce Christianity into this country have been carefully prevented, and the name of Christian proscribed. The Dutch are now the only Europeans whom they allow to trade with their country.

Language. The Japanese language is entirely distinct from the Chinese.

CHAP. XVII.

Bootan.

Boundaries. Bootan is adjacent to the northern frontier of the province of Bengal. It is bounded on the north by the Himalaya mountains separating it from Tibet; east, by China; south, by Assam and the frontier districts of Bengal; and west, by the river Teesta separating it from Sikkim.

Divisions. It has no divisions worthy of particular notice.

Rivers. Its rivers are numerous. The principal are the Teesta on the west; the Gudhadhur towards the centre; and Monas, or Goomaree, to the eastward; all flowing from the Himalaya range, the Teesta into the Ganges in the province of Bengal, the others into the Brahmapootra.

General Description.

The northern portion of this country consists of an irregular assemblage of lofty mountains, known by the general appellation of Tangustan, some covered with snow, others clothed with forests. Amongst these are populous villages surrounded by orchards and plantations; at the base of the hills, towards the Bengal frontier, is a plain of about 25 miles in breadth covered with luxuriant vegetation, and marshy forests abounding with elephants and rhinoceroses. From its mountainous character the climate of Bootan varies greatly, the inhabitants of the more elevated parts shivering with cold, while a few miles lower down the people are oppressed by intense heat. Every favourable spot is cultivated, the sides of the mountains being industriously cut into terraces.

Productions.

Its principal productions are wheat and other grains, numerous fruits and vegetables, including peaches, apricots, strawberries and other fruits; bees-wax, ivory and coarse woollen manufactures. In the forests there is a variety of useful timber, such as the ash, birch, yew, pine and fir, the last growing to a considerable size, and the hills yield abundance of limestone. Wild animals are not numerous, with the exception of those in the low country. Monkeys of a large and handsome kind abound and are held sacred. Bootan has also a peculiar breed of horses, noted for strength and activity. They are small and short bodied, seldom exceeding thirteen hands in height, but remarkably well proportioned and com-

Productions.

monly piebald. They are known in India by the name of Tangun or Tanyan, from Tangustan their native country, and numbers of them are brought to Rungpoor for sale by the annual caravans from Bootan.

Towns.

The principal towns are Tassisudon, Poonukka, and Wandipoor, towards the north, and Dellamcotta, Lukheedwar, Bukhsheedwar, and Kuchhoobaree, lying along the southern hills, nearly in a line from west to east.

Tassisudon, pronounced by the Natives *Tassjung*, which is the capital, stands in lat. 27° 5′ N. long. 99° 40′ E. about 100 miles north from the town of Kooch Bahar. It is pleasantly situated, and has a number of handsome buildings, and has a large manufactory for paper, which is fabricated from the bark of a tree named *dea*, growing in the neighbourhood.

Name.

In ancient Brahminical legends this country is denominated Madra. Its Native name, however, is Bhoot, or according to English usage, Bootan.

Inhabitants.

The inhabitants are styled Bhootiyas, or Bootanners. They are part of a numerous tribe of Tartar origin, which has peopled the greater part of the mountainous tract bordering upon the Himalaya range. In features they resemble the Chinese, and like the Chinese they are remarkable for cowardice and cruelty, though in person a very robust and active race. Their weapons are chiefly bows and arrows and swords; their ar-

Inhabitants. rows being generally poisoned. They have also fire-arms, but of a very inferior kind. There are also some thousands descendants of Bengalese and Assamese. The total population is believed not to exceed 150,000.

History. The government of this country is of a very peculiar character. There are in fact two sovereigns, one styled the Debor Deva raja, who exercises all the real authority; and a second styled the Dhurma raja, who is the legitimate sovereign. The Dhurma raja, however, being considered a sacred person and an actual incarnation of the Deity, never interferes in any but religious matters, leaving every thing else to the Deva raja, who is nominally his deputy. Of the early history of this country we know nothing. The first intercourse of its government with the British happened in 1772, when the Deb raja suddenly invaded and overran Kooch Bahar, before the authorities in Bengal were informed of his proceedings. The invaders were easily driven back by two battalions of Native infantry and pursued into their own territories, and their fortress of Dellamcotta was attacked and taken by storm. This alarmed the Deb raja for his own safety, and at his entreaty the teshoo lama of Tibet prevailed upon the British Government to conclude peace, which has since continued.

Religion. The religion of Bootan is the Booddhist system of Tibet, or as it is termed the lama religion.

Language. Four different dialects are spoken in different parts of this country. The whole are generally designated as the Bhootiya language, and it is believed to be derived from the language of Tibet.

CHAP. XVIII.

Assam.

Boundaries. This country lies on the north-eastern frontier of Bengal. On the north it has Bootan, and a range of lofty mountains dividing it from Tibet; on the east it is believed to be bounded by other ranges of mountains separating it from China; south it has the Shan Country, Moga-ong, and Cassay districts of Ava, and Kachar; and west, the district of Gentiapoor, adjoining the Silhet district of Bengal, the Garrow mountains, and Bijnee.

Divisions. It is divided into three provinces, Kamroop on the west, Assam in the centre, and Seediya on the east.

The province of Kamroop was formerly an extensive division in Hindoo geography, and included a large part of Assam, with the modern districts of Rungpoor and Rungamutty, part of Mymoonsing, Silhet, Munnipoor, Gentia, and

Divisions. Kachar. As the name is now used, however, it is restricted to the western division of Assam, and extends from the province of Bengal eastward about 130 miles.

Rivers. In number and magnitude the rivers of Assam probably surpass those of any other country in the world of equal extent, the total number being said to be sixty-one. The principal are the Brahmapootra, or as it is called in Assam, the Loohait; and the Dihong, Dibong, Dikho, and Diprong, all of which fall into the Brahmapootra, or some of its branches.

General Description. The whole of this country may be considered as forming the main valley of the Brahmapootra river, extending in its greatest dimensions, about 350 miles in length by 60 its average breadth.

It is enclosed on all sides by ranges of mountains. Those on the north and east particularly are very lofty, and have their summits constantly covered with snow.

There are hilly tracts covered with woods in different parts of the valley, and the mountains also are covered with forests.

Productions. The productions of Assam are much the same as those of Bengal, which country it greatly resembles in appearance. The principal articles are rice, mustard-seed, black pepper, chillies, ginger, betel, tobacco, and opium. The sugar-cane thrives, but is generally eaten by the

Productions. Natives fresh from the field; cocoa-nuts are very rare; oranges abound. The most remarkable produce of Assam, however, is silk. No fewer than four different kinds of silk-worms are reared. Silks of several varieties forming great part of the Native clothing, besides leaving a quantity for exportation. The Native women of all classes, from the raja's wives downwards, wear the four sorts of silk. The cultivation of tea has lately been introduced, and promises to become of much importance. Gold is found in all the rivers, particularly in the Dikrong, and there are probably other metals. Buffaloes and oxen are common, but horses, sheep, and goats are scarce, and there are no asses. The wild animals are generally the same as in Bengal.

Towns. The principal towns are Gaohati, Jorhat, Gerghong, Rungpoor, and Seediya.

Gaohati is situated on the south side of the Brahmapootra, in lat. 25° 55′ N. long. 91° 40′ E. It was in ancient times the capital of Kamroop, but is now a place of little consequence.

Jorhat, latterly the capital of the country, stands on both sides of the river Dikho, in lat. 26° 48′ N. long. 94° 6′ E.

Gerghong is also situated on the Dikho, and was for many years the capital of the Assam kingdom; but an insurrection of the people breaking out in 1794, ruined the town, and caused the seat of government to be transferred to Jorhat.

Rungpoor, the principal town of the country in point of size and importance, is situated on the Dikho, in lat. 26° 55′

Towns.

N. long. 94° 30′ E. It is a walled town, and contains several mosques and other buildings.

Seediya is little more than a village. It is situated at the mouth of a small river, named the Kondeil nulla, running into the Brahmapootra in about lat. 27° 52′ N.

Inhabitants.

The inhabitants of this country consist of numerous different tribes, some of Hindoo origin, others apparently from Tibet and China. The following are the names of some of the principal classes:—Ahams, Mismees, Mahamaris, Meerees, Singhpos, and Kolitas; all differing from each other more or less in language and manners. The whole are, however, commonly denominated by European writers by the general name of Assamese.

The amount of the population is doubtful, but it may be estimated not to exceed 150,000, including the petty states adjacent.

History.

Nothing satisfactory has been ascertained respecting the early history or religion of Assam. The first authentic notice of them is found in Mahomedan writers in 1638; from whom it appears, that during the reign of Shah Juhan, the Assamese sailed down the Brahmapootra, and invaded Bengal, but were defeated and driven back. Subsequently, in the reign of Aurungzeb, his general, Meer Joomla, attempted the conquest of Assam, which he entered with a large army; but being overtaken by the rains, and harassed by the Assamese, nearly

History. the whole perished, and the few who escaped spread such a report of the difficulties they had encountered, that the Mooghul government abandoned all further idea of its subjection, and it was for long afterwards held by the Mahomedans of Bengal in great horror, as a region inhabited only by infidels and evil spirits. After the introduction amongst them, however, of the Brahminical system, the Assamese seem entirely to have lost their former warlike character, and to have become exceedingly abject and pusillanimous towards foreigners, while they were filled with discord and confusion amongst themselves. About A. D. 1770, in consequence of a dispute between the priests and the government, an insurrection broke out, headed by a priest of the Mahamari tribe, which was at first suppressed, but afterwards burst forth with increased violence; and in 1793 the raja was driven out of his dominions, and compelled to solicit the protection of the British Government. A detachment of British troops in consequence entered Assam, and reinstated the raja in his authority, and the Mahamaris were driven out. After many years of disorder, the Bura Gohaing, one of the raja's principal officers, usurped the government, bands of free-booters established themselves in different parts, and the country was plunged into a state of the greatest misery and confusion until 1822, when it was subjugated by the Burmese, who had been called in as allies by one of the claimants to the throne. The Burmese general was now proclaimed

History. raja of Assam, subordinate to the emperor of Ava. Disputes shortly ensued between the new government and the British, in consequence of the aggressions of the former upon the territory of the latter, which brought on war; and in 1825, Assam was invaded and conquered by the British, with whom it has since remained.

Religion. Of the ancient religion of the Assamese, too little is now known to afford any clear idea of its nature. They had priests called Deodhaings, under whose guidance they were accustomed to worship an idol, named Chung, with much mystery and secrecy, and they had books called Bulonji, written in a character much resembling that of the Burmese sacred writings, but in a language which is not now understood. From the beginning of the 17th century, the Brahminical system appears gradually to have taken place of the original superstition, and about the year 1650 was embraced by the raja, when it became predominant, and may now be considered the national religion of the country. In the parts adjacent to Bengal, there are many Mahomedans, but of so degenerate a character, that they are not acknowledged as such by the Mahomedans of India.

Language. The common language of Assam is a corruption of the Bengalee, which was introduced with the Hindoo system of religion, and soon became so general, that the original Assamese is now nearly a dead language.

CHAP. XIX.

Arracan.

Boundaries. Arracan lies to the south-east of Bengal, between lat. 18° and 21° N., and is bounded on the north by the district of Chittagong, in the province of Bengal, from which it is separated by the river Nauf; east, by a chain of mountains dividing it from Ava; south, by the district of Bassein in Pegu; and west, by the Bay of Bengal.

Divisions. It is divided into the districts of Arracan, Ramree, Sandowy, and Cheduba.

The district of Ramree is an island separated from the mainland by a narrow creek.

Cheduba is also an island in the open sea, a few miles from the coast of Ramree. It is one of a small cluster, and is in length 30 miles, by about 10 in breadth. Limestone is found in these islands.

General Description. Between the mountains and the sea, this country is covered with thick jungles, inundated and intersected in all directions by small rivers, lakes, and creeks. In extreme length it may be estimated at 230 miles from north to south, by an average breadth of 50 from east to west.

General Description. The great chain of mountains forming the eastern boundary, commences at Cape Negrais, and runs northerly almost as far as the southern bank of the Brahmapootra in Assam. By the Natives these mountains are called the Yomadoung. Their general elevation seems to be from 3,000 to 5,000 feet.

In both Ramree and Cheduba are many small volcanoes, mostly of the description called mud volcanoes; generally when in their tranquil state throwing up greasy mud, mixed with petroleum, and strongly impregnated with sulphur; and occasionally also discharging flames, and quantities of iron pyrites. These volcanoes are worshipped by the Mugs, who think they are occasioned by the great Naga, or serpent, which supports the world.

Productions. The productions of this country are principally rice, salt, tobacco, indigo, cotton, hemp, ivory, timber, and beeswax. Lead is found in the mountains, and in the streams towards Bassein, small quantities of gold and silver.

The forests afford abundance of timber of various kinds, but although they produce the teak, it is generally found in places so difficult of access, that little advantage is derived from it.

The animals are in general the same as in Bengal, the principal being the elephant.

Towns. The principal towns are Arracan, Akyab, Ramree, and Sandowy.

Arracan is the capital, and is situated

Towns. inland about 40 miles from the coast, upon a river of the same name, which flows into the sea. Lat. 20° 30′ N. long. 92° 5′ E.

Akyab is the principal military station of the British troops. It is situated on the sea coast, about two hundred miles to the southward of Chittagong.

Name. This country is called by the Natives Rekhaing, and by Mahomedan writers "Urkhung," from the name of its capital, and from this last is derived the English name *Arracan*.

Inhabitants. Its inhabitants consist of Mugs, who are the original Natives, Mahomedans originally from India, and Burmese. The Mugs are called by the Burmese "Great Mrunmas," and are considered by them as the original source of their own race. The total population in 1826, including the islands, was estimated at not more than 100,000, of whom 60,000 were Mugs, 30,000 Mahomedans, and 10,000 Burmese.

History. According to Native historians, the dominions of Arracan formerly extended over Ava, part of China, and a portion of Bengal. Nothing, however, now remains to show that it was ever in a state of so much power and civilization; for when taken possession of by the British its condition was found to be exceedingly savage and barbarous. In 1783 Arracan was conquered by the Burmese. Many attempts were subsequently made by the inhabitants to expel the invaders, particu-

History. larly in 1811, under a chief named Kingberring, but without success. In 1825 it was conquered by the British, to whom it was finally ceded by the Burmese on the conclusion of peace in 1826.

Religion. The religion of the Mugs is that of Booddh, mixed with many Hindoo superstitions.

Language. The prevailing language is the Mug, which is written in the same character as the Burmese, though in other respects it differs, especially in its pronunciation. The principal Mahomedans generally speak good Hindoostanee.

CHAP. XX.

§ 1.

Ava, including the Shan Country.

Boundaries. Ava is situated to the eastward of India. It is bounded on the north by Assam, north-easterly by China; east, by Siam; south, by Siam and the sea; west, by the sea, Arracan, and Bengal.

Divisions. It is divided into the following chief provinces:—Ava, Pegu, Martaban, Ta-

Divisions. voy, and Tenasserim, of which the latter two are subject to the British Government.

The province of Ava extends to Prome, which was the southern boundary of the empire previous to the conquest of Pegu. Its principal districts are Cassay, Mogaong, Ava, and the Shan country.

Cassay, and the Shan country will be separately noticed.

Mogaong borders upon Cassay on the west, and Assam on the north.

Ava, so named from the capital, constitutes what was originally the whole extent of Burma proper, and comprises the remainder of the province.

The province of Pegu extends southward from Prome. Its principal districts are the following: Prome, Sarawadi, Henzawadi, Donabew, Bassein, Negrais, Syriam, Rangoon, Sitong, and Tongo.

The provinces of Martaban, Tavoy, and Tenasserim, follow in succession southward from Pegu, and embrace the whole of the coast from the south side of the Saluen river.

Rivers. The principal rivers are the Irawadee, Kienduem, Saluen or Martaban river, Pegu river, and Lokiang.

The Irawadee has its source in the southern mountains of Tibet, in about lat. 27° 30′ N. and flows southerly through the provinces of Ava and Pegu, into the bay of Bengal, below Rangoon. It is navigable for ships as far as Rangoon, which is about 28 miles from the

Rivers.

sea, and for large boats beyond Amrapoora, a distance exceeding 500 miles.

The Keenduem has its source in the northern mountains of Assam, and flows south into the Irawadee, which it joins opposite to Yandaboo, about 45 miles below the city of Ava.

The source of the Saluen is not correctly known. Its channel is broad but shallow, and not navigable for vessels of large size, except for a short distance from its mouth.

General Description.

This country may be described in general terms as consisting of the great valley of the Irawadee, intersected by several other smaller rivers and low hills, and having ranges of mountains along its northern and western sides, with another cross range separating it from the Shan country. The inland districts of Pegu are also generally hilly.

Productions.

The plains and valleys near the rivers are fertile and well cultivated, and yield abundance of rice, wheat, and other grains; sugar, tobacco, cotton, and indigo.

The tea plant grows in a district to the north of Amrapoora, named Palongmyoo, but its leaf is very inferior to that of the Chinese plant, and is seldom used except for a pickle.

The most remarkable product of the country is petroleum oil, an article of universal use throughout the provinces, and affording a large revenue to the government. Tin, antimony, iron, coal, and salt-petre, are also found in different

Productions.

parts; and it is said that in the mountains of the northern frontier there are mines of gold, silver and precious stones, but it does not appear that these have ever been in any great abundance.

There are quarries of excellent white marble a few miles from Amrapoora.

The forests abound with teak, and almost every description of timber known in India.

The animals are the same generally as in India, with the exception of the camel, which does not appear to be known to the eastward of India.

The elephant abounds most in Pegu, it is sometimes found of a white or sandy colour, the consequence, it is supposed, of some leprous disease. The white elephant holds a very remarkable place in the estimation of the Burmese, who consider it an indispensable part of the royal establishment, and the want of one would be deemed a sure sign of some great evil about to come upon the country. The residence of the white elephant is contiguous to the royal palace, and connected with it by a long open gallery, at the further end of which a curtain of velvet embroidered with gold, conceals the august animal from vulgar eyes. Its dwelling is a lofty hall covered with gilding, and supported by numerous gilt pillars. Its fore feet are secured by silver chains, and its hinder ones by chains of iron. Its bed consists of a thick mattress, covered with cloth, over which is spread another softer one covered with silk. Its trappings are of gold, studded with diamonds and other precious stones. Its

Productions.

betel-box, spitting-pot, bangles, and the vessel out of which it feeds, are also of gold, inlaid with precious stones, and its attendants and guard exceed a thousand persons. It ranks next in honor to the king himself, and all ambassadors attending the court of Ava are expected to show it their respect by offerings of muslins, chintzes, silks, &c.

The horses are small, but very active and hardy; those of Pegu especially are much valued. Amongst the wild fowl is one named the henza or braminy goose, the figure of which is used by the Burmese as the symbol of their nation.

Towns.

The principal cities are the following: In Ava—Umrapoora, Ava, Yandaboo, Pagam, Melloon and Meeaday, all situated on the banks of the Irawadee.

In Pegu—Prome, on the bank of the Irawadee, Tongo and Pegu inland, Sarawa, Henza, Donabew, Basseen, Negrais, Syriam, Dalla and Rangoon, all on the banks of the Irawadee and its branches.

In Martaban—Martaban, Amherst and Moulmein.

In Tavoy—Tavoy.

In Tenasserim—Merqui.

Umrapoora and *Ava* have both been the capital of the empire at different times, according to the caprice of the king. At present the seat of government is Ava.

Yandaboo is noted as being the place to which the British army had advanced, when peace was concluded with the Burmese, in February, 1826. It is distant 45 miles from Ava.

Towns.

Pegu, formerly the capital of the kingdom of Pegu, is situated about 90 miles from Rangoon. It was taken in 1757 by the Burmese under Alompra, who destroyed the city, leaving only the temples, and dispersing all its inhabitants. In 1790 the Burmese government ordered it to be rebuilt, but it has never recovered its former consequence, and is now little more than a large open village.

Rangoon, which on account of its trade may be considered as perhaps the principal city of the Burman empire, is situated on the Irawadee, about 28 miles from the sea. It is a dirty mean looking town, built of wood and bamboo, and surrounded by a weak stockade. Outside the town, and about two miles and a half from it, stands the Shoe Dagon Pagoda, built upon a small hill 75 feet above the road. It is 338 feet high, and is surmounted by a cap of brass 45 feet high, the whole covered with gilding.

Moulmein is the principal town of the British province, being the chief military station. It lies nearly opposite to the Burmese town of Martaban, and is 27 miles higher up the river than Amherst.

The town of *Martaban* is on the northern side of the Saluen river, which divides the Burmese from the British territories. It belongs to the Burmese.

Name.

By Europeans the country is generally called Ava, from the common name of the capital, but by the Natives themselves it is named Burma, which is a corruption of *Mrumma*, its original appellation.

Inhabitants. Its inhabitants are composed of the following principal classes:—Burmese, properly so called; Cassayans, Taliens, or the people of Pegu; Karens, also inhabitants of Pegu; and Shans. The total population of the empire is estimated at about 3,500,000.

History. The early history of this country, like that of most other eastern lands, is little known, as no dependence can be placed upon its records. It appears, however, that the Burmans were originally subject to Pegu until about the middle of the 16th century. A revolution then took place, and the Burmese acquired the superiority until 1740, when the Peguers revolted and a fierce civil war ensued, which was carried on with savage ferocity until 1752, when the Peguers captured the city of Ava, and completed the conquest of the whole country. The king of Pegu having then returned to his own capital, the Burmans again took up arms under the command of a man named Alompra, an individual of low origin, but of a brave and enterprising character, who not only succeeded in expelling the Peguers, but also invaded and conquered Pegu itself, which has ever since remained subject to Burma. Alompra, who was the founder of the present dynasty, died in 1760, and his successors following his example, actively employed themselves in extending their empire by the conquest of Cassay, Arracan, Cheduba and other islands, Tavoy, Tenasserim, Merqui and Junk Ceylon. Various foolish schemes were formed by

History. them at different times for the invasion of British India. In 1817 they conquered Assam, where they established a military force, threatening the frontier of Bengal. Various acts of aggression now took place on the part of the Burmese troops against the British territories. The remonstrances of the British Government were treated by the court of Ava with contemptuous silence, until in 1824 the British found it necessary to declare war. Ava was in consequence invaded in May of that year by a British army, composed principally of Madras troops, which defeated the Burmese in various engagements, and advanced to within fifty miles of the capital. In February 1826 peace was concluded, the king of Ava being compelled to renounce all claims on Assam, Cassay, Arracan, Martaban, Tavoy, and Tenasserim, and to pay a crore of rupees (10,000,000,) as an indemnity for the expenses of the war. The Burmese history of this war, however, is rather different from the above. In the national records kept by the king's historian, the following account of it is given:—"In the years 1186 and 1187, (Burman era) the "kula pyoor," (or white strangers of the west) fastened a quarrel upon the lord of the golden palace. They landed at Rangoon, took that place and Prome, and were permitted to advance as far as Yandaboo: for the king from motives of piety and regard to life, made no preparation whatever to oppose them. The strangers had spent vast sums of money in their enterprise, so that by the time they

History. reached Yandaboo, their resources were exhausted, and they were in great distress. They then petitioned the king, who in his clemency and generosity sent them large sums of money to pay their expenses back, and ordered them out of the country."

Religion. In regard to religion the Burmese are followers of Booddh, whose image is worshipped throughout this country under the name of Gaodhma, or Gaotoom. The Booddhist system is not much superior to mere atheism, as according to it the world and all its affairs are left to go on as chance may determine, the Deity not taking any concern therein.

The Booddhists therefore offer no worship to the eternal God, but say that from time to time men of surprising piety have appeared, who have in consequence, after their death, received power over the living, and these saints are the direct subjects of their worship.

This system has, notwithstanding, one advantage over Hindooism and Mahomedanism, as it leaves the people entirely free both from the absurd prejudices of caste and the evil feelings of ignorant bigotry. Christian missionaries have latterly gone amongst them, and many have embraced the Gospel, particularly amongst the Karens.

Language. The common language of this country is called the Burman, and is written from left to right in characters of a circular form. The language in which all their religious books are composed is called

Language. the Pali, and is written in the Sanscrit character. The Burmese use the palmira leaf, and for common purposes, the iron style; their religious and other books of value are written with lacquer, or sometimes with gold and silver, and the leaves are splendidly gilt and ornamented.

§ 2.

The Shan Country.

Situation. The Shan Country constitutes an extensive region centrally situated between China, Ava, and Siam, and occupied by a number of tribes; those on the frontier being tributary to these three kingdoms according to their contiguity, and those in the interior being independent.

Former writers were accustomed to designate this country as the kingdom of Laos, a name derived from that of one of the principal tribes.

Divisions. It is generally divided into the following:—Lao Shan Yoon Shan and Taroop Shan, lying in succession between Ava on the west, China on the north, and Tunquin on the east; Mrelap Shan, situated south of Lao Shan; Lowa or Lawa Shan, occupying the centre; and south-eastward, bordering upon Siam and Cochin China, Laos Shan.

Description. It is mountainous and woody, and is said to abound in metals, principally silver, lead, copper, antimony, and iron.

Inhabitants. By the Burmese the inhabitants of this country are called by the general name of Shans, but they style themselves T'hay. They form a number of distinct tribes under chiefs called Chobwas. In appearance and dress they bear some resemblance to the Chinese, and they are believed to be an active and ingenious people.

History. Little is yet known of this country, few Europeans having entered it. A body of 8,000 Shans formed part of the Burmese army opposed to the British in 1825. Besides their chobwas or chiefs, and other officers, the Shan troops were accompanied on this occasion by three young and handsome women of high rank, who were believed by their superstitious countrymen to be prophetesses, and invulnerable. These females rode on horseback at the head of the troops, encouraging them with the promise of victory. They were, however, utterly defeated, and two of the heroines were unfortunately killed in the action.

Religion. Their religion is believed to be a modification of Booddhism.

Language. Their language is that of Siam, and according to Shan accounts, abounds with books, some of very ancient date.

§ 3.

Cassay.

General Account.

Cassay, sometimes called Munnipoor from the name of its capital, is a mountainous and woody country, lying between the province of Bengal and Ava. By Europeans it is sometimes called Muklee, though neither of these names are used by the Natives, who style themselves Moitay. The Bengalese call them Muggaloo. Cathee, or Kasee, is the name given to the people by the Burmese. It was under the government of its own rajas until 1774, when after frequent invasions it was finally conquered by the Burmese. It continued to form part of the Burman empire until 1826, when by the terms of the treaty of peace with the English, it was restored to independence. It is now under its own chief, protected by the English. The Cassayers have more resemblance to the Hindoos than to the Burmese, and they follow the Brahminical system of religion.

Its principal town is Munnipoor, lat. 24° 20′ N. long. 94° 30′ E.

The Cassayers are considered good artificers, and formerly supplied all the gun-smiths of the Burman empire. Being also much superior to the Burmese in horsemanship, they furnished the only cavalry employed in the armies of Ava.

§ 4.

Islands connected with Ava.

ANDAMANS.

Situation and Description.

In the Bay of Bengal, opposite to the Tenasserim coast; and a short distance from it, between lat. 10° 32′ and 13° 40′ N. lie two islands called the Andamans.

The northernmost, or great Andaman, is about 140 miles in length by twenty in breadth. Though considered as only one, the great Andaman consists in reality of three islands, as it is divided in two places by very narrow straits. In the centre of the great Andaman is a mountain named Saddle Peak, about 2,400 feet high.

The southernmost, or little Andaman, is about 28 miles in length by 17 in breadth.

There are no rivers of any size.

Productions.

These islands produce various kinds of wood, amongst which are ebony, red wood, dammer, bamboo and rattans. The coasts abound with fish of every description.

In the woods are a few kinds of birds and fowls, and the shores abound with a variety of beautiful shells.

There are no other animals with the exception of swine. Within the caverns and recesses of the rocks are found the edible birds' nests, so highly prized by the

Productions. Chinese. The vegetable productions are few, and there are no cocoa-nut trees.

Inhabitants. The inhabitants of these islands are a very singular race, differing entirely not only from all the inhabitants of the neighbouring continent, but also from the Natives of the Nicobar Islands, though not a hundred miles distant. In appearance they resemble a degenerate race of Negroes, having woolly hair, flat noses, and thick lips. Their eyes are small and red, and their skin of a deep dull black. In stature they seldom exceed five feet, with large heads, high shoulders, protuberant bellies, and slender limbs. They go quite naked, their only covering being composed of a coat of mud, which they plaster all over their bodies, in order to protect themselves from the insects. Their heads and faces they paint with red ochre. They are an exceedingly savage and ignorant race, and have always evinced an inveterate hatred towards strangers; constantly rejecting all intercourse, and frequently attacking boats' crews landing for water. They do not appear ever to have made any attempt to cultivate the ground, but subsist on what they can pick up and kill. They are armed with wooden spears, and bows and arrows, which they use with much dexterity. As far as can be ascertained, they have no distinct ideas of religion. They appear to pay some sort of adoration to the sun, and to spirits whom they suppose to rule over the woods and waters and mountains. They were formerly supposed to be can-

Inhabitants. nibals, that is men who eat human flesh, but there is reason to believe that this is not the case.

The total population is supposed not to exceed 2,500.

History. The English formed a settlement on the great Andaman in 1791, near its southern extremity, which in 1793 was removed to Port Cornwallis, or Cornwallis Harbour, on the eastern coast.

The object of the English Government was to procure a convenient harbour in that part of the bay of Bengal, in which ships might find shelter during the north-east monsoon; and it was also intended to make a place of reception for convicts sentenced to transportation, but the settlement proving extremely unhealthy, it was abandoned in 1796.

Language. As far as is known of their language, it does not possess the least affinity with any spoken in India, or among the neighbouring islands.

BARREN ISLAND.

General Account. About 50 miles to the eastward of the northern Andaman is a small island, called Barren Island, about 1800 feet high, and of a circular form, in the centre of which is a volcano. The eruptions are frequent and very violent, stones of the weight of three or four tons being sometimes discharged.

NICOBARS.

Situation. These islands are situated in the south-

Situation. east quarter of the bay of Bengal, between the sixth and tenth degrees of north latitude, and occupy the space from the little Andaman to the north-western point of Sumatra.

General Account. These islands compose an extensive group, of which the islands named Nancowry, Car Nicobar, and little Nicobar, are the only ones which have been much visited by Europeans. They are generally hilly, and some have high mountains. Their chief productions are cocoa-nuts and betel, for which they are much resorted to by ships from India. The Natives are in a very rude state, and have sometimes attacked and murdered the crews of vessels visiting them for traffic. The Danes attempted to form a settlement upon them from Tranquebar in 1756, and many missionaries engaged in the undertaking; but the climate proved so extremely unhealthy, that after a great number of missionaries and other colonists had died, it was found necessary in 1787 finally to abandon the design.

There are also a number of small islands a few miles from the coast of Tenasserim, known by the general name of the Mergui islands, or the Mergui Archipelago. They are occupied merely by a few Burmese fishermen.

CHAP. XXI.

Cochin China.

Boundaries. Cochin China occupies the south-eastern corner of Asia, being bounded on the north by a range of mountains dividing it from China; east, by the Chinese Sea; south, by the Malayan Sea; west, by the Gulf of Siam, and a range of mountains separating it from Siam.

Divisions. Its divisions or provinces are Tunquin, Cochin China, Cambodia, and Siampa.

Rivers. Few countries are better supplied with water than Tunquin and the lower parts of Cochin China. In the first there are more than fifty rivers which flow into the sea. The principal are the Donnai or Tunquin river, and the Cambodia. The Donnai is said to have its source in the province of Yoonan in China, and receiving the addition of many others in its course, traverses nearly the whole extent of the kingdom, falling into the sea near Saigong, in lat. 10° 47′ N. The Cambodia is also said to rise in the same province, and flows southerly into the sea in about lat. 10° N. after a course of about 1500 miles, the greater part of which is navigable for boats. This is one of the largest rivers in Asia.

General Description.

This country may be described in general terms as consisting of long and well watered valleys, lying between two principal ranges of mountains running from north to south, the one on its western, the other towards its eastern side, besides other ranges traversing it from west to east.

Productions.

Taken altogether this is one of the most fertile countries in this quarter of the world, and abounds with valuable productions, such as rice in abundance, sugar, cotton, silk, tobacco, betel, indigo, cinnamon, pepper, ivory, and wax. A coarse kind of tea is also extensively cultivated. The forests are well supplied with teak, ebony, cedar, and various other woods, and they also yield stick lac and gamboge; which latter article derives its English name from a corruption of that of its native district, Cambodia. Mulberry trees abound, and supply food for the silk-worm. Iron ore is found in great purity, and it is said that there are also mines of silver and tin. Gold is procured in most of the rivers and mountain streams, and salt and saltpetre are plentiful. The animals are in general the same as are found in India, with the exception of sheep, asses, and camels, which are not common to this country. The flesh of the elephant is used for food.

Towns.

There are numerous towns, particularly in Tunquin, the principal of which are Cachao, the capital of Tunquin; Quinnong, Hue, and Saigon, in Cochin China; and Parompin, in Cambodia, all seaports.

The capital of the kingdom is *Hue-foo*,

Towns. or *Hue*, the word "foo," meaning "city." It is situated on a river of the same name, about 10 miles from its mouth, in lat. 16° 19′ N. long. 107° 12′ E., strongly fortified and armed, and containing about 40,000 inhabitants.

Saigong, which though not the capital is the largest and most important city of the whole, is situated on the banks of the Donnai, in lat. 10° 47′ N. long. 107° 5′ E. It is an extensive city, and well built, and has a fortress of considerable strength constructed upon European principles. It is the chief naval depôt of the empire, and has large arsenals, and numerous ship-builders. Its population is estimated at about 200,000.

Name. The derivation and meaning of the word "Cochin," applied to this country, are not known; amongst themselves each province retains its distinct name.

Inhabitants. The inhabitants, who are called by Europeans by the general appellation of Cochin Chinese, are properly speaking composed of two divisions. The Anams and Quantos. The Anams are of Chinese origin, and include Tunqinese, Cochin Chinese, Cambodians, and Siampese.

The Quantos, who inhabit the mountainous districts, are the original Natives, who were expelled from the low country on its being colonised by the Chinese.

In appearance and manners the Anams resemble the Chinese from whom they are descended. They are accustomed to redden their lips and stain their teeth

Inhabitants. black, considering white teeth to be fit only for dogs. Though remarkably indolent, they are a clever and ingenious people, and particularly skilful in ship and boat building. They have founderies for casting cannon, and manufactories of ammunition, as also of cotton and silk cloths, paper, brass and iron ware, &c.; but they have not yet been able to supply themselves with muskets, which they still import from Europe and America. The total population is estimated at about five millions.

History. The ancient history of this country is little known. It appears to have been conquered and settled by the Chinese at an early period; and to have constituted part of the Chinese empire until the Tartar invasion of China in 1644, when the governors of these southern provinces took advantage of the opportunity to make themselves independent; and in this manner Tunquin and the other provinces became distinct kingdoms, remaining so until towards the end of the 18th century, when they were finally subdued by Kaung Shang, the king of Cochin China, and the whole formed into one empire. Kaung Shang was one of the most remarkable men in the east. With the assistance of a French missionary, named Adran, he introduced many great improvements, and arranged his government upon a system far superior to any thing known in the countries around him. He encouraged cultivation, established schools and manufactories, disciplined his troops, and formed a considerable navy;

History. so that Cochin China may now be considered as one of the most advanced of the eastern states. Foreigners are admitted to the ports to trade, but none are permitted to settle. The Portuguese, Dutch, English, and French, had formerly factories in different parts, but they have all been abandoned, and none have since been allowed.

Religion. The religion of this country is a branch of the Booddhist system, though some of the mountain tribes are said still to follow the ancient idolatry, and to worship the tiger and the dog. The Romish religion was introduced by the Portuguese about the beginning of the 17th century, and subsequently carried on by French missionaries, and notwithstanding repeated and violent persecutions, it has made great progress; as according to the statements of the French missionaries, there are throughout the kingdom as many as 350,000 persons professing their religion.

Language. The general language is the Anam, which is of Chinese origin, though now so far changed as to be distinct. The character remains the same as the Chinese, and is written the same way. The Quantos have a distinct language of their own, which they write on leaves with an iron style. On the sea coast the people usually carry on their intercourse with foreigners in a very corrupt sort of Portuguese. Printing with wooden blocks is practised, but books are not numerous, nor do the Cochin Chinese possess any works of value, either in history or science.

CHAP. XXII.

Siam.

Boundaries. Siam is bounded on the north by China; east, by the dominions of Cochin China; south, by the sea, and by the Peninsula of Malaya; and west, by the sea, a range of mountains dividing it from the British province of Tenasserim, and the Saluen river separating it from the dominions of Ava.

Divisions. It consists of the following principal divisions:—Northward, the Shan Country; central, Siam Proper; eastward, part of Cambodia; southward, part of the Malay Peninsula, as far as lat. 7° N. where at Trang, on the western side, and Sungora on the eastern, commence the possessions of the Malay nation; and westward, Junk Ceylon, *(Jan Silan.)*

Rivers. It has one great river, the Menam, which rises in the Yoonan province of China, and flows southward through Siam into the gulf of Siam, watering the whole country in its course.

General Description. Siam Proper may be described as a vast plain, intersected by the river Menam, on the banks of which all the principal towns are situated. The other divisions are hilly and wooded.

Productions.

The productions of Siam are numerous and valuable. The land in the vicinity of the river is remarkably fertile, and yields rice in such abundance, that it is probably cheaper here than in any part of the world. It produces also sugar, pepper, tobacco, gum, gamboge, and cardamoms.

The Shan districts supply benzoin and stick lac. The fruits are in general the same as in India, as also the domesticated animals, but their horses are of an inferior description. In the jungles are tigers, rhinoceroses, and elephants, including those of a white colour, which here as in Ava are held in great estimation, and considered a necessary appendage of royalty. The most valuable woods are the teak, rose-wood, eagle, and sapan; of the latter of which large quantities are exported to China. In the interior, to the northward, are mines of iron, tin, copper, and gold.

Towns.

The principal towns are Yoodia and Bankok, and there are also several seaports in the gulf of Siam, chiefly on its western coast.

Yoodia is situated in lat. 14° 5′ N. long. 100° 25′ E., on an island formed by the branches of the river Menam. It is of great extent, and was the ancient capital, until its capture by the Burmese in 1767.

Bankok, which became the capital on the capture of Yoodia, is situated on the banks of the Menam, in lat. 13° 40′ N. long. 101° 10′ E. It is the chief seaport of Siam, and is a busy flourishing town,

Towns. containing about 40,000 inhabitants. It is built almost entirely of wood, the houses being all raised upon posts so as to place them above the rise of the tide and the periodical inundations. The greater part of the town floats upon the river, the houses being constructed upon bamboo rafts, and moved in rows of ten or more from each bank. The population forms a mixed assemblage of Siamese, Burmese, Shans, Malays, and Chinese, the last amounting to a half of the whole number. The principal manufactures are in tin, iron, and leather, carried on entirely by Chinese artisans. Nearly all the junks used in the eastern trade are built here.

Name. The names Siam and Siamese, which are given to this country and its inhabitants by Europeans, appear to be corruptions of the word *Shan*, the appellation by which they are known amongst the Burmese. The Natives style it the T'hay country, and call themselves T'hay. The Siamese nation, properly so called, consists of two races or tribes of people; the T'hay, and the T'hay J'hay. By the Burmese they are generally called Shans, and sometimes from the name of the ancient capital Yoodras. In manners and customs they greatly resemble the Burmese, and like them are distinguished by the most inordinate ideas of their national importance. The amount of the population cannot be correctly stated. It probably does not exceed 3,000,000, including 150,000 Chinese.

History. The Siamese records are said to contain minute accounts of all that has occurred in Siam and the adjacent countries for more than a thousand years past; but their country was not known in Europe even by name, until after the discovery of the route to India by the way of the Cape of Good Hope. About the year 1550 Siam was first visited by some Portuguese adventurers, and in 1662 French Missionaries established themselves in the country. In 1684 the king of Siam sent ambassadors to the king of France to solicit his alliance, which was granted, and several Frenchmen entered into his service. In 1688, however, a sudden revolution broke out, when the king was dethroned, and the French were expelled. A long period of internal war and confusion followed, but without any foreign interference, until 1754, when a collision took place with the Burmese. In 1767 Alompra, the emperor of Ava, invaded Siam, plundered and burnt the capital Yoodia, and left the country almost depopulated. The Siamese recovered their independence a few years afterwards, and they have since succeeded in maintaining it, though continually at war with the Burmese. Their government is a pure despotism, the monarch being absolute, and considered so sacred a character, that even his name is not allowed to be uttered. Heretofore the troops have been a mere rabble, badly armed, and without discipline; but latterly the government has directed its attention to the establishment of a regular army. Siam has

History. an extensive commerce with China and the Eastern Islands, and Bankok is also visited by European and American shipping. Until recently the Siamese carried on no foreign commerce in their own vessels, but they now venture to China and the straits of Malacca, and occasionally to India and Ceylon.

A commercial treaty was concluded between the British and Siamese governments in 1827, by which all Asiatic subjects of Great Britain "not being Burmese, Peguers, or descendants of Europeans," are allowed to travel through the interior of Siam from Tenasserim or other British provinces; and British subjects of all descriptions may proceed by sea to any Siamese port.

Religion. In religion the Siamese are Booddhists of the same sect as the Singalese, but all religions are tolerated.

Language. Their language is called by Europeans the Siamese, and by themselves the T'hay. It belongs apparently to the same general division as the Burmese, and is written from left to right.

JUNK CEYLON.

General Account. Junk, or Jonk Ceylon, properly *Jan Silan*, may be considered as an island, being connected with the mainland only by a sand-bank which overflowed at high water. It is situated on the western coast of Siam, near the northern entrance of the Straits of Malacca, in lat. 8° N. It is 40 miles in length by 15 in breadth

General Account. Inland the country is mountainous, but towards the coast low, well supplied with water, and fruitful. The hills are covered with large and useful timber, and the land produces every variety of rice. Tin of the best quality is found in great abundance, and forms a valuable article of commerce. The mines are worked entirely by Chinese settlers. The island is thinly inhabited, having been nearly depopulated in the course of the Burmese invasions; and from 14 or 15,000 persons, it is now reduced to not more than 2,000, including Chinese. The Natives are Booddhists as in Siam, but there are also some Mahomedans.

CHAP. XXIII.

Malaya.

Boundaries. This country occupies the southern extremity of the continent of Asia. It forms a peninsula extending from about lat. 8° 30′ to 1° 30′ N., bounded on the north by the Siamese territories; east and south by the sea; west by the straits separating it from Sumatra, called the Straits of Malacca, and by the Bay of Bengal. In length it may

Boundaries. be estimated at 800 miles from north to south, by an average breadth of 125 from east to west.

Divisions. It consists of the following principal divisions:—Queda, Province Wellesley, Perak, Salengore, Malacca, and Johore; with the islands of Penang, Singapoor, and Bintang, which will be separately noticed.

Queda occupies the northern part of the western coast, between lat. 8° and 5° N. This was formerly an independent principality, until 1821, when it was invaded by the Siamese, who drove out the king, and annexed his country to their dominions. Province Wellesley, which belongs to the British, was formerly a part of Queda, being a tract of the Queda coast about 35 miles long from north to south, and about four in breadth.

Perak and Salengore follow southward from Queda, and are both independent principalities.

Malacca occupies the coast towards the southern extremity, between Salengore and Jahore, and is about 40 miles in length by about 30 in breadth inland. It belongs to the British.

Johore occupies the south-eastern quarter of the peninsula, and forms an independent state.

General Description. This peninsula is composed of a central range of mountains traversing its whole length from north to south, leaving a tract of undulating low country on both sides to the sea, watered in every direction by small rivers, of which there

General Description. are about ninety altogether, and covered with forests and vegetation.

Productions. Its principal articles of produce are rice, rattans, canes, betel, ivory, and various kinds of useful wood. The forests do not, however, yield the teak. The animals, both wild and domestic, are the same as are found in India, with the exception of sheep and horses, which are not natural to the country. Tin is plentiful, and there is some gold.

Towns. The only towns upon the peninsula, worthy of notice, are Malacca and Johore.

Malacca, so named from a fruit called the Malka, produced in great abundance in its neighbourhood, was one of the first settlements of the Malays. It was founded by them in 1252, and in 1511 was captured by the Portuguese, remaining with them until 1640, when it fell into the hands of the Dutch. In 1795 it was taken from the latter by the English, but restored at the peace in 1801. It was again taken in 1807, and again restored in 1815; and in 1825 it was finally made over by the Dutch to the British, in exchange for some British possessions in Sumatra. It contains, including the adjacent district, about 25,000 inhabitants, composed of Malays, Hindoos, descendants of Dutch and Portuguese, and Chinese, almost all the cultivators and artisans being of the last nation. Lat. 2° 14′ N. long. 102° 12′ E.

Name. By the Natives this peninsula is called "Tana Malaya," or the land of the Ma-

Name.

lays. By the Siamese the Malays are usually termed "Khek," and by the Burmese "Masoo."

Inhabitants.

The inhabitants of this peninsula consist of two classes, the original Natives, and the Malays. The original Natives, (or *aborigines*) are of the class usually denominated oriental Negroes, and inhabit the mountains of the interior. They are of a diminutive stature, but in other respects resemble the Negroes of Africa, having woolly hair, black skins, thick lips, and flat noses. They are in a perfectly savage state, going quite naked, and subsisting upon roots and game. They form numerous little tribes, many of which acknowledge no chief and lead a wild wandering life. By the Malays they are called Samang.

The Malays were originally from Sumatra, from which island their tribe emigrated about 1160 to the southern part of the peninsula, and soon establishing themselves throughout, gave their name to their new country.

As a people, the Malays are noted for their ferocity, cunning, and treachery; never forgiving an affront, but always taking a cruel revenge. They are addicted to gambling of all kinds, especially to cock-fighting, to an extraordinary degree, and they are universally in the practice of intoxicating themselves with opium. Their vessels, which are called prows, are many of them very well built, and skilfully navigated; but it is only as pirates that they have ever shown activity or enterprise.

History. Nothing is known of this country prior to the time of the Malays, who colonised it in 1160. Since that time it appears to have been under the rule of various independent chiefs, continually at feud amongst themselves, and occasionally at war with the Siamese; and except on account of its situation for the purposes of commerce, never obtaining any importance.

Religion. The religion of the Malays is Mahomedanism of the Soonnee sect, which appears to have been introduced among them in 1260, and from them to have spread over the adjacent islands.

Language. Their language is termed the Malay. It is a compound of various others, including Sanscrit and Arabic, and is considered very soft and simple. It is written from right to left in the Arabic character, with a few slight alterations, and is general to all the adjacent islands. The purest Malay is said to be spoken in the Queda district.

Islands connected with Malaya.

PENANG.

General Account. Penang is situated opposite the coast of Queda, from which it is separated by a strait two miles broad.

It is of an irregular four-sided figure, containing about 160 square miles. It is

General Account.

mountainous and woody, well supplied with water, and well cultivated.

Its principal article of produce is pepper. It also yields betel, coffee, spices, sugar, rice, cayapooti oil, and caoutchouc, commonly named Indian rubber. In the forests there is also abundance of excellent timber.

The town of Penang, called by the English George Town, with a fort named Fort Cornwallis, is situated on the north-eastern corner in lat. 5° 25′ N. long. 100° 19′ E. The hill overlooking the town on which the flag-staff is placed, is the highest point in the island, its elevation being 2,248 feet above the sea.

This island, called by the English Prince of Wales' Island, and by the Natives Pulo Penang, was granted in 1785 by the king of Queda, as a marriage portion with his daughter to Captain Light, of an English country ship, and by him transferred to the British Government. In 1800 the king of Queda further sold to the British a tract on the main land opposite, now called Province Wellesley. Penang is believed to have been peopled by the Malays or others in early times; but when taken possession of by the British, it was one large forest, with no inhabitants excepting a few fishermen on the coasts. Its population is now about 50,000, comprising a mixed assemblage of almost all the nations of the east, about one half being Malays.

SINGAPOOR.

Singapoor, or Sinkapore, is a small island at the southern extremity of Ma-

General Account. laya. It belongs to the British, who obtained it by purchase from its Native chief in 1819, and on account of its situation commanding the navigation of the straits and its good harbour, it is considered a place of great commercial importance. It has a mixed population of about 15,000, of whom one-third or more are Chinese, and it is rapidly increasing. When taken possession of by the British, there were not more than 150 persons on the island.

The town of Singapoor stands in lat. 1° 15′ N. long. 104° E.

BINTANG.

Bintang is a small island lying off the south-eastern end of Malaya, in lat. 1° N. about 35 miles in length by 18 in breadth. It belongs to the Dutch, who have a town there named Rhio.

CHAP. XXIV.

Eastern Islands.

§ 1.

Situation. The Eastern Archipelago, as it is some times termed, comprises the largest assemblage of islands on the globe. It extends from long. 95° to 138° E. and from lat. 11° south to 19° north, and includes the following principal islands.

Situation. Northward, the Philippines; central, the Sooloo Isles, Borneo, Celebes, the Moluccas, and the Isles of Banda; east, Papua; south and west, the Sunda Islands; all which after a few general remarks, we shall separately notice.

Productions. The productions of the several islands will be separately noticed. Gold is general throughout, the total annual produce of the Archipelago being estimated at 150,000 ounces, or about 7,050,000 rupees. The diamond is also found in Borneo.

Inhabitants. These islands have two original but distinct races of inhabitants, a fair or brown complexioned people with lank hair; and a people of black complexion, with woolly frizzled hair.

Of the first class there are numerous different tribes, some tolerably civilized, others in a state of great barbarism. Some amongst them are addicted to cannibalism, that is the eating of human flesh, as the Battas in Sumatra; and in Borneo it is an invariable rule that no man may marry until he can show the skull of some man whom he has slaughtered; a man's wealth being estimated by the number of heads he has obtained.

The latter class, commonly designated as oriental Negroes, may be traced from one extremity of the Archipelago to the other. They are, however, few in number to the westward, from which the brown and more civilized tribes appear gradually to have expelled them; but are numerous to the eastward, the island of Papua being still almost entirely inhabit-

Inhabitants. ed by them. Of their origin nothing is now known. They are in a still more savage state than any of the brown race, and seem very little raised above the brutes.

Religion. They may also be divided into two principal classes in respect to religion. Idolaters of various degrees of ignorance, and Mahomedans.

Of the pagan tribes, many are altogether without any system of religion, having neither idols nor temples, nor any intelligible belief of the existence of a Supreme Being, though full of superstitious fears of evil spirits.

Mahomedanism of the Soonnee sect appears to have been introduced from Arabia about the year 1300. Hindooism also was formerly established by colonists from India; but is now hardly known except in the island of Bally, and amongst a few of the mountain tribes of Java.

History. These islands were first visited by European navigators in 1501, when settlements were made by the Portuguese. These were followed by the Spaniards and Dutch; in 1602 by the English, and in 1621 by the French.

Language. The languages, or rather dialects, of the Archipelago are numerous, but apparently derived from the same source. Of these, many are written in distinct characters, and others are merely colloquial. The Malay may be considered as the most general, and after it the Javanese, Buggess, and Macassar.

§ 2.

Philippines.

Situation. The Philippines, or Manillas, comprise a number of islands lying between the 5th and 19th degrees of north latitude, due eastward from Cochin China. The principal are Luzon, Mindoro, Samar, Salawan, and Mindanao.

General Description. These islands are mountainous, and there are in them several volcanoes, particularly in Luzon, the largest of their number, which has suffered some severe earthquakes. The latest great eruption took place in 1814, and occasioned great devastation.

Productions. They are exceedingly fertile, and yield all the ordinary productions of India; in addition to which they possess the breadfruit tree, as also the edible birds' nests or sea-slug, so much esteemed by the Chinese. Their domestic animals are also the same as in India, but they are believed to be free from tigers and other large wild beasts. There are mines of gold and iron, and abundance of excellent timber much used for ship-building.

Towns. The principal town is *Manilla*, in Luzon, situated in lat. 14° 38′ N. long. 120° 50′ E. This is the capital of the Spanish possessions, and contains about 175,000 inhabitants of all classes. In 1650 it was nearly destroyed by a severe earthquake.

Name.

These islands received the general name of Philippines in honor of King Philip the 2nd of Spain. By the English they are more commonly styled the Manillas from the name of the capital.

Inhabitants.

Besides Europeans and Chinese, the inhabitants consist of a number of distinct tribes, the most considerable of which are the Natives of Luzon, comprising both races, the brown and the Negro. The Natives of Manilla of European descent, are considered much superior to the others in intelligence, and are much employed in the country ships of India, being very active and clever sailors. The total population of the islands in 1820 amounted to 225,000, of which number 2,800 were Europeans, 6,000 Mestizos (mixed descendants of Europeans,) and 6,000 Chinese.

History.

These islands were first visited by the celebrated navigator Magellan in 1561, and were taken possession of by the Spaniards in 1565, at which time they were found under the government of numerous petty chiefs of the Malay race. The Spanish settlements have been attacked at different times by the Chinese and by the Sooloos, and in 1762 Manilla was captured by the English, but was restored to the Spaniards shortly after, and the islands have since remained under the Spanish government, though in continual conflict with various Native tribes, several of which have never yet been completely subdued. Mindanao in fact does not acknowledge the authority

History. of the Spaniards at all. They have a fort there, but the island may be considered to form a distinct Malay state under its own sooltan, and constantly engaged in piracy.

Religion. The religion of the Native inhabitants is principally paganism. Some of the tribes, however, are Mahomedans, and the Romish religion has been introduced by the Spaniards.

Language. Several distinct dialects are current in the islands, the principal of which are the Tagala, and the Bisayan, the former a written language.

§ 3.

Sooloo Isles.

General Account. These are a chain of numerous small islands situated between the western extremity of Mindanao the southernmost of the Philippines, and the north-eastern extremity of Borneo, and lying between the 4th and 7th degrees of north latitude.

Sooloo, which is the principal, and gives its name to the group, is situated about lat. 6° N. and long. 121° E., and is about 40 miles in length by seven the average breadth.

This island is fertile and well cultivated. It produces rice and the usual tropical fruits, and possesses the common domestic animals. It is believed to be free from the large sorts of wild beasts. The shoals round and between the islands

General Account.

yield abundance of pearls and mother of pearl, which are disposed of chiefly to the Chinese.

The inhabitants who are termed Sooloos, are of the Malay race. They are an exceedingly savage and treacherous people, and have always been noted as pirates.

They are under the government of a Malay chief, who has the title of sooltan.

Their religion is Mahomedanism of the Soonnee sect, and their language a mixture of Malay, Javanese, and Tagala, written in the Malay character.

§ 4.

Borneo.

Situation.

This island, which is the largest in the Archipelago, extends from lat. 7° N. to lat. 4° S. and from long. 109° to 118° E. In length it is estimated to be about 750 miles by an average breadth of 350.

Divisions.

It comprehends several distinct principalities, of which the principal and only one of note is Borneo, occupying the north-western coast along a line of about 700 miles. There are several rivers in the island, but none of them have as yet been explored by Europeans.

General Description.

Little is known of its interior, but as far as has been ascertained, the island is in general level towards the coast, and cultivated; and inland, mountainous and covered with forests.

Productions.

Its productions are abundant; rice, sago, pepper, camphor, cinnamon, wax, rattans, and many useful woods; and in the seas, pearls, mother of pearl, tortoise-shell, and sea-slug *(biche de mer.)* It has all the common domestic animals, and the forests swarm with wild beasts, including the elephant, rhinoceros, and leopard, but no tigers. It has numerous varieties of the ape and monkey tribes, amongst which is the ourang-outang, or "*man of the woods*," so called by the Malays from its great resemblance in size and figure to the human form. Gold is abundant, and diamonds frequently of a large size.

As sago, which has been mentioned above, is throughout the Archipelago an article of nearly as general use for food as rice is in India, it may be useful to give a more detailed account of it. It is produced from a species of palm, the trunk of which is filled with a spongy pith, which being extracted is ground down in a mortar and then passed through a sieve, by which means it is formed into grains, as it is seen when brought to India. One tree yields upon an average about 300 pounds of sago, and the tree is generally considered ripe for cutting down in fifteen years.

Towns.

The principal town is *Borneo*, situated on the coast, in lat. 4° 56′ N. long. 114° 44′ E. There was formerly an English factory here, but it has been abandoned for some years in consequence of the unsettled state of the country.

Name. By its inhabitants, and throughout the Archipelago, this island is called Pulo Klemantan; but Europeans have given it the name of Borneo, from "Boornee," the principal state, and the first visited by them.

Inhabitants. The inhabitants are composed of Malays, Sooloos, Javanese and others, on the coast, noted as rapacious and cruel pirates; and a number of savage tribes in the interior, of which the principal are the Dayaks and Biajos. These are of the original brown race, and are much handsomer and fairer than the Malays, to whom they are also superior in strength and activity. There are also great numbers of Chinese, more than 200,000 of that nation being settled at the gold mines. None of the Negro race have been seen in Borneo. The total population of the island is supposed to be about 4,000,000.

History. The Malays appear to have settled themselves on this island about the middle of the 13th century, and they now possess the coasts, which are divided into a number of petty Mahomedan states; the interior being left to the original savage tribes. The chief of Borneo has the title of raja. The Dutch have small factories on the west coast, the chief at Pontiana, lat. 3° S. long. 109° E.

Religion. Mahomedanism and Paganism.

Language. Principally the Malay.

§ 5.

Celebes.

Situation. This is a large island, of very irregular shape, extending from lat. 2° N. to nearly 6° S. and from long. 119° to 125° E. and lying east of Borneo, from which it is separated by the Straits of Macassar.

Divisions. It is divided into a number of independent states, of which the principal are Boni and Macassar.

Productions. Its principal articles of export are gold, cotton cloths, sago, cassia, pearls, and sea-slug. The small island of Bootoon, at the south-eastern extremity of Celebes, also produces the bread-fruit.

Towns. The principal towns are Macassar and Boni.

Name. By the Natives and by the Malays this island is called Negree Ourang Buggess, or the "Buggessman's Country," and sometimes "Thana Macassar." It received its European name of Celebes from the Portuguese.

Inhabitants. It contains several distinct tribes of inhabitants, of which the principal are the Buggesses and the Macassees.

History. It is not known that there was ever any intercourse between either India or China and the Celebes, prior to the year 1600, yet the Natives assert that they are descended from the Hindoos, and

History. many of the names of their ancient idols indicate a connection with India at a former period. The island was first visited by the Portuguese in 1512, followed by the Dutch, who established themselves at Macassar in 1660, and subsequently extended their rule over the island generally. Macassar was taken from the Dutch by the English in 1811, but restored in 1816, and it has since remained with them. The Native governments under the Dutch compose several distinct states, each having its own chief.

Religion. The prevailing religion is Mahomedanism, which was introduced in 1603. The Buggesses have the Koran translated into their own language. The central tribes of the interior are still pagan.

Language. The principal languages are the Buggess and the Macassar, both written.

§ 6.

Moluccas.

Situation. This group of islands is situated a little to the eastward of Celebes, and occupies nearly the same latitudes. The principal are Gilolo, Ternate, Tidore, Ceram, and Amboyna.

Productions. Their most important articles of produce are cloves and nutmegs. They abound with sago, and Amboyna yields also indigo and cayapooti oil. They are

Productions. free from beasts of prey, but possess the common domestic animals.

Towns. The principal towns are Ossa in Gilolo, and Amboyna, or Fort Victoria, in Amboyna, the capital of the Dutch possessions.

Name. These islands are now generally termed the Molucca or Spice Islands, although originally this name belonged only to the smaller islands of Ternate and Tidore, and some others westward of Gilolo and Ceram.

Inhabitants. They are inhabited partly by Mahomedans and partly by Pagans of the brown race. Mahomedanism was introduced in the course of the 16th century.

They are distinguished as the most civilized and enterprising people of the whole Archipelago, particularly the Buggesses, who have always been actively employed in navigation and commerce, and are noted for honesty and fair dealing.

These islands are considered to form the eastern boundary of the brown race of men, and beyond this line there are no horses, horned cattle, nor sheep.

History. These islands were formerly under the government of different independent sooltans, chiefly those of Ternate and Tidore, but have latterly become generally subject to the Dutch, who expelled the Portuguese, the first European settlers, and established themselves in different parts about the beginning of the 17th century. The Dutch possessions were twice taken by the English in 1801 and 1811, and finally restored to them at the peace in 1814.

Language. The general language on the coasts is the Malay.

§ 7.

Isles of Banda.

General Account. These form a small cluster situated about 120 miles south-easterly from Amboyna, the principal being the island of Banda.

They are almost exclusively appropriated to the cultivation of the nutmeg, which they produce in great abundance.

They belong to the Dutch, and in their history, inhabitants, religion, and language, resemble the Moluccas.

§ 8.

Papua, or New Guinea.

Situation. This is a large island commencing a little to the eastward of Gilolo, and slanting in a south-easterly direction as far as lat. 10° S. having the Pacific Ocean along its northern and eastern coasts, and separated by Torres Straits on the south from the continent of Australia.

Description and Productions. It appears to rise gradually from the coast to hills of considerable elevation, covered with palm trees and forests of large timber. It produces both the cocoa-nut and bread-fruit trees, but has no animals except dogs, wild cats, and hogs.

Inhabitants. The western part of the island is inhabited by the Negro race, and the eastern by a people approaching more to the appearance of the South Sea Islanders, that is, having yellow complexions and long black hair. Such of these Negro tribes as are known to Europeans are in an entirely savage state, and some of them are said to be cannibals. They wear their hair bushed round the head to a circumference of two and three feet, combing it out straight, and occasionally sticking it full of feathers; and from this practice they have received from Europeans the name frequently applied to them of "the mop-headed Negroes." They understand the manufacture of common earthen-ware and mats, and are so far civilized as to comprehend the nature of traffic, which they carry on with the Buggesses and Chinese, from whom they purchase iron tools, crockery, and cloths, in exchange for slaves, missoy-bark, ambergris, sea-slug, birds of paradise, loorees, and other birds which they dry and preserve with great skill. The origin of this race is not known. They formerly were found in all the islands of the Archipelago, and are still to be met with in the mountain districts; and the aborigines of Malaya, as well as the Natives of the Andamans, seem to be of the same stock, though much inferior to the Papuans, who are robust and powerful men. Their arms are chiefly bows and arrows.

Name. The word Papua is a corruption of Pua Pua, the term commonly used by

Name. the brown tribes to designate the Negro race. The name New Guinea was given to the island by the first European navigators, on account of the resemblance of its inhabitants to the Africans.

§ 9.

The Sunda Islands.

Situation. The Sunda Islands, or Sumatran chain, form the southern and western line of the Archipelago, comprehending Timor, Floris, Java, and Sumatra, with some smaller islands.

TIMOR

General Account. lies between about lat. 8° and 11° S. and long. 123° and 127° E.

Its chief productions are sandal-wood and earth oil. It also yields gold and copper. The principal article of food is maize. Rice is also cultivated, and a species of sago, and it has all the common domestic animals.

It is inhabited by a pagan race of dark complexion and frizzled bushy hair, but differing in other respects from the Papuans, and appearing to hold a middle place between them and the brown races.

This island belongs to the Dutch, who have a fort at Koopang at the southern extremity, in lat. 10° 10′ S. long. 124° 10′ E.

FLORIS

General Account. or Ende, is situated immediately to the westward of Timor.

General Account. Its productions are the same as those of Timor.

The town of Ende on the south coast possesses an excellent harbour.

It is inhabited by Buggesses and Malays on the coast, and by Negro aborigines in the interior. The Portuguese have a small settlement at Sarantooka, but the rest of the island is independent.

Java.

Situation. This is a large island lying westward of Floris, between the 6th and 9th degrees of south lat. and the 115th and 105th of east long., being about 660 miles in length, and of a breadth varying from 50 to 130 miles. It includes the small islands of Madura and Bally.

General Description. The interior of this island throughout its whole length is marked by an uninterrupted range of mountains, varying in their elevation from 5,000 to 12,000 feet, and many of them occasionally subject to volcanic eruptions. The rivers are numerous, and the soil remarkably rich.

Productions. Java abounds with all the productions, and swarms with all the animals, both wild and domestic, known in India. It also produces sago and the edible birds' nests.

Towns. The principal towns are Batavia, Samarang, Sooryakarta, and Soorabaya.

Batavia, which is the capital of Java and of all the Dutch possessions in the

Towns. east, is situated on the northern coast in lat. 6° 8′ S. long. 106° 54′ E. Its population of all classes is estimated at about 50,000. It was founded by the Dutch in 1619.

Name. By the Malays and Natives this island is named Thana Java.

Inhabitants. The inhabitants are called Javanese, there are also many Chinese, Malays, Buggesses, Arabs, and Indians. The total population amounts to about 4,500,000.

History. The early history of this country is unknown, as there are no records which can be depended upon prior to about the year 1200. It appears to have been divided into a number of petty states, which about A. D. 1600 were consolidated under the general government of the Sooltan of Sooryakarta, and in a few years after the whole fell under the dominion of the Dutch. In 1811 the island was taken possession of by the British, but restored to the Dutch in 1816, with whom it now remains.

Religion. The predominant religion is Mahomedanism, which was introduced in 1406 by a sheikh from Arabia, prior to which time, the Javanese followed the Hindoo systems both of Brahma and Booddh, but without observing the distinctions of caste. The Hindoo system, however, is still prevalent in the island of Bally.

Language. The language is called Javanese, and is written in a character formed upon the Sanscrit alphabet.

Sumatra.

Situation. This is a large island lying obliquely north-west and south-east between the 6th degree of north lat. and the 6th of south, and long. 95½° and 107° E. In length it may be estimated at 1,000 miles by 150 the average breadth.

Divisions. Its chief divisions are Acheen, the Batta Country, Menancaboo, Palembang, and the Rejangs.

Rivers. It has numerous rivers, some of them large and navigable, but not well known to Europeans.

General Description. Ranges of lofty mountains run through the whole extent of the island; many of them are volcanic, and lava is occasionally seen to flow from them. Earthquakes also are frequent, but generally slight. The highest mountain visible from the sea has been named by Europeans Mount Ophir, and is 13,842 feet in height.

Productions. In addition to all the productions of India which it possesses in remarkable abundance, this island produces camphor, cassia, nutmegs, cloves, benzoin, rattans, sago, the bread-fruit, and the edible birds' nests. The animals, wild and domestic, are the same as in India, the tiger growing to a very large size. There is also the ourang-outang. The horses are of a small and active breed generally known in India as the Acheen poneys. In the

Productions. Batta Country they are used for food. Gold is abundant, and there are mines of copper, tin, and iron. Earth oil and sulphur are also plentiful.

Towns. The principal towns are Acheen, Menancaboo, Palembang, Padang, and Bencoolen.

Acheen is situated at the north-western extremity of the island. This was formerly the principal trading port in this part of the world, and its sooltan was held in great respect throughout the east. It has since greatly declined, and is now a place of no consequence.

Menancaboo is the capital of the state so named, and was in former times considered the chief city in Sumatra, and the seat of all Malay learning and religious authority. The state of Menancaboo constitutes the original country of the Malays, and is entirely peopled with them at the present time. The Natives of this place are the expertest artists in the island, and are particularly noted for their gold and silver fillagree work.

Palembang on the eastern coast, an ancient Malay town, and *Padang* on the western, now form the two principal settlements of the Dutch.

Bencoolen, or *Fort Marlborough*, on the south-western coast, formerly belonged to the English, who made a settlement there in 1685, but in 1825 it was given over to the Dutch.

Name. By the Natives this island is usually called Pulo Purichoo, and by the Java-

Name. nese Thana Palembang; the origin of its European name Sumatra is quite unknown.

Inhabitants. Its inhabitants consist of various tribes of the brown race, of which the principal are the Malays and Battas. The Battas are addicted to an extraordinary system of cannibalism. According to their laws, all persons put to death for capital offences are cut up and eaten; as are also enemies killed or taken prisoners during any general war. Notwithstanding this savage practice, the Battas are remarkable as a quiet and timid people. In appearance they resemble the Hindoos. It is a general custom throughout Sumatra for both sexes to file down their teeth, and to stain them jet black, many also casing the two front teeth in gold. All classes are inveterately given to gaming and cock-fighting, and all are great opium smokers.

History. Of the early history of this country nothing has been satisfactorily ascertained, though the Natives commence their own history with the landing of certain persons from Noah's ark after the flood. It does not appear ever to have formed a single kingdom, but to have been composed of a number of petty states, in which condition it still remains; the Dutch now possessing the principal authority over the whole.

Religion. Mahomedanism is the religion of the Malay tribe, but the Battas and others are still pagans, without any regular

Religion. form of religion as they have no kind of worship, possessing little more than a confused notion of some superior and invisible beings, with very little idea of a future state.

Language. The principal languages are the Malay and the Batta. The Batta differs not greatly from the Malay, but is written in characters derived from the Sanscrit, from left to right, upon the inner bark of a tree and on bamboos.

GLOSSARIES.

GLOSSARY, No. I.

EXPLANATORY OF SUCH WORDS AS COMMONLY OCCUR IN HISTORY AND GEOGRAPHY.

Intended chiefly for the use of Native Students.

A

ABORIGINES, derived from the Latin *ab*, from, and *origine*, the beginning, and signifies the first inhabitants of any country.

ANNUAL, from the Latin *annus*, a year, signifies any thing that happens yearly, or once a year.

ANTÆCI, derived from the Greek *αντι anti*, opposite, and *οικεω oikeo*, to inhabit, are those who live in the same degree of longitude, and in equal degrees of latitude, but the one in north, and the other in south latitude. They have noon at the same time, but contrary seasons of the year. Those who live at the equator can have no antæci.

ANTARCTIC, derived from the Greek *αντι*, *anti*, against or opposite to, and *αρκτος arktos*, the bear, generally signifies southern, so called because it is opposite to the arctic or northern.

ANTIPODES, are those inhabitants of the earth who live diametrically opposite to each other, and consequently walk feet to feet; their latitudes, longitudes, seasons of the year, days and nights, are all contrary to each other. Derived from the Greek *αντι anti*, opposite, and *ποδας podas*, feet.

APHELION, derived from the Greek *απο apo*, from, and *ηλιος helios*, the sun. It signifies that part of the orbit of a planet or comet, in which it is at its greatest distance from the sun.

APOGEE, derived from *απο apo*, from, and *γη gē*, the earth, and signifies that point in the orbit of a planet, which is at the greatest distance from the earth. The ancients considered the earth as the centre of the planetary system, and therefore assigned to the sun with the planets an apogee. But the moderns reckon the sun as the centre, and therefore use the terms aphelion and perihelion. The sun's apogee therefore is in truth the earth's aphelion—apogee is properly applicable to the moon.

ARCHIPELAGO, supposed to be derived from the Greek *αρχος archos*, chief, and *πελαγος pelagos*, the sea, primarily signifies that part of the Mediterranean Sea, between Greece and Asia Minor. Its general import is a sea interspersed with many isles.

ARCTIC, derived from the Greek *αρκτος arktos*, a bear, and signifies northern, so called because the *bear* is generally called the northern constellation.

ASTRONOMY, derived from the Greek *αστρον astron*, a star, and *νομος nomos*, a law, or rule; it signifies the science which teaches the knowledge of the celestial bodies, their magnitudes, motions, distances, periods of revolution, aspects, order, &c.

ATMOSPHERE, from the Greek *ατμος atmos*, vapour, and *σφαιρα sphaira*, a sphere, and signifies the whole mass of fluid consisting of air, aqueous and other vapours surrounding the earth.

AXIS, derived from the Latin *axis*, an axle-tree, and signifies a straight line, real or imaginary, passing through a body on which it revolves, or may revolve, as the axis of the earth.

B

BAY—see page 3.

BOGS, signify wet grounds, which are too soft to bear a man. It is sometimes defined by marsh and morass, but differs from them as a part from the whole.

BREAKER, from the English word to break, is a rock which breaks the waves; it sometimes also signifies the wave itself, which breaks against a rock, a sand-bank, or the shore, exhibiting a white foam.

BROOK, signifies a small natural stream of water, or a current flowing from a spring or fountain, less than a river.

C

CANAL, is derived from the Latin *canalis*, a watercourse; this word is usually applied to those artificial watercourses which are made for the purpose of facilitating the conveyance of goods from one part of the country to another.

CANTONMENT, from the Latin *centum*, a hundred, and signifies a part or division of a town or village, assigned to a particular regiment of troops.

CAPE—see page 2.

CARDINAL, derived from the Latin *cardo*, a hinge, which is the principal support of a door, and that on which it turns. Hence it came to signify principal or chief, and in this sense is applied to the four chief points, north, south, east and west.

CATARACT, from the Greek *κατα*, *kata*, downwards, and *ρασσω*, *rassō*, to strike or dash, and signifies a great fall of water over a precipice, as the cataract, or as it is more generally called, the Falls of Niagara.

CELESTIAL, derived from the Latin *cœlum*, the heaven, and signifies any thing belonging to the heavens.

CENTRIFUGAL, from the Latin *centrum*, the centre, and *fugio*, to fly from, and signifies a tendency to recede from the centre.

CENTRIPETAL, from the Latin *centrum*, the centre, and *peto*, to seek, and signifies a tendency to draw towards the centre.

CHAIN, derived from the French *chaîne*, or from the Latin *catena*, and originally signifies a series of links or rings fastened to one another. Hence it comes to be applied to a continuation of mountains, which are linked as it were to each other, as the chain of the Andes.

CHAMPAIGN, derived from the Latin *campus*, a field, and signifies a flat open country.

CHANNEL, derived from the Latin *canalis*, a watercourse, and generally signifies a passage; but other meanings are attached to this word, as the deeper part or hollow in which the principal current of a river flows, as the channel of the Thames; or a part of the sea, as the British Channel, the Irish Channel.

CHART—see pages 7 and 8.

CIRCUMFERENCE, from the Latin *circum*, around, and *fero*, to bear—see page 5.

CITY, derived from the Latin word *civitas*, and signifies in England generally a large town, or a large number of inhabitants established in one place, and having a bishop.

CLIMATE—see page 26.

COLONY, from the Latin *colo*, to cultivate, and signifies a company of people transplanted from their mother-country to a remote land, in order to inhabit and cultivate it.

COMET, from the Greek *κομη* *come*, hair, and is an opaque spherical solid body like a planet, but accompanied with a train of light, performing their revolutions in an elliptical orbit. They are so called because in popular language they are represented as bearded, hairy, &c.

COMPASS—see page 8.

CONDUIT, derived from the Latin *con*, together, and *duco*, to lead, and signifies a canal or pipe for the conveyance of water. They are made of lead, stone, cast iron, &c.

CONFLUENCE or **CONFLUX**, both these words are derived from the Latin *con*, together, and *fluo*, to flow, and signify the junction or meeting of two or more streams of water, as the confluence of the Ganges and Jumna.

CONSTELLATION, derived from the Latin *con*, together, and *stella*, a star, signifies a cluster or group of fixed stars.

CONSTITUTION, derived from the Latin *con*, together, and *statuo*, to set, and signifies the established form of government in a state or country.

CONTINENT—see pages 1 and 2.

COUNTRY, from the Latin *con*, with, and *terra*, the earth, and primarily signifies land adjacent to a city, but is more generally applied to the land belonging to a kingdom or state.

CREEK or COVE—see page 3.

D

DALE, primarily signifies a low place, through which rivers run. Generally speaking it has the same signification with vale and valley, and is a poetic word.

DEFILE, from the Latin *de*, from, and *filum*, a thread, and primarily signified a narrow passage or way in which troops may march only in a file; hence it came to signify a narrow passage between two hills.

DELTA—see page 4.

DEPOT, derived from the Latin *de*, from, and *pono*, to place, and signifies a store or magazine for depositing goods or merchandise.

DESERT, from the Latin *desertum*, signifies an uninhabited tract of land. Sometimes applied to an uninhabited country covered with woods.

DESPOTISM, derived from the Greek δεσποτης *despotes*, a master, and signifies absolute power or authority unlimited and uncontrolled by men, laws, or any thing else.

DIAMETER, from the Greek δια *dia*, through, and μετριω *metrio*, to measure—see page 5.

DIOCESE, from the Greek δια *dia*, through, and οικησις *oikesis*, a residence, and is applied to the circuit or extent of a bishop's jurisdiction. Formerly it was a division of the Roman empire, for the purpose of civil government.

DISTRICT, from the Latin *distringo*, to draw tight, and signifies a limited extent of country.

DIURNAL, from the Latin *dies*, a day, and signifies any thing that happens daily, or every day.

DOCK, signifies a broad deep trench by the side of a harbour, or mouth of a river, where ships are built or repaired.

DOWNS, derived from the Saxon *dun*, and primarily signifies a hill or elevation. It is applied to a bank or elevation of sand thrown up by the sea, as the Downs, so called by way of eminence, off the S. Eastern coast of England. It also signifies a large open plain, primarily an elevated land.

DYNASTY, derived from the Greek δυναστης *dunastes*, a lord or chief, and signifies government, sovereignty, or rather a succession of kings of the same line of family, who govern a country.

E

EARTH, in its primary sense signifies fine particles. Its common signification is that globe or planet which we inhabit.

EARTHQUAKE, compounded of two English words, earth and quake, signifies a shaking or trembling of the earth, at other times a rocking or heaving of the earth.

ECCENTRIC, from the Latin *ex*, from, and *centrum*, the centre, and signifies deviating or departing from the centre.

ECLIPSE, derived from the Greek εξ *ex*, without, and λειπω *leipō*, to leave. An eclipse of the sun is an obscuring of part of the face of the sun, caused by the moon coming between the earth and the sun; consequently all eclipses of the sun happen at new moon time. An eclipse of the moon is a privation of the light of the moon, occasioned by the interposition (or coming between) of the earth between the sun and moon; consequently all eclipses of the moon happen at full moon.

ECLIPTIC, derived from the Greek εκλειπω *eklεipo*, to fail, is a great circle in which the sun makes his *apparent* annual progress among the fixed stars. But more properly it is the track which the earth would appear to describe, if viewed from the centre of the sun. It is called the ecliptic because eclipses can only happen when the moon appears to be in or very near this circle.

EMPIRE, derived from the Latin *imperium*, signifies supreme power in governing; also a large tract of land under the jurisdiction of an emperor. It is generally larger than a kingdom. As for instance the British Empire.

EMPORIUM, from the Greek εμποριον *emporion*, a market place, and is a place of merchandise, a city or town of extensive commerce.

EQUATOR, from the Latin *æquo*, to make equal—see page 5.

EQUINOCTIAL LINE—see page 5.

EQUINOCTIAL POINTS, are the two points where the equator and ecliptic intersect each other. The one being in the first point of Aries, is called the vernal equinox, (from the Latin *ver*, spring) the other in the first point of Libra, the autumnal equinox (from the Latin *autumnus*, autumn.)

EQUINOX, is the precise time when the sun enters one of the equinoctial points, or the first point of Aries about the 21st March, and the first point of Libra about the 23rd September, making the day and night of equal length.

ESTUARY, from the Latin word *æstuo*, to boil, and was originally applied to the sea when in a state of agitation. Its most common signification is a narrow arm of the sea, and signifies much the same as frith.

F

FEN, signifies low land overflowed or covered wholly or partially by water, but producing coarse grass or other aquatic plants.

FEUD, is of Saxon origin, and signifies right to lands or hereditary estates held in trust, or on the terms of performing certain conditions.

FEUDAL, usually means dependant upon a lord or chief.

FOREST, signifies an extensive wood, or a large tract of land covered with trees.

FORTRESS, signifies any fortified place, a place of defence or security.

FRIGID—see page 9.

FRITH, derived from the Latin word *fretum*, and its primary signification is the water that beats against the shore. Its more common signification is a narrow arm of the sea, as the Frith of Solway; or the opening of a river into the sea, as the Frith of Forth, the Frith of Clyde.

FRONTIER, signifies the border, confine, or extreme part of a country bordering on another country.

G

GEOGRAPHY—see page 1.

GHAUT—see page 25.

GLOBE—see page 1.

GULF, perhaps derived from the Greek κολπος *kolpos*, which signifies a bosom—see page 3.

H

HARBOUR—see page 3.

HAVEN—see page 3.

HEADLAND—see page 2—from the English words head and land.

HEMISPHERE—see page 5.

HILL, derived from the Saxon *hyl*, and signifies a natural elevation of land, or a mass of earth, rising above the common level of the surrounding land.

HILLOCK, diminutive of hill, and denotes a smaller eminence.

HORDE signifies a company of wandering people dwelling in tents, and migrating from place to place, to procure pasturage for their cattle.

HORIZON—see page 8.

I

ISLAND, compounded of the English words isle and land—see page 2.

ISLE and **ISLET**, these are the diminutives of island, and signify a small island.

ISTHMUS, from the Greek ισθμος *isthmos*, and in its primary sense signifies a passage—see page 2.

J

JUNGLE, is of Hindoo origin, and signifies a thick wood of small trees or shrubs.

L

LAKE, derived from the Latin *lacus*, and primarily signifies a reservoir for water, a basin—see page 4.

LATITUDE, means breadth, applied by the ancients to the measurement of the earth, north and south, because they thought it was less that way than from east to west.

LAVA, probably from the Latin word *lavo*, to flow. It is a mass or stream of melted minerals, or stony matter, which is thrown out from the mouth or sides of a volcano, and is often ejected in such quantities as to overwhelm cities; as Catana destroyed by the lava of Mount Etna, Herculaneum and Pompeii by that of Mount Vesuvius.

LINE, the—this term is applied by way of eminence to the equator, because it is the first and principal line by which latitude is measured. It is most commonly used by mariners.

LONGITUDE, means length, applied by the ancients to the measurement of the earth, east and west, because they considered it to be larger that way than from north to south.

M

MAP—see pages 7 and 8.

MARSH, signifies a tract of low land usually covered with water, and overgrown with coarse grass.

MART, is a contraction for the English word market, and signifies a place of sale or traffic.

MERIDIAN—see page 6.

MERIDIAN, BRAZEN, is the circle on which the artificial globe turns, and is divided into 360 equal parts called degrees. In the upper semicircle of the brass meridian these degrees are numbered from 0° to 90°, from the equator towards the poles, and are used for finding the latitudes of places. On the lower semicircle of the brass meridian they are numbered from 0° to 90°; from the poles towards the equator, and are used on the elevation of the poles.

MINERAL, is the general name for all metals, whether pure or compound. It is applied also to those things that are neither animal nor vegetable.

MONARCHY, from the Greek *μονη monē*, single, and *αρχη archē*, a government, and is a state or government in which the supreme power is lodged in the hands of a single individual.

MONSOON—see page 26—it is of Hindoo origin.

MOOR, signifies a tract of wet low ground, a marsh or fen.

MORASS, signifies a tract of low moist ground—it is the same as a marsh.

MOUNTAIN, derived from the Latin *mons*, is a large mass of earth, rising above the common level of the earth, or of the adjacent land. It is generally applied to larger eminences than hills.

N

NADIR, is a point in the heavens exactly under our feet.

NOMADE, from the Greek *νομας nomas*, pasturage, and signifies pastoral, wandering for the sake of pasturage.

O

OBLIQUE, derived from the Latin *obliquus*, signifies deviating from a right line, not perpendicular, not parallel, aslant.

OCEAN, from the Greek Ωκεανος *ōkĕanos*, and signifies a vast body of water—see page 3.

OFFING, derived from our English word off, and generally signifies that part of the sea which is at a good distance from the land, and where there is deep water.

ORBIT, from the Latin *orbis*, a circle, any thing round. It signifies the curved line which a planet describes in its periodical revolution.

P

PARALLELS—see page 8.

PASS, derived from the Latin *pando*, to open, and hence signifies an opening, or a narrow passage between mountains.

PENINSULA—see page 2.

PERIGEE, derived from the Greek περι *peri*, about, and γη *gē*, the earth, and signifies that point in the orbit of the sun or moon, which is at the least distance from the earth. It is the opposite term of apogee—see apogee.

PERIHELION, derived from the Greek περι *peri*, about, and ηλιος *helios*, the sun. It signifies that part of the orbit of a planet or comet in which it is at its least distance from the sun.

PERIŒCI, derived from the Greek περι *peri*, about, and οικεω *oikeo*, to inhabit, are those who live in the same latitude, but in opposite longitudes; when it is noon with the one, it is midnight with the other. The inhabitants of the poles can have no periœci.

PHASIS, from the Greek φασις *phasis*, a shining, signifies generally an appearance, but it sometimes also signifies any appearance or quantity of illumination of the moon or other planet.

PLAIN, derived from the Latin *planus*, level, signifies any smooth, even, level, or flat extent of ground.

PLANET, from the Greek πλανaω *planao*, to wander, they are celestial bodies which revolve round the sun or any other centre, and are so called because they have no fixed position in opposition to the fixed stars.

POLAR, from the Latin *polus*, signifies of or belonging to the poles.

POLE, from the Latin *polus*, and in its primary sense is the end of the axis round which the wheel turns—hence it has come to be applied to the extremities of that axis or diameter about which our earth revolves.

POLICE, from the Greek πολις, *polis*, a city, and signifies the government of a city or town.

PRECIPICE, from the Latin *preceps*, headlong—strictly signifies a falling headlong, hence a steep descent of land, and hence it comes to signify a steep descent generally.

PRESIDENCY, from the Latin *præ*, before, and *sedeo*, to sit, and signifies superintendence; but it also sometimes means the jurisdiction of a president as the British dominions in the East Indies.

PRINCIPALITY, from the Latin *princeps*, chief, and signifies sovereignty, supreme power; though sometimes it signifies the territory of a prince.

PROMONTORY—see page 2.

PROVINCE, from the Latin *provincia*. Among the Romans it signified a country acquired by conquest. Among moderns it is a state belonging to a kingdom, either by conquest or colonization.

Q

QUADRANT, derived from the Latin *quatuor*, four, because it is the fourth part of a circle. The quadrant of altitude is a thin flexible piece of brass divided, upwards from 0° to 90°, and downwards from 0° to 18°, and when used is generally screwed to the brazen meridian. The upper divisions are used to determine the distances of places on the earth, the distances of celestial bodies, their altitudes, &c. and the lower divisions are used for finding the beginning, end, and duration of twilights.

R

RANGE, commonly applied to a long continuation of mountains, as the range of Taurus or of Caucasus.

REPUBLIC, from the two Latin words *res*, affairs, and *publica*, public, and is a state in which the exercise of the supreme power is lodged in representatives elected by the people—of such a government is Switzerland.

RIDGE, applied to a continuation of hills, as the Ridge of Carmel.

RIVER, from the French *riviere*, or from the Latin *rivus*—see page 4.

RIVULET, derived from the Latin *rivulus*, and signifies a small stream. It is the diminutive of river.

ROADS, derived from a Saxon word *rade*, signifying to ride. It signifies a place where ships may ride at anchor, as the roads of Madras. It is sometimes called also roadstead, *i. e.* a place for riding, meaning at anchor.

ROCK, derived from the French *roc*, or *roche*, and primarily signifies something rendered rough by constant breaking. It however usually signifies a large mass of stony matter.

S

SATELLITES, from the Latin *satelles*, one who guards or defends a person, also an attendant. They are secondary planets, or moons, revolving round the larger planets.

SEA, primarily signifies a repository or basin—see page 3.

SHINGLE, derived from the Greek σχινδαλμος *schindalmos*, a piece of cleft-wood, signifies in its primary sense thin planks sawed off, but is sometimes used to signify round gravel, or roundish stones.

SHORE and BEACH, the former of these words which is of Saxon origin, signifies the coast or land adjacent to (*i. e.* lying near) the ocean or sea, or on the border of any lake, &c. The latter of these words is derived from the Russian *bok*, a coast, and signifies the same as shore.

SIDEREAL, from the Latin *sidereus*, belonging to a star, signifies any thing relating to the stars.

SOLAR, from the Latin *sol*, the sun, and signifies any thing relating or belonging to the sun, as the Solar system.

SOLSTICE, from the Latin *sol*, the sun, and *sto*, to stand. It is that point in the Ecliptic at which the sun ceases to recede (*i. e.* go back) from the equator, either north in summer, or south in winter. These two are therefore called the *solsticial points*, the one the summer solstice, the other the winter solstice.

SOUND, signifies a narrow passage of water, or a strait between the mainland and an isle, or a strait connecting two seas.

SPHERICAL—see pages 4 and 5.

STATE, from the Latin *sto*, to stand, and signifies much the same as kingdom.

STRAITS—see page 3—also applied to a narrow passage between two mountains, as for instance the Straits of Thermopylæ.

SUBURBS, derived from the Latin *sub*, under, and *urbs*, a city, and signifies those parts which lie without the walls and in the vicinity of the city.

SURF, derived from the French *sur*, upon, and signifies the swell of the sea which breaks on the shore, or it may be on sand-banks and rocks.

T

TABLE LAND, from the two English words table and land, and signifies elevated flat land, as the table land between the ghauts.

TANK, is of Japanese origin, a large basin or cistern, a reservoir of water.

TEMPERATE, derived from the Latin word *tempero*, to be moderate—see page 9.

TERRESTRIAL, derived from the Latin *terra*, the earth, signifies any thing belonging to the earth.

TERRITORY, from the Latin *terra*, the earth, and is the extent of land within the bounds, or under the jurisdiction of any state or city, or sometimes it signifies the land belonging to a kingdom, but lying at a distance from its parent country.

TORRID—see page 9.

TOWN, originally signifies a walled or fortified place. In England it properly means any collection of houses larger than a village, and having a market place.

TROPIC, from the Greek word *τροπη*, *tropē*, a turning. The tropics are two circles parallel to the equator, at the distance of 23° 28′ from it. The northern is called the Tropic of Cancer, and the southern the Tropic of Capricorn, forming the limits or boundaries of the Torrid Zone.

V

VALE, derived from the same root as valley, and has also the same signification, but the difference between them is this, vale is used in poetry, valley in prose and common discourse.

VALLEY, derived from the Latin word *vallis*, and signifies a hollow or low tract of land between mountains and hills. It is however sometimes applied to low lands watered by rivers, and enclosed by no mountains, as the valley of Connecticut.

VERTICAL, derived from the Latin *vertex*, point or summit, and is applied to any thing placed on the zenith or perpendicularly over our heads. Thus we speak of the sun's being vertical, when it is directly over our heads.

VILLAGE, derived from the Latin word *villa*, and signifies a small assemblage of houses, and inhabited chiefly by farmers and other labouring men. In England it is distinguished from a hamlet, as having a church in it.

VOLCANO—this word is generally supposed to be of Italian origin, viz. from Vulcan, a heathen deity. It signifies an opening in the surface of the earth, or more generally in a mountain, from which smoke, flames, stones and such like substances are ejected, (or thrown out) as Hecla, Etna, Vesuvius, &c.

W

WILDERNESS, signifies a tract of land or region uncultivated and uninhabited by human beings, whether a forest or a wild barren plain.

WOOD, signifies a large and thick collection of trees.

WORLD—see page 1.

Z

ZENITH, is a point in the heavens exactly over our heads.

ZODIAC, derived from the Greek ζωδιακος *zōdiăcos*, belonging to animals. It is so called because the signs of the zodiac are chiefly represented by the figures of animals. The Zodiac is an imaginary ring or broad circle in the heavens, in the form of a belt, or girdle, within which all the planets make their revolutions.

ZONE, derived from the Greek ζωνη *zone*, literally signifies a girdle, and is applied to a portion of the surface of the earth contained between two small circles parallel to the equator, and is synonymous to climate. There are only 5 zones—see page 9.

GLOSSARY, No. II.

EXPLANATIONS OF HINDOOSTANEE AND OTHER WORDS IN COMMON USE.

NOTE.—The words as usually written in English are entered in the first column, and according to their correct pronunciation in the second. The vowels to be pronounced as in the words below:—

a	e	ee	i	o	oo	u	ou	y *medial*	ye *final.*
mast—	nay—	keel—	kill—	cole—	boot—	but—	out —	tyke —	bye

The third column of letters denotes the language to which the words belong—A meaning Arabic—H Hindee—M Malay—P Persian—Po Portuguese—S Sanscrit—T Tamil—Te Teloogoo. The fourth column gives the signification of the words.

A

Adawlet	udalut	A	justice, equity—a court of justice, civil or criminal.
Ameer	umeer	A	nobleman, lord.
Ameen	umeen	A	guardian, arbitrator.
Amildar	amildar	A	collector, ruler.
Anna	ana	H	a silver coin, the sixteenth part of a rupee.
Annicut	unnye-kuttoo	T	dam.
Avatar	uvutara or outar	S	incarnation.

B

Baboo	baboo	H	equivalent to esquire.
Bajree	bajra	H	name of a grain.
Bang	bung bhung	P S	hemp, an intoxicating mixture made from the leaves of hemp.
Bangy	buhungee	S	a stick carried over the shoulder, with slings at both ends for burdens.
Banyan	bunya	S	shopkeeper, merchant.
Batta	butta	H	exchange, allowance to troops in the field.
Bazar	bazar	P	market.

Beastie	bihishtee	P	water carrier, *(who carries water in a skin.)*
Beebee	beebee	H	lady.
Begum	begum	P	Mahomedan princess, or lady of rank.
Bismillah	bismillah	A	in the name of God.
Brinjarry	birunjaree	P	carriers of rice.
Bungalow	bungla	H	a house, properly a thatched cottage.
Byraggy	byragee	H	a Hindoo ascetic, so called as having renounced the world.

C

Caliph	khuleef	A	vicegerent, successor, title of the first successors of Mahomed.
Canoongoe	kanoon-go	P	interpreter of regulations, name of a district officer.
Carcoon	kar-koon	P	the register of the collections under a zemindar.
Cawny	kani	T	a ground measure, equal to about $1\frac{1}{3}$ acre.
Cazee	kazee	A	Mahomedan judge.
Chenna	chenna	H	name of a grain.
Chickledar	sykul-gur	P	polisher.
Chokeydar	choukee-dar	P	a watchman.
Choultry	chavuri, or chavudi	S Te	a hall or other building for public purposes, as for travellers, for police, &c.
Chout	chout'h	S	the fourth—name of the tribute formerly levied by the Mahrattas.
Chunam	choona	H	lime.
Circar	sirkar	P	the government, district, superintendent.
Compound	campao, or campong	Po M	an enclosure.
Conicopilly	kunukkoo-pillye	T	accountant.
Cooly	kooli	T	hire, used by Europeans for labourer, porter.
Corge	kodi	T	a score (Portuguese, *corja.)*
Cossid	kasid	A	courier.
Coss	kos	S	a measure, averaging two miles.
Crore	kror	S	ten millions.
Cumbly	kumlee	H	a blanket.
Curnum	kurnum	S	village accountant.
Cusbu	kusbu	A	a small town.
Cutcherry	kuch' huree	H	town hall, court.
Cutwal	kotwal	P	chief officer of the police in a town.

D

Dacoit	dakayut	H	an attack made by robbers.
Darogah	daroghu	P	director, inspector, head-man.
Dawk	dak	H	post, for letters or bearers.
Dessaye	desaee	S	ruler, landlord.
Dewan	deewan	P	minister, steward.
Doab	dooab	P	any tract of country between two rivers.
Dobash	dobhasha	S	interpreter, (lit. *two languages*) used commonly for an agent or head servant.
Dooly	doolee	S	a light description of palankeen made of canvas.
Duffadar	dufa-dar	P	a rank equivalent to lieutenant.
Durbar	durbar	P	court, hall of audience.
Durgah	durgah	P	court, mosque connected with a tomb.

E

Eedgah	eedgah	P	place for the celebration of a festival.

F

Fakeer	fukeer	A	a Mahomedan devotee, literally *a beggar*.
Foujdar	foujdar	P	the military governor of a town or district.

G

Ganja	ganja	S	hemp, an intoxicating mixture used for smoking and drinking.
Ghee	ghee	S	clarified butter.
Ghurry	ghuree	P S	an Indian hour—24 minutes.
Gobrum	gobrum	S	the porch tower of a pagoda, a gate.
Godown	gidung	M	warehouse, store-room.
Gola	gola	H	granary.
Gomasta	goomashtu	P	agent.
Gooroo	gooroo	S	spiritual guide. (Hindoo.)
Gosain	goosaeen	S	holy person; applied to a particular sect of Hindoo devotees who never marry.
Guddee	guddee	S	seat, throne.
Guicowar	gaikowar	S	cow-herd, title of the chief of Guzerat.

H

Hackery	hankre	H	native bullock carriage.
Hakeem	hukeem	A	physician.
Hakim	hakim	A	ruler.

Haram	hurum	A	women's apartments.
Havildar	huwal-dar	P	equivalent to serjeant.
Hijra	hijrut	A	flight; the flight of Mahomed from Mecca, from which the Mahomedan era commences.
	hijree	A	adjective of above.
Hircarrah	hurkaru	P	courier.

J

Jaghire	jae-geer	P	land granted in the way of pension.
Jaghiredar	jae-geer-dar	P	a holder of land as above.
Jattra	jatra	S	festival.
Jemidar	juma-dar	P	equivalent to lieutenant.
Jheel	jheel	H	a lake.
Jogee	jogee, yo-gee	S	Hindoo devotee.
Jumma musjid	jooma musjid, jamiu musjid	A	the Friday mosque, or the assembly mosque; that is the principal mosque at which the Mahomedans assemble on the Friday.
Jurree putka	zuree putka	H	golden girdle, an ensign of authority amongst the Mahrattas.

K

Khan	khan	P	prince, a title similar to that of lord.
Khas	khas	A	noble, private.
Khelaut	khilat	A	a robe of honour.
Khootba	khootbu	A	the oration at the mosque after prayers on Fridays.
Killadar	kiladar	P	commandant of a fort.
Kist	kist	A	tax.
Kohistan	koh-istan	P	hill district, highlands.

L

Lack	lak'h	S	hundred thousand.
Lascar	lushkuree	P	literally, *an army man*, applied in India to men employed with camp equipage, ordnance, and stores.
Lubbie	lubbee		descendants of Arab settlers on the Coromandel coast.

M

Mahabharat	muha-bharut	S	name of a Hindoo epic poem, describing the wars of the descendants of Bharut.
Malgoozar	malgoozar	P	landholder, tenant.
Mamool	mamool	A	custom, usage.
Mantra	muntur	S	charm, spell.
Maund	mun	A	name of a weight.
Meerassy	meerasee	A	hereditary.

Meerassadars	meeras-dar	P	heritors.
Minar	minar	A	turret, minaret.
Mirza	mirza, or meerza	P	prince, also secretary.
Mofussil	moofussul	A	the country, in opposition to *town.*
Moochy	moochee	H	saddler, applied to a bookbinder or other who works in leather.
Moollah	moolla	A	learned man, *answering to the word,* DOCTOR.
Moonshee	moonshee	A	secretary, *commonly used for a teacher of languages.*
Moulavy	mouluvee	A	see *moolla.*
Munsif	moonsif	A	judge.
Mufti	mooftee	A	one whose office is to pronounce decrees.
Musjid	musjid	A	mosque, lit. *place of adoration.*
Musnud	musnud	A	throne.

N

Nabob	nuwwab	A	governor of a district, deputy.
Nackodah	nakhooda	P	captain of a ship.
Naick	naik	S	a chief, also used to designate a rank equivalent to corporal.
Nizam	nizam	A	administrator, governor.
Nulla	nala	H	streamlet, watercourse.
Nunja	nunjye	T	dry cultivation.

P

Paddy	unknown		rice in the husk.
Padshah	padshah	P	king.
Pagoda	unknown		a Hindoo idol temple, also name of a coin.
Palankeen	palkee	H	*originally,* litter or sedan.
Parcherry	puriyur-cheri	T	a Pariah village.
Pariah	puraya	S	stranger, used to designate outcasts.
Pattemar			small Native coasting vessels on the Malabar Coast.
Peer	peer	P	saint, spiritual guide (*Mahomedan.*)
Peon	peewun	S	footman, used for foot-police or irregular foot-soldiers.
Pergunnah	purgunu	P	a subdivision of a zilla.
Perwanah	purwanu	P	pass, permit, warrant.
Peshcush	pesh-kush	P	tribute, present.
Peshwa	peshwa	P	leader, foreman, (a Mahratta title originally applied to the prime minister.)
Pice	pysa	H	a small copper coin, one-twelfth part of an anna.

Pindarry	pindara (*plural*, pindare)	S	plunderer.
Pollam	paliyum	T	district of a feudal chieftain, camp.
Polygar	paliyukarun	T	chief of a pollam.
Poonja	poonjye	T	wet cultivation.
Potail	putel	S	chief, head-man of a village.
Puckally	pukhalee	P S	water-man (*the water being carried in a* PUK'HAL, *or large leather bag, on a bullock.*)
Punchayet	punchayut	S	court of arbitrators (from its consisting of *five* members.)
Pundit	pundit	S	learned, title of a Brahmin lawyer.
Putta	putta	S	title deed of land.
Putwary	putwaree	H	land steward.
Pyke	pyk	S	footman, irregular foot soldiers, courier.

R

Rajah	raja	S	Hindoo prince or king.
Rahdary	rah-daree	P	collection of duties (on roads.)
Ramayum	Ramayunum	S	an epic poem describing the exploits of Rama.
Rana	rana	S	Hindoo prince or king.
Ranee	ranee	S	Hindoo queen or princess.
Rao	rao	H	Hindoo prince.
Razinamah	razee-namu	P	acknowledgment of settlement.
Rowanah	ruwanu	P	passport, permit.
Rupee	roopye	P	a silver coin whose value is about two shillings.
Rutt	rut'h	S	car, chariot.
Ryot	rueeyut	A	tenant (of land,) subject.
Ryotwarry	rueeyut-waree	H	revenue collection by direct settlement with the tenants.

S

Sahib	sahib	A	master, sir, lord.
Sanyogy	sunyogee or sunjogee	S	a Hindoo devotee, who does not give up his family.
Sanyassy	sunyasee	S	Hindoo devotee.
Sayer	sair	A	tax on personal property.
Seaconny	sookkanee	P	helmsman, (sookkan, *helm.*)
Sebundy	sibundee	P	militia soldier.
Seer	seer	S	name of a weight or measure, usually about 2 lbs.
Sepoy	sipahee	P	soldier.
Serishtadar	sur-rishtu-dar	P	(*office-holder,*) title of a revenue officer.
Shastras	shastru	S	Hindoo sacred books and laws.

Shastry	shastree	S	an expounder of the Hindoo laws.
Sheikh	shekh	A	chief, elder, a title assumed by descendants of Mahomed.
Shiah	sheea	A	a follower of the sect of Ali, heretic.
Shroff	surraf	A	money-changer, banker.
Sirdar	sirdar	P	chief, commander.
Soobah	soobu	A	province, governor of a province.
Soonnee	soonnee	A	lawful, applied to the sect of Mahomedans who acknowledge the four successors of Mahomed, in opposition to the Shiahs, who reject three and acknowledge only Ali.
Soukar	sahoo-kar	S	merchant (of the first rank.)
Sowar	suwar	P	horseman.
Subahdar	soobu-dar	P	governor of a province, also a rank in the Native army.
Sudder	sudur	A	chief, supreme.
Sultan	sooltan	A	monarch.
Sungum	sungum	S	conflux.
Sunnud	sunud	A	deed, document bearing a magistrate's seal.
Suttee	sutee	S	chaste, virtuous, a woman who burns with her husband's body.
Syrang	surhung	P	captain, overseer.
Syed	sy-yud	A	lord, prince, a title assumed by relations of Mahomed.

T

Tahsildar	tuhseel-dar	P	collector, tax-gatherer.
Talook	talook	A	a manor, division of land.
Tanadar	thana-dar	S P	station-man, police officer.
Tanna	t'hana	H	the head place of a district, a watch-house.
Tappal	tuppal	H	post, for letters or bearers.
Thakoor	t'hakoor	S	lord, chief.
Thug	t'hug	H	robber, cheat.
Topass	topee (hat)	H	name given to Native Portuguese sepoys, from their wearing *hats*.
Tusser	tusur	S	silk of the wild silk-worm.

V

Vakeel	wukeel	A	ambassador, agent.
Vizier	wuzeer	A	minister of state.

Y

Yug	joog, or yoog-um	S	a period, an age.

Z

Zemindar	zumeen-dar	P	landholder.
Zillah	zila	A	district.

GLOSSARY, No. III.

TERMINATIONS OF NAMES OF PLACES.

N. B. The first column gives the termination as used in English—the second gives the proper termination in the original languages—the third column of letters points out the language to which they belong, as in the former glossary—the fourth the meaning of the terminations—and the fifth gives examples.

A

Abad	abad	P	abode, town	Hyderabad.
Ar	aroo	T	river	Pal-ar, Pan-ar.
Ab	ab	P	water, river	Doo-ab, Punj-ab.

B

Baddy Barry	padi	T	village	Vaniambaddy.
Bar Var	var	S	region	Malabar, *Mulya-var.*
Baug	bagh	P	garden	Hazribaugh, *Hazreebagh.*
Baukum Vaukum Paukum	pakkum	T	village	Cauveripauk.
Bhoom	bhoom	S	land	Beerbhoom, Singhboom.
Bunder	bundur	P	sea-port	Muchleebundur (Masulipatam.)
Bund	bund	P	embankment	Sunderbunds.

C

Cherry	cheri	T	village, town	Pondicherry, *Poodoo-cheri.*
Coil	kovil	T	temple	Permacoil.
Conda Condah	konda	Te	a hill	Gurrumcondah.
Coond Koond Khoond	koond	S	spring	Seeta-koond, *the spring of Seeta.*
Cottah, or Kota Kote Cote	kotha kottye	H T	fort	Palamcottah, *Palyum-kottye.* Poodoocottah, *Poodoo-kottye.*

Coopam	koop-pum	T	village	Ariancoopam.
Courchy	koorsee	P	seat	Pandalamcourchy, *Pund-lum-koorsee.*
Cullum	koollum	T	tank	Periacullum, *Peria-kool-lum.*
Cund	k'hund	S	country, district	Rohilcund *Rohilk'hund* the country of the Ro-hillas. Bundelcund *Bundul-khund* the country of the Boon-delas.

D

Dar Dur	d'har, dhur	S	a house, city	Deodar, *Deo-d'hur.*
Doon	doon	S	valley	Deyradoon.
Droog	doorg	S	a hill fort	Nundydroog, *Nundi-doorg.*
Dwar Dwara	d'hwar d'hwara	S	gate, en-trance	Hurdwar, *Huri-dhwar.*

G

Gaum Gong	gaon	S	town or village	Mulligaum, *Mali-gaon.*
Ghaut	ghat	H	pass or ford	Ram-ghaut, Pal-ghaut.
,,	bala ghat	P H	above the passes.	
,,	paeen ghat or tulghat	P H	below the passes.	
Gire Gherry	giri	S	hill, moun-tain	Neilgherries, *Neela-giri.*
Gola	gola	H	granary	
Gul or kul,	kul	T	rock, rocky hill	Dindigul.
Gunge	gunj	P S	market, granary	Saibgunge, *Sahib-gunj.*
Gunga	gunga	S	river	Wynegunga, Ramgunga.
Gurry Gherry	gurhee	H	fortress	Kistnagherry, *Krishna-gur-hee.*
Gur Ghur	gurh	H S	fort, castle	Futtighur, *Futih-gurh.*

H

Haut	hat	S	market	Jorhat.

I

Istan	istan or stan	P	land, place	Hindoostan, *Hindoo-stan,* the land of Hindoos.

K.

Kera Kerry	k'hera	H	village	Arsikera.

M

Maha	muha		great	Mahanuddy, *Muha-nudee.*
Mahal Mal	muhul	A	district, quarter	Baramahal, *Baruh-muhul*, the twelve districts.
Malee Mally	mulye	T	hill, mount	Trinomalee, *Tiroonamulye.*
Mandel	mundulum mundulu	S	orb, region, circuit	Coromandel, *Chola-mundulu.*
Mangalum	mungulum		place	Satimengalum, *Suttimunglum.*
Mere	meer		region, district	Ajmere, Cashmere.

N

Nagore Nagur Naghur Nugger Nagram	nuggur nugrum	S	city	Chandernagore, *Chundurnuggur.* Vizianagram, *Vijuyu-nugrum.*
Naud Naad	nad	S	district	Ramnad.
Naut	nath	S	master, lord	Jaggernaut, (*Jugga-nath, lord of the world.*)
Nuddy	nudee	S	river	Mahanuddy, *Muha*, great, *nudee*, river.

O

Ore	oor	T	country	Bangalore, *Bungul-oor.*

P

Patam Patnam	puttun puttunum	S	city	Seringapatam, *Sree-rungaputtun.*
Pauk Paukum	pakkum	T	village	Caverypauk.
Pet Pettah Put	pent'h	H	suburb	Chinglepet.
Pollam	paliyum	T	district under a feudal chief	the Chittoor Pollams.

Poondy	poondi	T	village	Goomarapoondy.
Pore, Pooree, Poora, Pura, puram	poorum, pooree	S	town	Shikarpore, *Shikar-poor.*
Prayag, Prayaga	pruyagu	S	confluence of any two sacred rivers	Prayaga.

S

Serai	surae	P	choultry	Mogulserai, *Mooghul-surae.*
Shire	shuhur	P	city	Anoopshire, *Unoop-shuhur.*

INDEX.

In using this Index it should be borne in mind how very differently the same words are often spelled in various books and maps; and therefore, if a word is not found under one spelling, it should be looked for under another. The following instances will give some idea of the variety of spelling, and be some guide to the student in using an index or gazetteer. The letters a and u, c and k, oo and u, o and u, s and z, e and a, ee and y, e and i, ei and ee, c and g, n and ng, oor and ore, i and y, ei and y, u and w, are frequently used the one for the other, with many other variations. Thus, Umritsir is also spelled Amritzir—Cabul, Kabool, or Kabul—Gondwana, Gundwana—Selem, Salem—Goomtee, Goomty—Penang, Pinang—Bassein, Basseen—Singapore, Sincapore—Nankin, Nanking—Velloor, Vellore—Hyderabad, Heiderabad—Kuch, Kutch—Gualior, Gwalior—Monghir, Monghyr—Guzerat, Gujerat, or Goojrat—Nepal, Nepaul. The letter h is frequently left out or added—as Bootan, Bhootan—Mooghul, Mogul—Cuddapah, Cuddapa.

A

THE END.